EVIL IN CONTEMPORARY POLITICAL THEORY

Edited by

Bruce Haddock, Peri Roberts and Peter Sutch

EDINBURGH
University Press

First published in 2011 by
Edinburgh University Press Ltd
22 George Square, Edinburgh EH8 9LF
www.euppublishing.com

This paperback edition 2013

Typeset in 11/13 Palatino Light by
Servis Filmsetting Ltd, Stockport, Cheshire, and
printed and bound in Great Britain by
CPI Group (UK) Ltd, Croydon CR0 4YY

A CIP record for this book is available from the British
Library

ISBN 978 0 7486 4196 3 (hardback)
ISBN 978 0 7486 6859 5 (paperback)

CONTENTS

NOTES ON THE CONTRIBUTORS

David Boucher is Professor of Political Theory at Cardiff University.

Kerstin Budde is Lecturer in Political Theory and Ethics at the University of Birmingham.

Mark Evans is Reader in Political Theory at Swansea University.

Eve Garrard is Honorary Research Fellow in the Department of Philosophy, at the University of Manchester.

Bruce Haddock is Professor of European Social and Political Thought at Cardiff University.

John Horton is Professor of Political Philosophy at Keele University.

John Milbank is Professor in Religion, Politics and Ethics at the University of Nottingham.

Peri Roberts is Senior Lecturer in Political Theory at Cardiff University.

Richard Shorten is Lecturer in Political Theory at the University of Birmingham.

Peter Sutch is Senior Lecturer in Political Theory and International Relations at Cardiff University.

Chapter 1

INTRODUCTION

Bruce Haddock, Peri Roberts and Peter Sutch

The concept of 'evil' has a long history in the western tradition, extending from early theological debate, through tortured discussion of the relationship between moral and religious issues, to a contemporary context in which moral and political theory have domains of discourse in their own right. The religious roots of the idea of 'evil', however, have often made it difficult to accommodate in predominantly secular cultures, especially in multicultural contexts where deeply held beliefs may not be widely shared. Indeed, there has been a tendency in recent decades, especially among political theorists, to set the notion aside as outdated or inappropriate. Yet, at an intuitive level, the idea that some things are especially wrong, beyond toleration, still has significant currency. 'Evil' is undoubtedly a complex and controversial notion, but it continues to capture something that resonates across cultures in the modern world. We can grant that 'evil' is a dangerous and loaded term, readily open to abuse. The simple fact that it remains in currency in so many areas of discourse demands philosophical attention. While there is a small (but growing) philosophical literature on evil, political theory has not revisited the idea systematically.[1]

It is clear that 'evil' as a concept is taken seriously in ordinary political debate. Politicians and the press recognise the power of describing something as evil. This is clear in accounts of 'evil regimes', an 'axis of evil', of evil people such as Josef Fritzl and other abusers of children. While different people or regimes may not always agree about the precise character of evil, there is little doubt in their minds that something is evil, that the concept labels something important. The label is reserved for institutions, people or behaviours that are not simply wrong, but appear to be especially horrible, or so bad that they warrant another moral category altogether.

1

In contrast, contemporary political theory has found little use for the concept of evil. Liberals have often been suspicious of its religious pedigree, not wanting to import a moral category that undermines claims to impartiality. Critics of liberalism have generally been equally wary of evil, uncertain about the status of the moral judgement it conveys. Indeed, communitarianism, multiculturalism and social constructivist positions more broadly have often attacked the possibility of objective or universal moral judgements that seem to characterise attributions of evil altogether, regarding judgements about right and wrong in contextual or interpretative terms. Rather than condemning practices on partial grounds, the claim is that we should recognise 'difference' and embrace a pluralist politics. In doing so it will become clear that what appears to be evil from one perspective may be much more ambiguous from another.

More recently, many political theorists have expressed a concern that some things may not be simply 'different', but wrong. Approaching the issue in very different ways, theorists argue that there are important questions to be asked about the extent of a reasonable pluralism. It is this concern that we address, focusing on the limits of politics from the nasty end. It is here, at the boundaries of politics where our tolerance is stretched to breaking point, that the concept of evil may prove useful. Where the term amounts to more than a rhetorical device, the ordinary use of evil points to the importance of a boundary to acceptable politics. There turns out to be surprising agreement in modern cultures on the substantive evils that confront human communities (genocide, torture, slavery in its various guises), but much less consensus about the criteria being invoked when these (apparently confident) judgements are made. This book explores the actual and possible roles of evil in contemporary political theory. It turns out that whether in outlining criteria for the limits of toleration, in understanding the development of humanitarian international law, in theorising post-conflict situations, or in making sense of political rhetoric, that the notion of evil has an important contribution to make.

Our substantive chapters begin (John Milbank, 'Darkness and Silence: Evil and the Western Legacy') with a comprehensive analysis of the relationship between religious and secular accounts of value. Milbank challenges the basic assumption that conceptions of value can be effectively articulated within the terms of reference of secular discourse. Secular rationality can manage instrumental (and especially pair-wise) comparisons of value very effectively. Treatments of absolute value are quite another matter. Milbank contrasts the richness of theological discussions of evil with the paucity of effective accounts in the secular tradition. Even Kant, whose sensitivity to the concept of evil is unusual in the liberal tradition, and whose moral philosophy defends a conception of absolute value, finds himself, in political terms, dependent on a sovereign state as an enforcer of political and legal order, ultimately linking freedom and autonomy among individuals to the arbitrary exercise of power. In Milbank's analysis, the fate of liberalism, even in the hands of its best exponents, highlights the failure of a secular theory of value. If we cannot do without the term 'evil' in our ordinary discourse, the implication is that we have to look beyond secular (largely instrumental) rationality for a grasp of the importance of human life.

This is a challenge to normative political theory at the most basic level. Temperamentally wary of the tone of strident moral condemnation implicit in casual use of the term 'evil', political theorists have generally exercised discretion, avoiding the loose use of language of tabloid journalists and the less cautious political speech writers. Widespread acknowledgement of the reasonableness of pluralism has contributed to this wariness. Human flourishing is understood to come in many different forms and the values these forms embody are, in some important sense, contingent. Peri Roberts ('Constructivism and Evil') argues, however, that a notion of evil represents a necessary limiting conception for a defensible politics. Much of contemporary liberal theory is constructivist in a way that is usually taken to rule out categorical moral judgements that draw on notions of objective good and evil. Roberts, in contrast, explores the role that a properly developed conception of evil can play in liberal constructivism. Firstly, theories of evil are an important basis for a cross-cultural understanding of wrongness that can be framed in a liberal manner. Secondly, the content of theories of evil appears much less partial than ideas of the good that predominate in liberal discussion. Liberal constructivism, often castigated for offering an inadequate understanding of human goods, is thus well placed to outline a sparser notion of human evil that can anchor discussions of value.

Contingency remains a problem for any secular (and especially liberal) theory of value. Bruce Haddock ('Systemic Evil and the Limits of Pluralism') confronts this issue directly. Pluralism is a fact of life for us. We have accepted that communities can flourish in a remarkable variety of ways. But it does not follow that human beings can flourish in any and every context. Human beings are creatures who do things, not creatures to whom things simply happen. They are agents engaged in complex patterns of interaction. Initiating activities, however, pre-supposes at least minimal conditions. Individuals will have to be recognised in consistent ways. They need to be able to predict how others will respond to them, at least in rough-and-ready terms. These are institutional presuppositions of agency that cannot be taken for granted. The project, for Haddock, is to understand the necessary insti-tutional conditions for human flourishing and, more significantly, to identify conditions in which those conditions are willfully denied. The key is a conception of systemic evil that Haddock argues can be devel-oped as a radical revision of the natural law tradition, which identifies an evil regime with a legal order that systematically denies people the opportunity to plan and lead fulfilling lives.

Fulfilling lives are led in co-operation with others. Kerstin Budde ('Unreasonable or Evil?') explores the implications of a denial of a capacity to co-operate. Budde accepts the link between reasonable-ness and justice, and focuses on the ramifications of unreasonable-ness in social worlds that must necessarily be co-operative, however specific terms of co-operation might be worked out in particular contexts. Rawls saw his own work as a defence of a realistic Utopia that held out at least the prospect of the eradication of many of the great evils that disfigure human life. He specifically links political and social evils (injustice in the broadest sense) with unreasonableness. Budde accepts that this is a problematic move. We can easily grant that evil is (among very many other things) unreasonable, but no one would contend that unreasonableness should always be equated with evil. Unreasonableness, however, always undermines basic reciprocity between human beings. Sometimes this will be little more than a trivial irritation. In other contexts much more is at stake. We may feel outrage at the denial of fully human status to a fellow human being. The fact that unreasonableness offers us a spectrum of positions, with evil at one extreme, actually highlights the seriousness of ordinary engagements in which free and equal status is denied.

Budde has exposed genuine tensions in Rawls's work. In a wider theoretical context, it may be that attachment to theoretical system is part of the problem. Peter Sutch ('Evil in Contemporary International Political Theory: Acts that Shock the Conscience of Mankind') rejects the systematic approach to theorising evil from cosmopolitan first principles. He argues, instead, that if we are looking for an international conception of evil, we should engage in an exposition of the idea of 'acts that shock the conscience of mankind', drawing on the rich material available in international law. This is a public repository of genuine concern, encompassing both moral reflection and clear recognition of the practical limits of state action in a complex world. When we attend to the history of this developing notion closely, according to Sutch, what we find is not the codification of a shared cosmopolitan account of evil but rather a critique of sovereign state power. In this view, the international community of states (loosely specified) has already gone beyond the standard assumptions of old-style realist theory. States can collectively respond to humanitarian catastrophe and crisis. When they do so, they create new norms and expectations which involve deep commitments that, by slow degrees, change the terms of reference of international relations.

Evil has always been a central issue in just-war theory. Mark Evans ('Doing Evil Justly? The Morality of Justifiable Abomination') argues, however, that just-war theory has been so preoccupied with justice in the declaration and conduct of war that it has neglected the implications of recognising that even just warriors unavoidably do evil. If just war is often characterised as the lesser of two evils, it is still an evil, and one that must be confronted as a tough consequence of morality in a non-ideal world. This focuses attention on the neglected notion of *jus post bellum*, justice in the ending and aftermath of war. *Jus post bellum*, Evans argues, obliges just warriors to set just terms for peace, recognise their responsibility for a fair share of the burdens of war, and to take a full part in processes of forgiveness and reconciliation. Even the most just war involves the wilful infliction of moral evils. Innocents and combatants alike are killed, and long-term consequences are not easily assessed. In a literal sense, once we embark on war, we know not what we do. Focus on the inescapable evil of war is a salutary reminder of an overwhelming burden of responsibility.

The language of evil is not easily accommodated across the conventional political spectrum. Groups on the Left, in particular, have often resisted the term, not least because they are often focused on the contingent (often economic) constraints on ordinary lives. Eve Garrard ('Evil and the Left') urges a reassessment in the light of the very real evils that blight lives. The fact that people's lives may not go well, for no fault of their own, is a matter of serious concern. To hold back from judgement, however, is especially worrying for anyone who positions themselves on the Left. We take a particular stance precisely because we want to remedy identifiable abuses. Garrard acknowledges that the term 'evil' is easily abused, readily and almost unthinkingly from some perspectives on the political spectrum. Yet real abuses remain to be addressed. Where they are serious and knowingly inflicted, it may be appropriate to use the term 'evil' to describe them. When that is the case, left-inclined reservations should be set aside. It is much harder to confront abuses if we fail to describe them adequately.

Thus far in this volume, the obvious wrongness of evil has not been questioned. In secular cultures, however, the absolute values that once warranted sweeping moral condemnation are not readily available as a shared public resource. Feelings may be strong, but arguments vastly different, pointing to cultural and moral worlds that may be barely intelligible from particular perspectives. It would be very odd in the modern world not to be aware that one's deepest convictions might be reprehensible from someone else's point of view. John Horton ('The Glamour of Evil: Dostoyevsky and the Politics of Transgression') confronts the ambiguity of judgement directly. Far from repelling us, evil might even have its own shocking allure for us. We read books and watch films that bombard our senses with atrocities. But even in conventional institutional contexts, the perverse attraction of evil might be very vivid. The Easter service of the Roman Catholic Church asks congregations 'do you reject the glamour of evil?' What this glamour might involve needs to be unpacked, suggesting images of temptation, fascination, and the spell of evil as an illusionary good. We might declare (almost wallow in) our weakness. Horton highlights an undeniable fascination with the excitement and vitality of the transgressive, the rule-breaker, as recognised by Nietzsche, Freud and their followers. He explores whether it is possible to give a theoretical account of the 'illusion' that evil can ever be in our interest. The alternative is to recognise that the fascination with evil not only has deep cultural and psychological roots but may also throw into question the wrongness and undesirability of evil. From where we stand, these are difficult judgements to make. Philosophy may be too neat and tidy to help us very much. Horton draws on Dostoyevsky's analysis of character and motivation to highlight what are, in fact, everyday psychological perils. In the end, our ordinariness may be our strongest resource. Good, no less than evil, might be irredeemably banal.

Undermining the distinctiveness of evil is a characteristic of political, as well as cultural, discourse. Ordinarily judgements of evil are a tool of political condemnation. As such they take their place alongside judgements of wrongdoing of varying degrees, from forgivable lapses to wrongful acts justified by necessity to criminal wrongdoing. But one feature of political rhetoric is that distinctions between degrees of wrongdoing are often undermined by claims of 'moral equivalence' that aim to blunt, revise and unsettle them. Richard Shorten ('The Rhetoric of Moral Equivalence') is concerned to sort through exactly what is going on when public speech about wrongdoing is treated as a distinctive kind of political action, to examine moral equivalence as a feature of *persuasive* political language. His aim is to understand the conditions that inform the allocation, weighting and distribution of properties that convey wrongdoing in a political, rather than a strictly philosophical, context.

A clear presence throughout this volume is Hannah Arendt's controversial characterisation of evil as banal. Arendt's *Eichmann in Jerusalem: A Report on the Banality of Evil* has always divided critics, and for a time dominated discussion of her wider work.[2] In retrospect it is still surprising that a report on a trial, with no pretension to offering a theory of evil, should remain an indispensable point of reference for theoretical discussion. David Boucher ('Banal but not Benign: Arendt on Evil') fittingly concludes our volume with a full account of the text and its reception. Arendt did not intend to belittle the horrific evil of the holocaust, but her account of evil-doing still has an unnerving quality. Boucher focuses on the banality of the evildoer, Eichmann himself, just getting on with his job. What emerges is a picture of an ordinary man who simply went about his daily tasks, seemingly barely aware of what he was actually doing. And, of course, behind the figure of Eichmann we can imagine a host of ordinary folk, attending to their banal tasks, which just happened to contribute to the slaughter of human beings on an industrial scale.

This is unnerving enough. Behind Arendt's account, however, is a darker story of the status of human beings as vulnerable rights-bearers, dependent on political protection if they are to enjoy any rights at all. Boucher highlights dark implications of what a 'right to have rights' (Arendt's phrase) might commit us to, given that we are essentially rightless outside political orders. We must ask ourselves (and Arendt) what qualifies us to be right-holders. Boucher shows that Arendt's own attitude privileged the fortunate citizens of established polities, leaving inhabitants of the underdeveloped world almost defenceless. He stresses a residual racism in Arendt's thought that must make modern citizens deeply uncomfortable. More important still, he leaves us with the worrying thought that all our judgements are made from partial positions.

The early chapters of this book emphasise possibilities for the systematic theorising of evil in contemporary political and international theory. Steps are made to carve out a continuing role for the notion of evil. Indeed, it may be that something like a concept of evil can do vital work in enabling us to be clearer about the limits of a legitimate politics. Later chapters focus attention on the way evil presents itself up close, in complicated political situations of war, for example, and to politicians in the process of political condemnation. What becomes clear, whether from the point of view of the perpetrators of necessary evil, of the victims of evil, or of political actors making judgements about evil, is that it demands understanding. Political theory should not sidestep such a demand but rather explore ways of meeting it.

Evil is a fundamentally cross-disciplinary concept. It would not be appropriate, given the range of the literature, to advance anything like a definitive theory of evil. It is clear, however, in political theory, ethics, history and cultural studies more broadly, that the assumptions we unthinkingly employ in everyday normative judgement demand closer scrutiny in light of our experience of the terrible things that are done to people. This book is part of a general move in contemporary theory to explore the grounds of the judgements we seem driven to make, especially in the context of deeply divided societies.[3] Whether we need to insist on the universal status of judgements in order to negotiate this difficult terrain is, of course, open to question. At the very least, however, doing political theory effectively involves coming to grips with the range of ordinary experience. The term 'evil' continues to convey something that is all too real in many lives. Our suggestion here, from our different perspectives, is that focus on 'evil' obliges us to address fundamental issues in normative judgement. This is unavoidably controversial work. Our hope is that analysis of extreme issues generates conceptual clarity.

Notes

1 See Susan Neiman, *Evil in Modern Thought: An Alternative History of Philosophy* (Princeton: Princeton University Press, 2004); Richard Bernstein, *Radical Evil: A Philosophical Interrogation* (Cambridge: Polity, 2002); Richard Bernstein, *The Abuse of Evil* (Cambridge: Polity, 2005); Phillip Cole, *The Myth of Evil* (Edinburgh: Edinburgh University Press, 2006); and Claudia Card, *The Atrocity Paradigm: A Theory of Evil* (Oxford: Oxford University Press, 2002).

2 See Hannah Arendt, *Eichmann in Jerusalem: A Report on the Banality of Evil* (Harmondsworth: Penguin, 1965).

3 See Anne Phillips, *Multiculturalism without Culture* (Princeton: Princeton University Press, 2007); Seyla Benhabib, *The Claims of Culture: Equality and Diversity in the Global Era* (Princeton: Princeton University Press, 2002); Seyla Benhabib, *Another Cosmopolitanism* (Oxford: Oxford University Press, 2006); Amartya Sen, *Identity and Violence: The Illusion of Destiny* (London: Allen Lane, 2006); Bruce Haddock and Peter Sutch, eds, *Multiculturalism, Identity and Rights* (London: Routledge, 2003); and Bruce Haddock, Peri Roberts and Peter Sutch, eds, *Principles and Political Order: The Challenge of Diversity* (London: Routledge, 2006).

Chapter 2

DARKNESS AND SILENCE: EVIL AND THE WESTERN LEGACY

John Milbank

A

Traditionally, in Greek, Christian and Jewish thought, evil has been denied any positive foothold in being. It has not been seen as a real force, or quality, but as the absence of force and quality, and as the privation of being itself. It has not been regarded as glamorous, but as sterile; never as more, always as less. For many recent philosophers, however (for example, Jacob Rogozinski, Slavoj Zizek, J.-L. Nancy) this view appears inadequate in the face of what they consider to be the unprecedented evil of the twentieth century: the mass organisation of totalitarian control and terror, systematic genocide, and the enslavement of people who are deliberately worked to the point of enfeeblement and then slaughtered.[1] Such evil, they argue, cannot be regarded as privative, because this view claims that evil arises only from the deliberate pursuit of a lesser good. Power directed towards extermination, however, suggests destruction and annihilation pursued perversely for its own sake, as an alternative end in itself. Such a motive towards the pure negation of being, as towards the cold infliction of suffering – that may not even be enjoyed by its perpetrators – suggests that the will to destroy is a positive and surd attribute of being itself and no mere inhibition of being in its plenitude.

This supposed positive evil for its own sake is often dubbed 'radical evil' following a term used by Immanuel Kant in his book *Religion within the Boundaries of Mere Reason*.[2] With some plausibility, Kant's account of evil is seen as encouraging a break with the traditional privation view focused upon being in general in favour of a view focused purely upon the finite human will. This new view comprehends evil as a positively willed denial of the good and so as a pure act of perversity

10

without ground. The development of such a position is traced from Kant, through Schelling, to Heidegger.

In this way, a specifically modern *theory* of evil is held to be adequate to account for a specifically modern extremism of evil *practice* – which the theory, nonetheless, predates. Despite this predating – which might suggest some causal link – the modern practical extremity of evil is held to be, at least in part, the outcome of a far older western tradition of metaphysical reflection on evil which trivialises it and underrates it. So not only is evil as privation refuted by Auschwitz, it is also indicted by it as responsible for such an outcome. Evil denied as mere denial leaves us unvigilant against its real positivity.

This position, then, traces no lineage to the Holocaust from the specifically German and modern accounts of radical evil, yet asserts, perhaps all too vaguely, a lineage from the age-old western metaphysical understanding of evil as privation. Here, however, the advocates of 'radical evil' (or 'postmodern Kantians' as I will henceforth describe them) have to face the diametrically opposite alignment of theoretical and practical evil proposed by Heidegger's pupil, Hannah Arendt – and arguably against her former teacher.[3] For Arendt, famously, the mass murderer Albert Eichmann, on trial in Jerusalem, discloses not a pre-satanic will to evil, nor a lust for horror, but instead 'the banality of evil', an incremental and pathetic inadequacy of motive which escalated imperceptibility into complicity with unimaginable wickedness. It has now been shown, against those (for various reasons) prone to doubt this, that Arendt's account of evil as 'banal' is most certainly linked with her Augustinian predilections, and support for Augustine's account of evil as negative.[4] Thus the horror of Auschwitz, for Arendt, is not the revelation of evil perpetrated for its own sake, but rather a demonstration that even the most seemingly absolute evil tends to be carried out by people who imagine, albeit reluctantly, that they are fulfilling the goods of order, obedience, political stability and social peace.

In this fashion, Arendt implicitly sees the western metaphysical account of evil as privation as confirmed, not denied, by the Holocaust. A fortiori, therefore, this traditional theory of evil is not for her complicit with the modern practical excess of evil. In addition, Arendt established very astutely certain links between a debased Kantianism, and the co-operation of many of the German people with the implementing of the final solution.[5] To this degree she also raised the question of a link between the modern theory of evil and the modern excessive practice

of evil. And where she did, in her political theory, deploy Kant favourably, she adverted to social convergence in judgement, which is linked,
by Kant, with the beautiful, and not to the common experience of the
natural sublime, that for Kant, has profoundly to do both with respect
for the formal law, *and* with radical evil.[6]

Despite this opening of the issue concerning the relation between
modern theory of evil and modern evil as practised, Arendt veered
well away from any indictment of Kant as such. *Debased* Kantianism
is culpable, not the real Kantian philosophical legacy. Thus, while in
relation to the Holocaust, the ancient view of evil is confirmed and
therefore exonerated, the modern, positive view of evil is not accused
of a certain responsibility. And yet this intellectual lineage would seem
to be, at least prima facie, more plausible in terms of time locality and
proximity than the supposed genealogy which traces back to western
metaphysical ontotheology. It would also allow some significance to
the pre-dating of the modern practice of evil by the modern theory of
evil. After all, the opponents of the privation theory have already contended for the profound alignment of radical evil with the Holocaust,
since this theory alone is held adequately to interpret it. Supposing,
instead, that *privation theory* can interpret the Holocaust, then this
alignment would appear very differently: not as the retrospective match
of event to detached theory, but as the prior perverse attempt to enact a
false theory. Instead of the view that the negation of evil that fantasises
its mere negativity permits its positivity to erupt, one would have the
view that the false assertion of evil as positive leads to an impossible
quest to enact such positivity, which can in reality only unleash a bad
infinite of further and further privation, since *being* will not permit any
final solution, any finished or perfected evil.

One can see immediately, from this formulation, however, why
Arendt could not have traced the genealogy it expresses, quite apart
from her residual respect for Kant. To ascribe causality to the pursuit of
the satanic illusion, the illusion of the pursuit of evil for its own sake,
appears clean contrary to the invocation of the banality of evil behaviour. And Arendt, as many have pointed out, had all too little to say
about the psychology of the *instigators* of the final solution rather than
those of people who must be judged its mere executives, albeit para-
mount ones, like Eichmann. All the same, this is not to say that a privation theory, nor even aspects of a banality theory, cannot apply also to
the instigators. Hitler and his henchmen were not exactly satanists and

their articulations of their motives were not like that of the Californian Charles Manson or the 'Moors murderer' Ian Brady, a close student of de Sade and decadent literature. In these extreme cases one has something like the illusion of the belief that evil is being performed for its own sake – although privation theory is able to discern amid this vaunted satanic glory the pathetic desire for control, of those whose high self-esteem has been in no way socially confirmed.[7] Something of that may, indeed, have been operative among the Nazi cohorts, but they still articulated their defective desires more positively, in terms of promotion of the racial health and excellence of humanity: indeed, in their paganism or atheism they remained all too humanist, and Hitler sought avowedly to produce a human being worthy of worship.[8] Likewise, the suppression and finally liquidation of the Jews were not articulated in nihilistic terms, but could be viewed as 'rational' given that one's objective was to secure a German power absolutely untainted by socialism and the influence of international commerce, and a German identity based on cultural uniformity and demotion of the Christian and biblical legacy in favour of a Nordic one.

The Nazis did not, therefore, like Charles Manson, avowedly elect radical evil, saying 'Be Thou my Good'. Such satanism discovers itself to be an illusion at the point where it finds it can establish no stable positive kingdom of evil, nor encompass absolute destruction of being, but instead can only unleash an ever-escalating slide of deprivation which will usually cease with self-destruction. Clearly, the theory of radical evil is not implicated in the Holocaust in this extreme satanic fashion. In a much more subtle fashion, however, it may after all, be implicated. Here one can claim first of all (as I will later demonstrate) that Nazi concepts of universal power and legality were much more compatible with, and even derived from, the Kantian categorical imperative, than Arendt allowed. In the second place, one can claim that, if the Nazis still affirmed a Kantian free will as their good, then they also intended the aporias of this free will, as half admitted by Kant in *Religion within the Boundaries of Mere Reason*. For these aporias, there is no clear way of distinguishing between the will which genuinely wills freedom, and the will which wills against itself, restraining freedom – this self-opposition for Kant characterises the evil will.[9] As we shall see, these aporias arise because of the lack, in Kant, at this highest level, of any teleology which can discriminate the good substance of what is willed, from a deficient instance of such substance. Here, instead, the only thing willed is the law of free willing itself, which defines legality as untrammelled autonomy – and it might seem that the free will to bind oneself equally instantiates such autonomy. At the very least one can ask, exactly how is one to discriminate between the will binding itself to be free, and the will binding itself in unfreedom, if there is no desirable content here to prove the goodness of the genuine good will to freedom?

But if this is really the case with Kant, then one must face up to something which seems at first sight highly unlikely: namely that political totalitarianism and terror really could, with a certain plausibility, pose as the fulfilling of the categorical imperative, just as much as the most stringent code of personal self-denial. Later we shall see how these opposites can indeed converge and mutually reinforce each other. In effect, the promotion of formal freedom can become akin to the systematic promotion of the inhibition of freedom by an imperceptible slide. And such self-deceiving espousal of evil would be in practice very like the setting up of a satanic organisation. Here also, no stable realm of evil would result but, instead, the pace of privation of being would be horrendously quickened.

In what follows I shall offer, in the first place, a further defence and exposition of the view of evil as privation and banality. I shall therefore argue that it can apply also to modern extreme evil, and is in no sense responsible for this evil. In the second place, beyond Arendt, however, I shall argue that the modern, positive theory of evil *is* in a measure responsible for the modern actuality of evil.

B

To begin with, however, I must offer a much fuller exposition of the modern theory of evil as positive and 'radical'.

Contemporary proponents of this view start with the proposition that totalitarian phenomena of the previous century, and in particular the Holocaust, exhibit something uniquely evil. And this is, indeed, more than arguable. For in these instances, not just executive forces became poisoned but sovereign law itself consented to criminal principles and dedicated systemically the resources of the state to mass murder on a legal, organised and bureaucratic basis. In particular, sections of the population deemed difficult or surplus to requirement were not simply oppressed or incarcerated; they were literally worked to death and discarded. So, whereas previous slave economies still preserved some sense of the human status of the slaves, here this was denied in the context of a new hierarchical humanism which restricted full humanity to certain racial, physical and mental ideals.[10]

For the postmodern Kantians, this new degree of malevolence suggests in effect a will towards evil for its own sake – not merely evil as a lack of reality, or a lack of power, but evil as an alternative and viable exercise of power, whereby some human beings can devote themselves primarily to the destruction of others. This is now revealed as a possibility: it worked; scarcely any Jews now inhabit Germany. And if evil is not revealed as having equal potency with the good – an equal potency which proceeds to an equal actuality – then it is also shown as proceeding entirely from the rational will. It would be, surely, unthinkable to proffer any excuses for the Holocaust, or to lay out a set of mitigating circumstances. Yet the postmodern Kantians suggest that privation theory proceeds precisely by offering mitigating circumstances for all evil, so allowing radical evil to slip through its theoretical net. What it amounts to, they argue, is a kind of justification of being, an ontodicy (by analogy with theodicy), which also exonerates all creatures who exist, including human beings. For privation theory, all being as being is good, and because all power in order to be effective manifests the actuality of being, all power, as power, is good, and evil not only is impotent but can even be defined, at least, in one valid way, as weakness and impotence (this is underscored most heavily by Dionysus the Areopagite).[11] It follows that, since the will is a potency, it is only actual and effective when it wills the good – hence for both Dionysus and Augustine, it is not exactly the case that evil can be willed; rather there is evil precisely to the degree that there is an absence of willing. No one, as willing, wills anything but the good, and evil affects the will only to the extent that a deficient good is being willed.[12]

This exoneration of the will as such, suggests, to the postmodern Kantians, that thereby the will is excused, and evil displaced from human origin. Instead of a primary referral of evil to potency and will, in terms of a kind of immanentised Manicheaism, privation theory seems to imply a root of evil prior to power and will, in impersonal ontological circumstances, or rather in neontological circumstances.[13] For, according to Jewish and Christian tradition, at least up to Maimonides and Aquinas, being in its pure self-origination is infinite, and if being as such is good, then, also, the infinite as such is good, indefeasibly good, beyond the possibility of swerving. Hence it would seem that goodness is a property of non-limitation, and not a derivative of personal election. Conversely, if evil is possible only for finite creatures, the finitude can always be proffered as something of an excuse: the will falls into evil by choosing the lesser good (since to will at all it must will *some* good) but here it is a victim of its finite partiality of perspective, and its finite lack of power to affirm. Indeed, even St Paul appears entirely to exonerate the will, lamenting that he does what he hates, the opposite of what he wants to do (Romans 7: 15, 18; Gal. 5: 17). Thereby he blames the incapacity of his flesh but not exactly the purity of his intentions. For where the will has failed to will what it should, then, for this traditional metaphysical perspective, it has failed to will in some measure, and the will is held captive by something prior to will: either, for the ancient Greeks, materiality as such; or else for Jews and Christian, certain perverse habits that hold our materiality and psychic passions in their grip.[14] Thus, while it might seem that privation theory, by defining evil as lack of being, prevents any rooting of evil in the ontological, in fact it does affirm such rooting. For, because evil is here tied to finitude, and the finite is caused by the infinite, the infinite is the real ultimate source of lack – the ontological of the neontological. And, because the infinite is essentially impersonal, freedom as the origin of evil is here subordinated to ontological *cause* as the origin of evil. In this way, it is argued by the postmodern Kantians, human evil is mystified, and blame shifted to a metaphysical scenario. Yet at the same time, their apparently more humanist account involves also an *alternative* metaphysical scenario. They wish to regard the alternative good/evil in preontological terms as entirely prior to the distinction between infinite and finite. This means, for them, that the finite will as such, in willing the good of the other, can manifest the extreme of goodness – an infinite good, if you like.[15] But conversely, as they concede, following Schelling, this must also mean that the infinite can manifest the extreme of evil.[16] Thus for Schelling, the good will of God is the result of a radical decision within the dark indifferent ground of the infinite – and this alone ensures that God *really* is good, according to any fashion of goodness that we can understand. God's goodness also is a loving decision; it is an offer, a free gift, not an inevitability. Were it the latter, how could we be grateful, how could we feel infinitely loved? (Schelling has a certain point here, even though I shall later dissent.)

C

In articulating their post-Holocaust alternative to privation theory, the postmodern Kantians draw primarily upon Kant's account of radical evil, which they see as explicitly or implicitly developed by Schelling and Heidegger.

In Kant's account, evil is not really referred to finititude and so not primarily to any sort of lack or deficiency. He produces instead a theory of the pure 'self-binding' of the will, which is sometimes seen as his qualification of the enlightenment and retrieval, or even purer expression of, a biblical, Pauline and Augustinian thematic.[17] But this is a mistake; radical evil is *not* original sin (even though Kant sees it as the rational rethinking of the latter) and it *is* an enlightenment substitute for original sin, in a fashion that I shall demonstrate. First of all, one should recall my invocation of St Paul. In his understanding of will, he still assumes a biblical and Hellenic teleology: human beings are created to will the love of God as their final end and beatitude. As created they have a certain foretaste of the vision of God, and sufficient power to pursue this vision as they ought. When the will does pursue this vision, it is free from perverse, unnatural restrictions of its appointed nature, which thereby inhibits its freedom as such – for the inner reality of creaturely freedom is just this passing beyond given finite nature in diverse ways towards the infinite. Will is nothing other, as Augustine makes clear in *De Libero Arbitrio*, than the site of the *dynamism,* of the participation of the finite in the infinite, in the case of rational creatures (angels and humans).[18] Thus 'will' arises where an as-not-yet-fully accessible rational vision lures forward through our desire, our finite potency. It follows that will as such cannot fail of the choice of its final end without in some measure slipping away from its freedom. And this slipping away *cannot* – either for St Paul or Augustine – be accomplished by a surd choice of will alone, since will is nothing but the impact of infinite reason upon finite power. Instead, the slipping must involve either or both an unnatural restriction of intellectual reason and of forceful capacity. St Paul dwells upon the latter, Augustine on both: for Augustine we cannot will what we will to will, because the inherited sin of Adam has impaired both our vision and our potency. If there was any pure 'sin of the will' (unknown to the Greeks) then this was the original sin of Adam himself, who, enjoying perfect vision and perfect capacity and so perfect freedom, nonetheless freely and without ground willed these things away.[19] This act, for Augustine, is strictly baffling and incomprehensible. It is not at all *explained* by free will, because free will in its natural created state knows only the willing of the good, under the compulsion of the vision of the good, and no choice between good and evil at all. To the contrary, the very (as it were) 'fictional' notion, that there is such a choice, was invented by Adam at the Fall (or by Satan in the Angelic Fall). The problem of the Fall is the sheer apparent impossibility of this invention – the imagining of a false simulacrum within the repleteness of reality. This imagining alone erects an illusory autonomy, or self-governance of the will, since it is precisely the will of a creature to hold sway over itself, in disregard of its appointed substantive end. That is to say, it is the will to prefer the identical repetition of emptiness of rule for no purpose, but rather for its own sake, over submission to the natural superiority of the infinite which must be perceived in ever-renewed, non-identical repetition. Indeed, finitude alone renders this delusion possible –yet finitude here is not really, as critics of privation theory imagine, invoked as an excuse – since the entire life of the finite, as created out of nothing, resides in its orientation to the infinite. Thus to assert the pure self-governing of the finite entity, over against the infinite – which, as boundless, *cannot* be self-governing in this fashion – is also to deny what sustains its bounds and specific substance, in favour of an emptiness (an *infinite* emptiness) which alone belongs to it solely.

Since Adam's choice was for the illusion of a finite autonomy of the will (that is to say, for the idea of a groundless free choice between good and evil as expressing the very essence of freedom) it is not at all true to say that, for Christian theology, the descendants of Adam inherit a tendency to evil which is primarily a tendency of *the will*. To the contrary, this would be to perpetuate Adam's fantasy. Instead, the *reality* of Adam's election is revealed primarily as loss of the vision of God and as physical death and incapacity of the body. As a result of this twin impairment, will as desire lacks both vision and capacity and degenerates into concupiscence: the original sin of Adam which we *do not*, as concupiscence, inherit, but through ignorance and weakness tend to *repeat*.

But then how, it might be asked, if the will is so inhibited, does St Paul think he can even *will* the good, although not carry it out? The answer is provided by Augustine in *De Libero Arbitrio*. Matching the aberrant leading role taken by the will at the Fall is the aberrant leading role taken by the will under grace. The miracle of grace consists *precisely* in our capacity to desire truth beyond our intellectual and forceful inhibitions.[20] To be sure, for Augustine following Plato, all human knowing is an interplay between always-already knowing something and not yet knowing it, which amounts to the thesis that for us, fully knowing something is *always* in some measure the desire to know it. In this way, it has to be understood that, in Augustine, the vision which 'governs' the will, is nonetheless a vision only secured to a degree *through* right will. Moreover, since effective will must be enacted, a true and unimpaired potency is also essential for the enjoyment of vision (in the much later *De Trinitate*, such 'Trinitarian' equality of power, understanding and will is much more emphatically expressed) and yet a loss primarily of vision and impulsion (rather than will/desire) after the Fall implies the cessation or at least inhibition of the interplay between the already and the not yet of cognition. Just as, before the Fall, the lure of true vision pulled desire towards itself, so, now, after the Fall, the loss of vision weakens drastically the impulse of desire (while the loss of power equally impairs its capacity to express itself). Yet God does not restore our plight by proffering us primarily true vision and power once more; rather his new accommodation remains appropriately true to our finitely necessary interplay of already and not yet, by now *accentuating* the role of desire upon which such interplay depends. Hence what God, by grace, restores to us, in the face of the loss of the magnetic poles of the already of power and the not yet of fully attained knowledge, is precisely the 'middle' of interplay between them, the middle of desire which reintegrates their magnetism.

It will be seen from the above that it is not at all the case, for Augustine, as in post-Reformation misreadings of his work, that, after the Fall, human beings are left with a will to the good and to salvation which they cannot enact, thereby becoming aware of original sin, and an impotence that is only cured after the Incarnation.[21] To the contrary, Augustine affirms that the original justification assured to humans by divine grace before the Fall is seamlessly continued as the offer of redeeming grace through Christ which becomes immediately available by typological anticipation after the Fall.[22] In consequence, for Augustine (and he never retracted this) *no one*, after the Fall, is *guilty* on account of original sin; people are guilty only if they refuse the offer of grace and remain content with their deficient inheritance.[23] And this grace arrives precisely *as* our immediately renewed capacity for a free willing of submission to God. Thus, if we experience original sin as the frustration of our will, then this is only because this will to fulfil the law is itself grace, and therefore, as James Alison has argued, original sin is only disclosed in the light of our salvation in Christ.[24] It is clear that in no way are grace and free will here set against each other in a Lutheran fashion. Instead, the gift of grace consists in a miraculously restored desire for God, despite the loss of original vision and capacity.

But if will operating properly as will is guided, for Augustine, by a true vision, how is it able to take the lead over vision in our restoration? How can purification of vision and capacity first of all be induced by a true desiring? To understand this, we have to understand the complex double hierarchy of will and virtue, which Augustine explains in the *De Libero Arbitrio*. He declares there that possessed intellectual and moral virtues lie hierarchically above the will, since virtue *as* virtue can only be good, while the will can be good or bad (meaning that the will can perversely inhibit itself). Nevertheless, he also asserts that the will wills a good *beyond* the good of virtue (beyond, therefore, one can note, the pagan conception of good).[25] What is this good beyond virtue? Augustine describes 'a virtue' as the possession of an individual, which *as* virtue he cannot lose, since virtue lost is vice. By contrast, the will desires, beyond virtue, an inaccessible divine good, which can never belong to an individual, and can only be enjoyed in common. This superabundant good is shared between us, and never possessed – just like sunlight, says Augustine, which is more truly precious than gold, even though gold can be held through private ownership. This good, since it is infinite and above us, and held securely by God, *can* be lost by us, unlike virtue as virtue. Nevertheless, insecure will, which should be guided by secure virtue, still takes the lead over virtue, because virtue is less fundamentally a possession than it is a sharing in the common good. Such sharing in what surpasses us is only ever to be attained by desire, even if a true desire, for Augustine, is also a kind of true, but inchoate, envisaging.

Moreover, if desire exceeds virtue in the direction of the more common and universal, then it also, according to *De Libero Arbitrio*, exceeds virtue in the direction of the more individual and particular. For the will is linked not just to discrimination of right from wrong, and the following of truth rather than falsehood, but also with idiosyncratic, but equally valid moral and aesthetic preferences. Thus, Augustine says, some in a landscape will admire more the'height of a mountain', others the'verdure of a forest', others'the pulsing tranquility of the sea'; and in like fashion the cleaving of desire to the good refracts it according to our specific local affinities.[26] In this way, the will for Augustine at once directs us beyond private virtue to the common good, and yet at the same time does so through a desire necessarily more individuated than virtues like patience, taken in the abstract, which though privately possessed, like gold, show, also like gold, the same identical quality in all instances. This is why'will', in Augustine, names the drastic participatory tension between the infinitely general and the finitely particular. And it is clear that this tension has for him also a political dimension, because it implies the equipoise of the'aristocracy' of virtue, with the 'democracy' of will and varied affinity. Thus, towards the end of Book I of *De Libero Arbitrio*, Augustine affirms clearly that theology requires a politics economically adapted to times and places: monarchy or aristocracy should be the norm where few are virtuous, and therefore the good is not much refracted; but democracy should be the norm where the good is widely (and we can infer, variously) distributed. This same tension indicates also an'economic' dimension in every sense: enjoyment as common does not inhibit individual expression – rather each is the precondition of the other.

In this light, one can see that Adam's error was to deny this ontological tension which validates at once both individual expressiveness and collective sharing, in favour of a confinement to 'virtue' or to merely *private* possession of the nonetheless *abstractly general* (whose abstraction travesties the real superabundant infinite varied specificity of the true divine universal). His error was, by an act of will, to deny the aspect in which will is hierarchically superior to virtue, and instead to affirm only the one-sided hierarchy of virtue over the will, or desire. This is tantamount to denying the participatory aspect of virtue, and imagining that one can entirely possess, with absolute security, one's own virtue. Where the security of virtue depends upon oneself, however, this is simply because one wills virtue, entirely out of one's own volition, with a will poised, like the post-Kantian will, equally between good and evil. Self-possession of virtue, which ranks above will, because it can only be good, nonetheless entirely depends upon the self-possession of the will. Adam's error was to imagine that he could possess his own will. And the legacy of this error is that human beings think of the highest good, in stoic fashion, as that which can be self-possessed, and is not subject to external erosion. The good is now thought of as the exercise of the most autonomous, which is free will.

By contrast, for Augustine, free will is only returned to us, as the arrival from outside of grace, and as the restoration of a good that we can only enjoy in common, and yet must receive according to our own unique affinities. To will, here, means to be moved beyond oneself towards a sharing and ontological distribution (according to real requirement, not formal equality) of the inexhaustible common good. It is through this moving that desire attracts once more to itself true vision, and draws along with it new resources of power for self-realisation.

D

Turning back now, to Kant, one finds instead an entirely different picture. He is not concerned with a lack of power to do good because, for him, this would be contradictory; 'ought implies can'. Nor is he concerned with a lack of guiding vision, because he has defined the good *as* a good will, or more precisely as the law which freedom gives itself, and which secures freedom. Because the good is primarily in this fashion law, it first of all concerns the form or manner in which things are done, and is indifferent as to content. To introduce some substantive good or aim towards such good into one's *primary* understanding of what is 'right' is, for Kant, actually to subvert morality.[27] 'Ends' are only admissible for Kant as a secondary consideration, and they concern first our willing of our perfect submission to the *formality* of duty, and second, our willing of the happiness of others, where 'happiness' means a mere empirical state, and *not* something inherently consequent upon virtue.[28] It is true that, owing to the conditions of our understanding, we cannot fully grasp the noumenally formal in itself as unmediated by the phenomenally substantive; but this ensures that freedom and its law remain for us an ineffable idea. Thus, both as formal and as ineffable, the Kantian 'right' which orientates the good, entirely exceeds all envisaging. And in no sense could radical evil for him connote loss of vision of the infinite, since the bounds between the finite and the infinite are permanently fixed and permit of no participatory mediation. For Kant, we will, adequately, as finite creatures with reference only to our finitude; at the same time, we do invoke a noumenal infinitude in which our spirits are truly at home; yet this infinitude only impinges on the finite as the empty and incomprehensible formality of freedom which is inexplicably able to interrupt the fatedness of phenomenal causality.

Therefore Kant does not regard the will as bound by incapacity or blindness in the intellectualist and historical fashion of St Paul and Augustine – which is as biblical as it is Greek. To the contrary, he regards the will as self-bound, as mysteriously unable to will, or as willing against itself, pathologically. He is not concerned with a Pauline acting contrary to what one wills but with a habitual failure of the will itself to will freedom. This failure has, for Kant, two aspects. First of all, we tend to adopt non-moral maxims instead of moral ones: this means that where one's actions should embody in their most immediate meaning and palpability a maxim that we could will to turn into a universal law – for example the imperative to tell the truth – they tend, instead, to be contaminated by a pragmatic and egoistic concern for individual or collective material survival and well-being: hence we usually succumb to the temptation to lie.[29] Now it might seem that here Kant does, indeed, see freedom as trammelled by the flesh in the manner of St Paul. This is not the case, however, because, in the Pauline instance, as developed by Augustine, there is a certain continuity between the lower passions and the higher desire for God. (Were it not so, for St Paul, then sexual union with a prostitute would not be able to contaminate our collective bodily union with Christ.) Correctly orientated and disciplined, the lower passions should encourage and give way to the higher desire and, indeed, this mediation is essential such that, given corrupt passions, given corrupt *flesh*, no person can truly love God – and St Paul spilt much ink denying such a self-deluding dualistic illusion. For Kant, however, there is no such sphere of participatory mediation between the physical and the psychic. For him it is rather a given that the sensory is neither moral nor immoral but, instead, amoral and so naturally orientated towards self-preservation and self-enjoyment. In consequence morality is *not* for him primarily a matter of the reorientation of the feelings, or the passions: for him a necessary 'moral feeling' is the paradoxical feeling of 'the sublime' which is the feeling of a break with feeling, or the counter-attractive attraction of self-sacrifice.[30] This sublimity also mediates, by rupture and not by participation, between the sensory with its natural egotism and the noumenal or spiritual with its equally natural and inevitable upholding of the freedom of self along with the freedom of others. Given that we are free as noumenal, and that this freedom is both intellectually and competently sufficient unto itself (as not for St Paul and Augustine) there is, in principle, absolutely no reason for it to be externally contaminated. Thus, in no way, as for the Greeks, the Church fathers and high scholastics, might sensory passions inevitably pull downwards the good will in Kant, unless entirely by its own perverse volition this will elects to substitute contingent for categorical ends.

In this way, Kantian 'radical evil' is a far more unsoundable mystery than Augustinian 'original sin' and a second aspect to our failure to will freedom redoubles the mystery. Here we do not adapt non-moral maxims but rather dilute our adoption of moral ones.[31] Kant avers that the dilution is always present, and even that the degree of such dilution is radically undecidable. This situation arises from the necessary role of 'moral feeling' in his account of morality. For, given that morality is the law of the noumenal, outside the bounds of our understanding which is confined to the noumenal, practical reason requires to be sensorily 'schematised' (or 'pictured' with an intrinsic appropriateness) and yet, unlike the categories of theoretical understanding, which are *orientated* to the phenomenal, it cannot, as reason, which is concerned with what lies beyond the phenomenal, be schematised in any truly legitimate sense.[32] Normally, Kant declares, it is improperly 'symbolised' according to a mere formal analogy, and schematised only at the curious point where we register, negatively, and yet still sensorily, a break with the phenomenal when it becomes sublimely infinitised. Such a break, Kant associates with heroism and self-sacrifice. Now in so far as these human phenomena belong with the natural sublime, they are not in any way for Kant necessarily moral: to the contrary, they concern our pride in, and awe at, a natural resistance to, and transcending of, nature. By contrast, Kant declares that the moral law in itself has nothing to do with sacrifice and admiration for sacrifice, which we tend to associate with the superogatory. Instead, the moral law commands only duty, and no one deserves admiration for fulfilling the minimum of duty; only disdain if they fail to do so.[33] And yet, according to Kant, we have *no* immediate access to this stringency and purity of duty – because for us the law of freedom is an essentially unknown idea which, indeed, we can affirm only through 'rational faith'; we are assured of freedom only at the point where we feel the attraction of giving up phenomenal well-being, or are led to admire such renunciation. Hence the moral law is only registered improperly as moral feeling, or the strange attraction of sacrifice.

This state of affairs, however, also drives the entire Kantian theory of ethics into irresolvable aporias, as he half concedes. We are supposed to know the moral law a priori, without recourse even (as with theoretical reason) to the application of categories to sensible intuition. And yet, if the moral law is registered only through the schematisation of the natural sublime, then Kant is forced to supplement his case for the a priori status of the moral law, as he does in the *Critique of Judgment*, through illegitimate appeal to the admiration of all men in all ages for the heroism of sacrifice, as an inchoate registering of the categorical imperative. (The problem here being, why has something the most humanly vital and so democratically knowable by all, even the most theoretically stupid, namely the categorical imperative, only just been discovered – by Kant.)[34]

But then, of course, the problem ensues, how is one ever to know that sacrificial motives are pure? How is one sure that even a Thomas More died for the moral law, and not out of self-pride or the love of admiration?[35] And how is one to discriminate within oneself, if only a feeling of love of self-sacrifice registers the law, and yet *even this feeling* contaminates the purity of duty and is valid only insofar as this feeling constantly negates itself, sacrificing even the love of sacrifice? If this sacrifice even of sacrifice is still, nevertheless sacrifice, how to distinguish a diminution of love of sacrifice, and denial of self, from a subtle increase of love of sacrifice and affirmation of self?

This is the aporetic situation more or less admitted by Kant in *Religion Within the Bounds of Reason Alone*. Here it is notable that some of the empirical instances he gives of 'radical evil' namely horrific slaughter in wars conducted for their own sakes, lie all too close to the instances of heroism practised for its own sake which he had earlier seen as evidence for the universal but inchoate registering of the categorical imperative.[36] The case, in Kantian terms, however, for regarding 'radical evil' as a priori, appears stronger than the case for the categorical imperative, since the a priori character of radical evil resides in the very undecidable uncertainty regarding human motivation as just described. If radical evil is more clearly a priori than the categorical imperative, then this implies, beyond Kant, that the reality of freedom itself, and its law, must remain uncertain (within the terms of a Kantian perspective).

As the self-binding of will, radical evil is a given fact precisely in the sense of an a priori. It is not, for Kant, like original sin, a biologically or socially inherited reality, because for him nothing in the causal order can affect the order of freedom. Nor, like original sin, is it a contingent event which distorts the created order, and one can note here that original sin, by remaining with narrative and an endless regress, is really *less* hypostatic and ahistorical than radical evil. Instead, radical evil is a co-given along with freedom as an inherent possibility of freedom. This makes sense because, if what defines freedom is not its willing of an infinite goal which allows the flourishing of the free creature but rather the willing of freedom as such, then freedom can be free only if it might will against itself. For this reason, radical freedom is *implied by* enlightenment autonomy and does not qualify it – though only Kant was clever enough to see this. Pure freedom is as free in self-denial as in its self-affirmation. And we have further seen that actually, under these conditions, self-denial becomes indistinguishable from self-affirmation.

In point of fact, though, Kant does not admit the pure positivity of the evil will. He retains a minimal attachment to privation theory, by distinguishing *Wille* from *Wilkur* – however much the latter, acting will may elect the unfree, it can never entirely pervert the pure faculty of will which is orientated to its own freedom and not its own destruction.[37] Nevertheless, this Kantian distinction appears unstable, precisely because Kant regards evil as an original possibility constitutive of freedom as such. For Christian tradition, this was not the case: to the contrary, it regarded evil as the very *invention* of counter-possibility – of possibility in the drastic sense of an alternative to the actual. Therefore, by making such counter-possibility a surd dimension of the will, Kant lodges possibility within being as co-equal with actuality. In order for freedom to be actual, the capacity for self-destruction must lurk; in consequence, freedom appears more original than either actuality or possibility, indeed prior to being and non-being. It was this implication of radical evil which was developed by Schelling, and we can now see that the problem with his de-ontologisation and de-infinitisation of the good, is that thereby it inherits the Kantian problem of an undedicability between good and evil.[38] If God decides to share a neutral infinite with us, what renders this a gift rather than a kind of establishing of empire via a grant of being? How might the gift of being not be perhaps disguised domination, unless the infinite we are granted to share in is in itself unshakeable, as infinite peace and harmony according to a substantive aesthetic measure? Since peace and harmony and affinity make sense only as subjectively experienced and judged, there is really no danger that the ineluctable infinite good might be merely impersonal.

After Schelling, the God beyond God of a ground of freedom prior to good and evil is transmuted by Heidegger into the ontological identical with nothing and indifferent to the resolute ontic decision for actuality.[39] Indeed, the ground for the authentic autonomy of this decision which fully admits its contingency remains a preserving of the sense of the equal validity of cancelling such a decision: this preserving constitutes our necessary 'guilt' in the face of being. Jean-Luc Nancy rightly worries that both this ontic humanist affirmation and its reverse face of resignation to the indifference of fate – whereby the ontological can manifest itself only in occluding itself (as apologetically resorted to by the later Heidegger, at the end of the Nazi era) – are both complicit with the Holocaust.[40] And yet Heidegger is logical within the terms of the legacy of radical evil: to desire, like Nancy, that the will to affirmation have ontological priority, is, in effect, to reassert the vision of good as ontological and evil as privative. If Nancy were able to admit this, then he would also be able to admit that it is perverse to suggest that the extremity of modern evil reveals the co-primacy of evil in power and in being. For this renders all being and all power superior either to good or to evil, and therefore ensures that any act of power is legitimate and 'good' as undecidably good or evil. (Or to put it in another fashion: where good is not identical with being as such, willed good has only an 'ironic' fictional status – and in the end no one acts in the name of a fiction. This is one crucial reason why there *cannot* really be a secular privation theory: secularity will not see being as such as good and so will have to identify the good in terms other than full presence of the actual. The nearest one gets to such a secular theory is Spinoza – and later Nietzsche – but Spinoza still has an immanent God and being and power as good. Nonetheless, his immanentism means that evil in the cosmos, which is deficient weakness, is fated and inevitable: but in this way it would seem that evil does get lodged in being and privation is compromised, unless the perspectives of becoming have no true reality. One can conclude, therefore, that privation theory does require transcendence and creation *ex nihilo*.)

Where being is rendered as indifferent to good and evil, Auschwitz is falsely accorded the status of a revelation; in this way taking evil seriously by granting it positive status passes over into resignation to the sway of evil itself. In this way Hitler enjoys a ghostly theoretical victory.

E

It will be recalled that the main objection of the postmodern Kantians to privation theory was that it provides an ontological excuse for evil which diminished the responsibility of freedom. Now, however, it can be seen that this charge should be thrown back at them. For on their view, the decision for evil is referred to a prior possibility for such freedom – to a freedom prior to freedom indifferent to good and evil, which alone establishes freedom as freedom. The demonic breaking in of such a radical pre-personal freedom which is *prior* to decision (Schelling's 'dark ground') surely cannot be blamed on the person so possessed? This is once more an ontological excuse. Moreover, worse still, where one starts by asserting that the good has its ground in freedom *rather than* in being, one inevitably winds up by saying that being, as neither good nor evil, itself trumps freedom. Even if at first it allows it, it must in the end obliterate it, since without participatory mediation between a partially good finite, and an absolutely good infinite, the finite good will arises only through a concealment of being with which it is essentially in conflict.

By contrast, the privation theory avoids all excuses, by denying that evil is lodged in any reality, power or being whatsoever. Somehow, it is impossibly instigated by will alone. If it is true, as we have seen, that it is not really *caused* by freedom, since freedom, as free, causes only the good, then this shows that the bad will cannot *even* blame a possibility lodged within the order of causality (within which freedom, for the tradition, as not for Kant, itself lies). And as for the idea that finitude is an excuse, this may apply to the ancient Greeks but not to Augustine and Dionysius. For them, there is nothing defective in finitude as such, and nothing in finitude to encourage moral evil: rather what is defective is the disallowing of finite things from reaching their own proper finite share of perfection. (For Dionysius, it should be noted, privation is more the removal of the good than the removal of being, since the good for him lies beyond being; this detail does not really affect the present argument, however.)[41]

Thus, evil for the Christian tradition was radically without cause – indeed, it was not even self-caused but rather the (impossible) refusal of cause. Since inherited evil was held to have already impaired our finitude, there was, indeed, in us a causal bias to evil; yet, because grace renews our will, our evil decision to refuse grace is as groundless and causeless as Adam's original sin. For this reason, according to Augustine, the origin of evil must be passed over as 'darkness and silence' as if there were a dreadful *apophasis* of evil that parodied the apophasis of the Divine.[42] Since evil is uncaused, there is, indeed, a sense in which it possesses us like an anti-cause proceeding from a satanic black hole (as J.-L. Marion argues – the non-existence of the Devil *is* the existence of the Devil).[43] But when it possesses us, not only are we responsible for this possession, it is also that this possession delivers the very phenomenon of autonomous responsibility. Evil is just that for which alone we are solely responsible. Evil is self-governing autonomy – evil *is* the Kantian good, the modern good.

Since evil is for privation theory so radically uncaused, it does not require to be justified by an ontodicy. Indeed, the rise of theodicy, and so of ontodicy, is much more correlated with a post-Scotist univocity of being, and a sense that, if the finite equally *is*, as much as the infinite, then even the lacking that is evil equally *is* along with the good: in consequence, the presence of evil must be 'justified' in terms of providential design.[44]

F

From such theodicy and ontodicy, the theory of radical evil is, in fact, by no means immune. If, for Kant, human good will is only evidenced in resistance to suffering, then certainly non-moral evil in nature plays for him a providential role. But, in addition, the most 'signal' virtue is for Kant displayed in our resistance to other human beings. Here moral evil, also, is a providential training ground for virtue, because Kant explicitly states that only the exercise of heroism in warfare (which, it will be recalled, is a sublime schema of the moral law) could have gradually trained up the strength of the will, such that it is finally able to resist its own self-denial, and to arrive at the moral preconditions for the establishing of 'perpetual peace' among the nations.[45] The passage to moral virtue via the sublime also traverses to exercise of radical evil, just as the path to civilised peace lies dialectically through warfare.

We have already seen, however, how this theodicy and ontodicy comes unstuck: the purportedly moral self-overcoming might still be the natural heroic will – at once sublime and radically evil, or one might well say, Miltonically satanic. How is one to decide? As Jacques Lacan pointed out, the Sadean sadistic will also wills only its own freedom, and is also prepared to sacrifice comfort, security and survival for the sake of its own exercise.[46]

But Kant was near to conceding this problem. How did he try to cope with it? The answer is that he sought to supplement morality with grace. Supposedly, Kant brings religion within the bounds of reason by reducing it to morality but we have already seen how practical reason problematically transgresses the bounds established by theoretical reasons, since it claims knowledge of noumenal freedom. And we have also seen how, when moral knowledge is brought back within the schematic bounds of the phenomenal, our claim to know the noumenal as moral is rendered uncertain. Thus, practical reason, if it is to be saved, must on the grounds of its own rational demand, be *supplemented* by religious faith. *Religion within the Boundaries of Mere Reason* should really be entitled 'reason outside its own bounds in the sphere of religion'. For it turns out that ethics, the essence of religion, cannot after all dispense with the mere 'inessentials' or *parerga* of religion which exceed, for Kant, the ethical. Thus, it cannot dispense with unmerited grace, with the sacraments, with the organised Church.[47] Grace must be invoked because we can only distinguish the will to freedom from radical evil if we have faith that our aspiration to a good will is graciously taken by God as equivalent to his infinite and ineluctably Holy Will (here Kant clearly has not gone as far as Schelling). And to have this faith is also to have faith in an eschatological discrimination when the good wills will finally be divided from the bad wills, and the mere empirical pursuit of egoistic happiness will be finally subordinated to freedom since the virtuous will be rewarded with happiness and the vicious with unhappiness. Moreover, this faith cannot merely be entertained by individuals because radical evil arises for Kant (here influenced by Rousseau) only from cultural association which gives rise to envy and greed and so forth, and contaminates a supposed 'private' exercise of moral autonomy.[48] One can contrast Augustine here, for whom the good will is enjoyment, according to a specific refraction that is not in rivalry with other specific refractions, of an essentially common good. The only way, according to Kant, to combat this corruption of the inward by the social, is to set up, not merely a state founded on a social contract and directed by a general will but also a church which seeks really to overcome and not to inhibit the inner desires of egotism. A church is supposed, for Kant, to engender a kind of 'general moral will' and its sacraments, though arbitrary signs, are necessary reminders of the hope of the eschaton, without which morality remains uncertain.[49]

And in this fashion, the theory of radical evil, which is supposed to locate evil within human limits, must after all, as Kant admits (though not his contemporary heirs) in order to avoid antinomianism, invoke divine grace. Kantian free will is not the Augustinian free will, however, identified with grace as the gift par excellence of grace. Instead, for Kant, freedom is no gift, but an inert *given*, and equally given along with it, is radical evil: so if it is a gift, it is a poisoned one. And as for Luther, free will as such cannot aspire to God; this Lutheran legacy is part of what leads Kant to conclude that finite will simply in itself is 'bound'.[50] Thus, bizarrely enough, Kantian grace is *far more* positivistically and pietistically irruptive than Augustinian or Thomist grace. For it does not give free will but juristically supplements its (ontologically) *given* deficiency since here the will to the good has reduced to the mere will to have a good will in the hope that God, by grace, will *impute* to us a good will.

If the Kantian account of grace and free will as it were parodies the Augustinian one, then so also does his account of the Church. For the Augustinian, as for the Pauline vision, the ecclesia aspires to and partially realises a real harmony of differentiated persons by blending together a diversity of characters and roles according to a beautiful and analogical affinity that is rooted in the Church's manifestation of the incarnate Logos. Kant seems almost to come near to this, and yet the diverse persons in his Church are only united under the abstract formal resemblance of their wills, and only aspire to be 'one body' according to a just matching of happiness to freedom. It is not that here the specific happiness which is also the specific freedom of one (within a scheme of teleological flourishing) is concretely blended with the specific free happiness of another, according to the advent of affinity under grace, as for the Pauline view which Augustine elaborated. (Not seeing this distinction, Arendt, like many others, overrates the anti-liberal potential of 'beautiful' reflexive judgement in the third critique.)[51]

And in this way it becomes apparent that radical evil does *not* offer a secular view of evil, but only an alternative theology which is an alternative account both of theological reason and of divine revelation to the traditional account provided by Christian privation theory. Now, then, we can attempt a theological discrimination between the two. And what is apparent is that, paradoxically, only privation theory (plus original sin and satanic possession) allow for a *human* discrimination of good and evil in the here and now, and so the possibility of a substantively just social order. By contrast, the theology of radical evil is also a theology of radical eschatological postponement of a guaranteed good and a guaranteed justice. And this theology cannot really allow any *anticipation* of the eschaton.

G

It is finally the political implications of the Kantian legacy which I wish to explore. I have already defended at length the view of evil as privation which undergirds the view of evil as banal. The two views are not, however, identical: it is possible for negativity to take a sublime, quasi-heroic form. Nevertheless, one can extend Arendt's theory of banality by arguing that the political quasi-satanism of the perpetrators of state horror is usually prepared by an incremental piling up of small deficient preferences which gradually and 'accidentally' (as Aquinas argued) produce the monstrous. (Aquinas after Dionysius speaks of 'accidental' causing of evil, where Augustine seems to speak of no causing at all. By this, however, they mean that pursuit of a too limited good 'accidentally' causes the lack of good that should ensue. This is an odd sort of accidentality because it really brings nothing about and involves not merely a non-intended consequence but also an overlooked one.)

To give an example of this 'accidental' process: in the seventeenth-century colony of Virginia, female servants proved at once unruly and overdependent upon their masters in circumstances of instability and great reliance on women's labour.[52] It proved harder and harder to grant them relative independence after their apprenticeships, and also harder and harder to ensure the legitimacy of their offspring. Gradually, their servitude drifted into legal slavery, and inheritance for slaves was directed for obvious reasons of convenience through the female line (though the irrelevance of paternity also gave savage licence to rape and seduction by masters). Soon there were more black female servants and slaves than white. Soon after that, there were only black female slaves, and then their children, female and male, were all members of a black slave class. I exaggerate deliberately but one can see the point: there was no original satanic monster who intended initially to enslave black people because they were inferior but, in the end, there were such monsters with such intentions, retrospectively legitimating an appalling outcome which had resulted from inadequate, but scarcely unambiguously malicious, intentions within the narrow light of their day.

Likewise with the Holocaust, the satanism of the final solution was the outcome of a long drift of deficient science, deficient philosophy, deficient politics and deficient sociality. To take the converse view, and to imagine that Hitler was a deliberate satanist or even that a Manson can attain a fully satanic perspective, is to lend credence to that saddest of all the errors of evil (and of Satan) whereby it always imagines that it is yet more evil than it really is. For evil to be at all, it must still deploy and invoke some good, yet it would like to forget this: evil as positive is evil's own fondest illusion. Insisting this way upon the pathos of evil and upon its creeping and incremental character by no means, as many fear, amounts to a taking away from the responsibility of individual wills. On the contrary, this insistence points to the gravity of even the smallest responsibilities; the dangers of apparently good intentions (which it does *not* quite deem as tragically unavoidable); also it does not excuse or regard as inevitable the long-encouraged emergence of 'monstrous' wills. Nor does this insistence tend to deny the unprecedented character of the Holocaust: all that it denies is the notion of a metaphysical revelation of an unexpected ontological status for evil. By contrast, it points to the Holocaust's real disclosure of the terrible capacities of an ancient depravity whose character, nonetheless, remains tediously as before.

But if the final solution was the outcome of a long incremental drift, then we must finally ask, was the Kantian legacy itself part of this process?

Hannah Arendt in part considered this to be the case. Albert Eichmann did, as she noted, have a self-admitted Kantian habit of mind insofar as he thought sovereign law must be obeyed; must be obeyed without exception; and must be obeyed beyond the call of duty in the spirit of the letter.[53] For Arendt, it is this popularised Kantianism which explains how the utterly inefficient Nazis were nonetheless able to co-opt the internalised efficiency of the German people.

Arendt, however, took Eichmann's Kantian habits to be a parody of Kantian nobility – and, indeed, it appears that Eichmann himself had thought so. Thus, she says that, for the ineffability of the sovereign law of free will as such, Eichmann had substituted the sovereign will of the Führer. This is not to be confused with the command of the categorical imperative. But is it not? And was Eichmann merely parodying?

Politics, for Kant, though rooted in the moral law, had to deal

mainly with the contingent, empirical imperatives of material well-
being. We have seen, however, how the categorical imperative has to
be schematised and symbolised in terms of these lesser imperatives.
And the Kantian account of the just polity suggests indeed that the
self-governing state symbolises the self-governing moral individual
according to a formal analogy ('symbol' for Kant, always denotes a
mere common ratio, which is also how he understands 'analogy'). This
analogy involves nothing more nor less than *the division of power*. At the
centre of the state should stand an unchanging sovereign power whose
issuing of laws without enacting them renders it akin to the transcend-
ent law of freedom in the individual. Kant himself makes this analogy
when, in *Religion within the Boundaries of Mere Reason*, he compares
God the Father, who is the ultimate source of the moral law, to a political sovereign.[54] God the Son is then compared to a political executive,
and also to the individual will which is incited by moral feeling to obey
the ineffable law. Thus, we see that, for Kant, the political executive is
akin to individual moral activity, inspired by moral feeling. Finally, God
the Holy Spirit is at once like the political judiciary and the individual
judgement. These two are akin because they both seek to apply the
law to particular circumstances, and to match freedom to happiness,
according to extrinsic desert, not intrinsic co-belonging. In this way
Kant, according to his logic of essential inessentials (*parerga*), reveals
that his hierarchy of cold duty over warm feeling is grounded in a het-
erodox and Arian Trinity. At the same time, he reveals how the same
Trinity secures a political sovereignty which can be taken as absolute and persisting over and above what is enacted and judged in its
name.

To be absolutely fair to Kant here, he is clear that tyranny results
when the powers are confused with each other and especially when the
executive usurps the sovereignty.[55] By this measure Hitler would surely
have been deemed a tyrant. Kant allows for the popular overthrow of a
corrupt executive and judiciary, and this was the basis for his qualified
support for the French Revolution. Nevertheless, in his famous footnote
on regicide in *The Metaphysics of Morals*, Kant ferociously disallows
overthrow of the sovereign power as utterly contradictory.[56] So where
sovereign and executive have coalesced, albeit through usurpation (as
in the Nazi case) what Kantian basis remains to support resistance and
non-obedience, even if the original usurpation was denounced, since
the *de jure* basis of sovereignty in Kant seems to reduce to the de facto?

For Kant, sovereign political authority *is*, in fact, the point where moral and political rule, categorical and contingent imperative, actually come together. Since the sovereign power embodies the collective general will, and is the absolute source of all legality, to will against the sovereign power in person is to will against political legality. This cannot be universally willed, under the maxim 'I will to destroy a corrupt sovereign power' because it removes the very basis of legality, just as lying for Kant destroys the possibility of trust and thus of all free association. Hence regicide *does* fall foul of the categorical imperative, and to oppose the political sovereign *is* to oppose the moral sovereign. This conclusion really results because the ground of legitimacy in Kant is entirely one of immanent consent and procedural emission from a consensually established centre: thus he cannot allow that a substantive natural law would remain, even in the absence of sovereign power. To the contrary, the only political law of nature for Kant is that there must be an earthly sovereign centre if there is to be collective justice. Here the closed bounds of human reason which disallow a mediation of the infinite, also absolutise established human authority. This absolutisation is very extreme in Kant since he describes regicide as the *supreme* instance of radical evil and of sublime horror, almost displacing the crucifixion of the Son of God in this respect. Here the only thing that prevents regicide as an act of freedom from being seen as an act of moral liberation is the identification of the sovereign idea of freedom we must respect, with a *given*, established, specific exercise of freedom by a political ruler. But then how else, short of the eschaton, *are* we now to discriminate a good will from a bad one? Even though Kant never commits himself to this conclusion, it seems to follow if one thinks through his aporias to their ends. Kantian morality, deconstructed, says, you know your will is good when you obey the law of the state without exception and beyond the call of duty. Eichmann had it more right than he knew.

If this analysis is correct, then the Nazi episode casts suspicion not just upon Fichte or Muller or Nietzsche or Heidegger but on the main lines of the Germanic philosophical legacy to which the second half of the twentieth century has remained in some ways perhaps too dangerously subservient. This is not, however, to indict an entire culture, because Kant's most decisive and insightful opponents – Jacobi, Hermann, Herder – were also German and also strongly informed a later Germanic legacy. Moreover, in relation to the Nazis, many other currents are equally culpable, including an originally British evolutionism in some of its manifestations.[57] But the ambiguity of the Kantian legacy does raise, specifically, the question which must still haunt us, of the collusion between liberalism and totalitarianism. Moral liberalism tends to engender an uneasy oscillation between absolute promotion of one's own freedom for any goal whatsoever, and absolute sacrifice to the freedom of the other, again without any conditions as to the goals that others should pursue. Writ large at the level of the state, this tends to produce a large-scale oscillation between a present collective identity as an end in itself, and the endless self-sacrifice of individuals for the sake of a better future. Thus, political liberalism itself engenders today an increasingly joyless and puritanical world in which we work harder and harder towards increasingly obscure ends while 'surplus' populations of the young, the old, the cultural misfits, the foreign and the poor are increasingly marginalised, disciplined, put to degrading work, or indeed simply destroyed. The liberal state already exhibits a certain totalitarian drift and may always become really totalitarian at the point where its empty heart is besieged by an irrational cult of race, class, science, style or belief.

This slide of liberalism towards totality confirms that where free will as such is identified with the good, the promotion of self-respect and autonomy will be simultaneously and indistinguishably the promotion of self-inhibition and radical evil. But for privation theory it is this very promotion of abstract free autonomy that itself enshrines what is evil, and radically deficient.

Notes

1 See Joan Copjec (ed.), *Radical Evil* (London: Verso, 1996); Jean-Luc Nancy, *The Experience of Freedom*, trans. Bridget McDonald (Stanford: Stanford University Press, 1993); Slavoj Zizek, *For They Know Not What They Do: Enjoyment as a Political Factor* (London: Verso, 1991). See also, to some extent, Jacques Derrida, 'Faith and Knowledge: The Two Sources of "Religion" at the Limits of Reason Alone', in J. Derrida and G. Vattimo (eds), *Religion* (Cambridge: Polity, 1988), pp. 1–79.

2 Immanuel Kant, *'Religion within the Boundaries of Mere Reason'*, trans. George di Giovanni, appearing as a chapter in Immanuel Kant, *Religion and Rational Theology*, trans. and ed. Allen W. Wood and George di Giovanni (Cambridge: Cambridge University Press, 1996), pp. 57–213.

3 Hannah Arendt, *Eichmann in Jerusalem: A Report on the Banality of Evil* (London: Penguin, 1992).

4 See Hannah Arendt, *Love and Saint Augustine* (Chicago: Chicago University Press, 1996) and the introduction by J.V. Scott and J. C. Stark, 'Rediscovering Hannah Arendt'.
5 Arendt, *Eichmann*, p. 137.
6 See Michael Halberstramm, *Totalitarianism and the Modern Conception of Politics* (New Haven: Yale, 1999).
7 For a good account of this, see Roy F. Baumeister, *Evil: Inside Human Cruelty and Violence* (New York: W. H. Freeman, 1997), esp. pp. 375–88.
8 See Jacob Rogozinski, 'Hell on Earth: Hannah Arendt in the Face of Hitler', in *Philosophy Today*, 37: 3/4, 1993, pp. 257–74, esp. p. 267.
9 Kant, '*Religion within the Boundaries of Mere Reason*', 6: 20–6: 53, pp. 69–97.
10 See Richard L. Rubinstein's classic text, *The Cunning of Reason: Mass Death and the American Future* (New York: Harper and Row, 1975).
11 Dionysus the Areopagite, *The Divine Names*, Book 4, pp. 19–35, 716D–736B, esp. p. 31: 'it is not principles and powers which produce evil, but impotence and weakness'.
12 Dionysus, *The Divine Names*, Book 4, 20: 'Abolish the good and you will abolish being, life, desire, movement, everything'; Augustine, *City of Good*, XIV, II: 'The choice of the will . . . is genuinely free, only when it is not subservient to faults and sins'.
13 See Slavoj Zizek, 'Selfhood as Such is Spirit' in Copjec, ed., *Radical Evil*, pp. 1–30. In the same volume, see Jacob Rogozinski, 'It makes us wrong: Kant and Radical Evil', pp. 30–45. See also Jean-Luc Nancy, *The Experience of Freedom*, chapter 12, 'Evil: Decision', pp. 121–41.
14 Both Paul Ricoeur and Pierre Watté interpret Kant as offering the finest interpretation of a Pauline 'Self-Inhibition', in a fashion that 'frees' the theme of liberty from cosmology, and discovers the seed of evil to be purely in the will taken as a *positive* assertion of self. The whole of this present essay is designed in part to demonstrate that such a view is historically false, pseudo-profound, and profoundly dangerous. Ricoeur also sees such positivity of evil as anticipated in primitive 'symbolisation' of evil as visible taint or disorder. This aspect of aesthetic disharmony, however, was rightly viewed by Dionysus as also privative: nothing that *appears* to us lacks beauty – rather what offends the eye is a deficiency of appropriate, requisite order that should pertain variously in any given instance. Thus, evil for him, while negative is also 'an inharmonious mingling of discordances': *Divine Names*, 4, 31. The invocation of an aesthetic aspect to privation does, nonetheless, serve to emphasise that evil as privation is not pure and simply nothing: as 'substance' it may be nothing, but in its effect of removal and deficiency it engenders a distorted positive act, even though, as positive, this act is not distorted. See Pierre Watté, *Structures, Philosophiques du Péché Originel: S. Augustin, S. Thomas, Kant* (Gembloux: J. Duculot S.A., 1974) and

the preface by Paul Ricoeur, esp. p. 8 and Paul Ricoeur, *The Symbolism of Evil*, trans. Emerson Buchanan (Boston: Beacon, 1967), pp. 70–100.

15 At this point these thinkers are incorporating a Levinasian thematic.

16 See Zizek, 'Selfhood as Such is Spirit'. Also see F. W. J. Schelling, 'Philosophical Investigations into the Essence of Human Freedom and Related Matters', in *Philosophy of German Idealism*, ed. Ernest Behler (New York: Continuum, 1987) and F. W. J. Schelling, *Of Human Freedom*, trans. J. Gutman (Chicago: Open Court, 1936).

17 See Watté, *Structures Philosophiques*, pp. 128–215.

18 Augustine, *On the Free Choice of the Will*, trans. Thomas Williams (Indianapolis: Hackett, 1993), Book I, 1, 4, 12, 13, 25; Book II, 14, 16, 13, p. 57: 'This is our freedom when we are subject to the [infinite] truth.'

19 Augustine, *City of God*, XIV, 13; *On the Free Choice of the Will*, Book I, 8.

20 Augustine, *On the Free Choice of the Will*, Book I, 11: once 'inordinate desire' has gripped the mind after Adam, it takes 'false things' for true, and becomes a prey to 'fear' and 'anxiety'. See further Book III, 3, 4, 18, p. 106: '. . . as it is [since the Fall] they [humans] are not good, and it is not in their power to be good, either because they do not see how they ought to be, or because they lack the power to be what they see they ought to be'; 'because of our ignorance we lack the free choice or the will to choose to act rightly'; 'or – even when we do see what is right and will to do it, we cannot do it because of the resistance of carnal habit'. Here Augustine is commenting on Romans 7: 18: 'To will the good is present to me, but I find no way to do it', and Galatians 5: 17, 'You do not do what you will, as flesh and spirit lust against each other.' Augustine continues, 'thus we who knew what was right but did not do it, lost the knowledge of what is right, and we who had the power but not the will to act rightly lost the power even when we have the will'. He then has to face the objection that if our free will is so inhib- ited by loss of vision and incapacity, then we are not to blame for failure to will the good. But he answers (p. 107), 'Perhaps their complaint would be justified if there were no victor over error and inordinate desire. But in fact there is one who is present everywhere and speaks in many ways through the creation that serves him as Lord. He calls out to those who have turned their backs on him, and instructs them who believe in him.' Desire of the good remains possible through grace, and so our lack of vision and incapacity are exceeded and potentially overcome (since the Pauline impotence, recognised *after* grace, is not really seen by Paul as an absolute check). See also Book II, 16, where it is made clear that the discernment of truth by will/desire is also the kenotic descent of divine wisdom towards us. At section 52 of *On the Spirit and the Letter* Augustine stresses that free will itself is the supreme gift of grace.

21 See Martin Luther, 'The Bondage of the Will', in *Martin Luther's Basic*

Theological Writings, ed. Timothy F. Lull (Minneapolis: Fortress, 1989), pp. 178–9.

22 See note 20, above and the passage quoted from *On the Free Choice of the Will*, Book III, 18, p. 107.

23 *On the Free Choice of the Will*, Book III, 18, p. 107: 'You are not to blame for your unwilling ignorance [the legacy of Adam's sin], but because you fail to ask about what you do not know. You are not blamed because you do not bind up your own wounds [the post-Adamic incapacity], but because you spurn the one who wants to heal you. For no one is prevented from leaving behind the disadvantage of ignorance and seeking the advantage of knowledge, or from humbly confessing his weakness, so that God, whose help is effortless and unerring, will come to his assistance. When someone acts wrongly out of ignorance, or cannot do what he rightly wills to do, his actions are called sins because they have their origin in that first sin, which was committed by free will. The later sins are the just result of that first sin.' This shows that Augustine's account of original sin is objective, collective, historical and realist, and involves no contorted doctrines of subjectivity which concern an inevitable willing of the bad for which we are to blame. These rather descend to us from Luther and Kant.

24 James Alison, *The Joy of Being Wrong* (New York: Crossroad, 1998).

25 *On the Free Choice of the Will*, Book II, 19.

26 *On the Free Choice of the Will*, Book II, 9, p. 49. Augustine associates the common true/good with light, enjoyed by all sight at once, unlike a touchable object, which we can only touch one at a time, in turn. However, it seems to me implicit in Augustine that in the Eucharist 'sight' and 'touch' are fixed since here the most intimate touching of eating, is a simultaneous and collective eating of a body not 'used up', and not enjoyed exclusively 'one at a time' by eating. So here a body is like light and in this fashion the Eucharist supremely combines the most common and the most intimate. Therefore the Eucharist most exemplifies true writing or desire, and participation. Augustine in this dialogue also figures the dialectic of common and particular with the co-belonging of 'wisdom' with 'number'. Here he is not always easy to follow, but roughly it seems that 'number' is at times associated with the eternal divine ideas, and at other times with the diversity of the creation: as in God numbering sparrows and the hairs on our head. By contrast, wisdom is associated with the kenotic 'reach' of omnipotence to the ends of the earth, as with the figure of personified wisdom rushing to meet us, which Augustine alludes to. In this way the eternal numbers reach to the created numbers, and Augustine indicates that the diversity of instance and preference is not alien to the common, universal, eternal and measured.

27 Immanuel Kant, *The Metaphysics of Morals*, trans. Mary Gregor (Cambridge: Cambridge University Press, 1991), p. 183 [378], p. 193 [389]; *Critique of*

Practical Reason, trans. L. W. Beck (Upper Saddle River, NJ: Prentice Hall, 1993), Part I, Book I, chapter I, II, pp. 65–8; *'Religion within the Boundaries of Mere Reason'*, 6: 22, p. 72; 6: 24–6 :31, pp. 73–8.

28 This is why the 'revisionist' attempt to read Kant as a virtue ethicist cannot be rendered plausible.

29 *'Religion within the Boundaries of Mere Reason'*, 6: 29, p. 77; *Groundwork of the Metaphysics of Morals,* trans. H. J. Paton (New York: Harper and Row, 1964), Preface vi–viii, p. 57 [389–90].

30 *Metaphysics of Morals,* pp. 201–2 [400]; *Groundwork,* pp. 128–9 [460], *Critique of Judgment,* trans. J. C. Meredith (Oxford: Oxford University Press, 1989), Part I, § 4, pp. 46–8 § 6, p. 51; § 26 p. 103; § 29, p. 120.

31 *'Religion within the Boundaries of Mere Reason'*, 6: 30, p. 77.

32 *Groundwork,* pp. 128–9 [460]; *Critique of Practical Reason,* Part I, Book I, chapter I, pp. 32–3, 43–52; chapter II, pp. 70–4; *Critique of Judgment,* Part I § 29, p. 121; § 30, p. 134; § 59, pp. 221–5.

33 *Groundwork,* p. 128 [460].

34 *Critique of Judgement,* Part I, § 29, pp. 112–13.

35 *Critique of Practical Reason,* Part II, pp. 161–3.

36 *'Religion within the Boundaries of Mere Reason'*, 6: 33, p. 80.

37 *'Religion within the Boundaries of Mere Reason'*, 6: 36, p. 82.

38 Schelling, *Of Human Freedom.*

39 See J.-L. Nancy, *The Experience of Freedom,* § 4, 'The Space Left Free by Heidegger', pp. 33–43.

40 Nancy, *The Experience of Freedom,* § 4. and 'Evil: Decision', pp. 121–41. Nancy also gives analyses of freedom highly compatible with Augustinianism, which describe it as that which 'surprises us, rather than as something we control, and as primordially 'sharing', since every free expression must 'give' something of oneself to others. See § 3 'Impossibility of the Question of Freedom: Fact and Right Indistinguishable', pp. 21–32.

41 For example, Dionysus, *The Divine Names,* Book 4, 26: 'there is no evil nature – rather evil lies in the inability of things to reach their *acme* of perfection'.

42 Augustine, *City of God,* XII, 7: 'To try to discover the causes of such defection . . . is like trying to see darkness or to hear silence.'

43 Jean-Luc Marion, 'Le Mal en Personne', in *Protégomenes à la Charité* (Paris: La Différance, 1986), pp. 11–43.

44 For Scotus and after, see Catherine Pickstock, *After Writing* (Oxford: Blackwell, 1999), pp. 121–67. Privation theory plays little role within Leibniz's, *Theodicy.* See G. W. Leibniz, *Theodicy,* ed. Austin Farrer (La Salle, IL: Open Court, 1985).

45 See, for example, Augustine, *On the Free Choice of the Will,* Book III, 15, pp. 100–1.

46 Jacques Lacan, 'Kant with Sade', trans. James Swenson, *October 51,* winter, 1989. See, for example, Augustine, *On the Free Choice of the Will,* Book III, 15, pp. 100–1; Slavoj Zizek, 'Why is Sade the Truth of Kant?'; Lacan in *For They Know Not What They Do,* pp. 229–41.

47 *'Religion within the Boundaries of Mere Reason'*, Parts III and IV, pp. 129–215.

48 *'Religion within the Boundaries of Mere Reason'*, 6: 94–5, pp. 129–30.

49 *'Religion within the Boundaries of Mere Reason'*, 6: 151–6: 202, pp. 175–215 esp. 6: 153, p. 176.

50 Luther, 'The Bondage of the Will', pp. 178–9.

51 See Halberstramm's discussion of Arendt's use of the *Critique of Judgment* in *Totalitarianism.*

52 See Kathleen M. Brown, *Good Wives, Nasty Wenches and Anxious Patriarchs: Gender, Race and Power in Colonial Virginia* (Chapel Hill, NC: University of North Carolina Press, 1996).

53 Arendt, *Eichmann in Jerusalem.*

54 *'Religion within the Boundaries of Mere Reason'*, 6: 139–43, pp. 165–8.

55 *Metaphysics of Morals,* Part II, section I, § 44–§ 48, pp. 123–8.

56 *Metaphysics of Morals,* Part II, section I, § 49, pp. 129–33, and Immanuel Kant, 'Perpetual Peace', in *Kant: Political Writings,* trans. A. B. Nisbet (Cambridge: Cambridge University Press, 1991), p. 124.

57 See the magnificent book by David Depew and Bruce H. Weber, *Darwinism Evolving: Systems Dynamics and the Genealogy of Natural Selection* (Cambridge, MA: MIT Press, 1997).

Chapter 3

CONSTRUCTIVISM AND EVIL

Peri Roberts

Constructivism in political theory is opposed to both scepticism and foundationalism. Against the sceptic the constructivist hopes to defend the objectivity of at least some political principles. Against the foundationalist the constructivist hopes to show that the defence of objectivity need not appeal to any account of the necessary and unchanging foundations for moral reasoning. Evil has traditionally been seen in foundationalist terms, as a theological concept depending on the existence of God or as depending on some alternative scheme of absolute moral judgement, in order to mark out a special sort of wrongness. When these foundations have been challenged by sceptical attack the idea of evil has seemed deprived of its sense. Many contemporary accounts seek to 'debunk' evil, to relativise it or to recast it as just a tool in the armoury of politicians. Given constructivism's non-foundationalism, must it be similarly sceptical towards evil, or can a place for the notion of evil be found in constructivist theories?[1]

After briefly laying out several contemporary sceptical positions that are keen to see evil in purely political and instrumental terms, this chapter will argue that evil can play three distinct roles in constructivist accounts and in doing so will defend an understanding of evil that goes well beyond the instrumental. Constructivism can make space for:

1. *Judgements of evil:* constructivist accounts of political morality get off the ground by reference to what are regarded as paradigmatic instances of moral reasoning. Our specific judgements about what constitutes evil can play this role.
2. *Conceptions of evil:* constructivist accounts of political morality aim to identify principles of justice that should be regarded as

especially weighty. Various conceptions of evil can be regarded as making claims about the content of such principles of justice.

3. *The concept of evil:* central to the idea of evil is the idea of the distinctly wrong, different in character from other wrongs. This notion of a 'threshold' within wrongness marks an important distinction for political constructivism. The idea of such a threshold makes possible the idea of a thin universalism that is important to plausible notions of political constructivism.

THE 'INSTRUMENTAL' USE OF EVIL

Some contemporary writers on evil, rejecting the straightforward religious account of evil, hope to expose talk of evil for what they think it really is, a rhetorical tool that is potentially very dangerous.[2] To this end Richard Bernstein opens his short book, *The Abuse of Evil*, with two quotes. The first, from George W. Bush immediately after the events of 11 September 2001, claims that, 'Today our nation saw evil, the very worst of human nature.' The second is from Moktada al-Sadr when it became clear what sort of response to 9/11 Bush had managed to mobilise; 'America has shown its evil intentions and the proud Iraqi people cannot accept it.'[3] Of course, there is no formal reason why both of these attributions of evil cannot be appropriate but the ease with which each adopts the language of evil to describe 'the enemy' has prompted some commentators to ask whether evil, like beauty, is in the eye of the beholder. Bernstein certainly thinks so and argues that evil 'tends to be used in an excessively vague and permissive manner in order to condemn whatever one finds abhorrent'.[4] Emotive and motivating claims about evilness are central to attempts to mobilise a population by identifying and demonising an enemy. Bernstein argues that the language of evil is used as an instrument of strategy.

> The religious and moral talk of good and evil is best understood as a *political* means for distinguishing ourselves from our enemies ... That is precisely what the United States has done; it has *constructed* an all-inclusive, threatening enemy – 'the Servants of Evil'. And in constructing this enemy, it has played on and manipulated people's fears and anxieties.[5]

Obviously, understanding conflict in terms of this simplistic Manichaean identification of the forces of good and evil is a strategy available to, and utilised by, both sides of any conflict. Certainly, no one argues that it is they who represent the servants of evil battling diabolically against the defenders of all that is good.

Similarly, Phillip Cole, in *The Myth of Evil*, seeks to generalise this approach to questions of evil.[6] The language of evil, he argues, generates imaginary monsters that are used by the powerful and by those seeking power to build 'communities of fear'. Fear of an evil enemy that threatens to destroy the community, in the form of either outsiders or an enemy within, reinforces the shared sense of community and encourages it to place its defence in the hands of the only people who can save it, the wise and powerful people who spotted the enemy for them in the first place.[7] Evil, for Cole, is a mythological, rather than a philosophical, concept that is a tool in the construction of narrative mythologies wherever you need to identify the person or group that is playing the bad guys in the story you are telling.[8] It has found its uses not only in conflict in the Middle East but also, for example, by the Nazis in their portrayal of the Jews, in the seventeenth–century eastern European 'epidemic' of vampirism and in the western European and North American witchcraft crazes. None of these incidents provides an edifying account of the narrative of evil. Recognising this, Cole argues, 'we ought to dispose of the concept of evil', 'abandon' it as 'a highly dangerous and inhumane discourse and we are better off without it'.[9]

These positions intend to 'debunk' evil, to expose its use as at best subjective and at worst partial and dangerous. When we describe something as evil, no matter what we think we are doing, our language is best understood instrumentally. Where evil has traditionally identified a special wrong or injustice that is especially awful from any point of view, these sceptical positions relativise evil to the interests of particular groups. On this understanding, attributions of evil are instruments that serve a purpose, and that purpose is to advance group interests. So, is this what evil is, just a vilifying word that we use to identify 'the other' as a threat, either to reinforce social ties, to justify our bad behaviour towards them, or simply to name our fears or temptations?

THE CONSTRUCTIVIST USES OF EVIL

Although sceptical accounts that highlight the instrumental use of evil are extremely plausible, it may not pay to dismiss a more straightforward understanding of evil so quickly. Even if we successfully and convincingly debunk many cynical uses of evil, this does not mean that all uses of evil are cynical. Evil may continue to identify something important that can only be captured by an account that picks out a set of wrongs that are qualitatively different from other wrongs. If political theory sets evil aside as a category it may be doing so prematurely. Evil is traditionally a religious idea, however, and this is a time when the mainstream of contemporary political theory has become increasingly wary of the foundational premises of religious reasoning. Religious reasoning is not singled out here. This wariness marks a wider suspicion of the claims of foundational accounts to be suitable grounds for general justifications or explanations. Foundational claims may serve to justify policy or action to those already within the cultures and traditions that are their source, or to those who are already committed to the appropriate religious beliefs, but fail to offer reasons to those who are not. To some extent, we appear to be generalising the sceptic's point, that notions of evil are very definitely limited in scope and relativised to groups who accept the foundational assumptions they depend on. If we accept this sort of understanding, it looks difficult to retain the idea of evil as a special sort of wrong that is also wrong cross-culturally. On the other hand, contemporary political theory has generated a distinctive and non-foundationalist approach to general justification: constructivism.[10]

While not necessarily arguing that foundational justification is impossible, constructivism maintains that it is not at all necessary if we are concerned with the possibility of objectively justifying principles. Rather than 'discovering' foundations, constructivism argues that objectively justified principles can be thought of as 'constructed' by human beings in their exercise of practical reasoning and without their having to make controversial foundational assumptions. The objectivity of principles is a consequence of their ability to withstand a process of constructive critical reasoning that constantly challenges claims to impartiality and generality. Principles that survive this critically reflective process are treated as (always only provisionally) justified until their claim to impartial and objective status is weakened by new ideas or new encounters that highlight a partial or subjective element that had previously gone unnoticed.[11]

Constructivists do not deny the pluralism that has often impressed critics of foundational justifications. They accept the 'fact of pluralism' and regard this recognition as the starting point for reflection rather than the end point of a discussion.[12] They argue that an increased sensitivity to the claims of diversity does not prevent the justification of a 'thin universalist' commitment to the idea of at least some objective reasons that are generally justifiable and apply to all persons. This involves constructing the principles of justice that set justifiable limits to tolerable forms of political organisation and morality, using thin but universal principles to outline an account of a 'principled pluralism'.[13] Constructed principles are 'universal' in that they apply to everybody. They are 'thin' because they neither rely on thick and controversial foundational assumptions nor do they aspire to lay down the detail of political institutional orders but rather justify basic principles of political justice that all polities must embody, whatever else they are also committed to. Such thin universal principles constitute a primary constructivist account that sets limits to, but does not dictate the content of, a plurality of secondary constructions, the thick and particular cultures and communities we inhabit day to day[14]

Given this understanding of constructivism, it may seem odd that it can find room for a historically religious concept, but what this paper hopes to show is that constructivism can find a role for the notion of evil. More accurately, it can find distinct roles for judgements of evil, for conceptions of evil and for the concept of evil. Let us take each in turn.

1. Judgements of evil as paradigmatic moral reasons

We commonly judge some activities or people to be evil. These judgements about evil are intended to identify something unquestionably wrong, whenever or wherever it occurs. Where we can often feel comfortable with people doing things very differently from us, we are much less comfortable if these things are ones that we regard as evil. Although we have become increasingly sensitive to pluralism these sorts of cross-cultural normative judgements persist. Some practices just seem different from ours; others we judge to be evil. What use can constructivism make of these judgements?

The first argument of this chapter is that our particular judgements about what is evil can inform the constructivist process of critical reasoning. This role for our judgements of evil becomes clear if we think about the account of constructivist critical reflection with which we are most familiar, Rawls's notion of reflective equilibrium. Here, to get our critical thinking going we need to identify what Rawls calls our 'considered judgements about justice'.[15] These are necessary to kick start formally the critical process of justification that generates an account of justified principles of justice. We have to start our thinking somewhere and these considered judgements are those judgements about political values in which we have the most confidence, that we are most sure pick out important considerations of right and wrong, justice and injustice. Isn't this exactly what our judgements of evil do? Judging the Holocaust or child sex abuse to be evil is like saying, 'if these aren't wrong then nothing is'. Any theory of justice, yet alone a theory of evil, we might think would need to capture these things and treat them as about as wrong as it gets. So, evil has a role here in identifying what we regard as paradigmatic instances of moral reasoning. More generally, constructivism orients itself by reference to certain paradigmatic instances of moral reasoning in order 'to ensure that the theory is focused on the right subject matter'.[16] Examples of such instances might be that slavery is wrong, as is torturing for amusement and the unnecessary suffering of children. These act as 'fixed points' to ensure that 'questions which we feel sure must be answered in a certain way' are answered in that way.[17] Constructivism is, in this way, constrained by 'obvious moral truths'.[18] It is also clear, however, that, while constructivist thinkers feel free to regard these as 'fixed points' in the justification of principles, they are not regarded as foundational as they are only provisionally fixed and are, in principle, open to revision. Thus, Rawls is clear that he regards certain things as 'great evils of human history' and includes poverty, religious persecution and slavery among them.[19] So, although 'even firmly held convictions gradually change ... slavery ... is rejected as inherently unjust ... these convictions are provisional fixed points that it seems any reasonable conception must account for'.[20] He goes on to say, 'certainly we may have been mistaken, but does anyone doubt ... that it is wrong to have abolished slavery? Who seriously thinks so? Is there any real chance of a mistake?'[21] But, this level of confidence in judgement doesn't endanger the provisional nature of the judgements of slavery's evil. It is clear that, when Rawls treats a rejection of slavery as a fixed point, it is because he has trouble imagining what sort of reason could make him, or us, think again about the merits of slavery. Recognising that the Greeks had equal confidence in their positive judgements about slavery, however, means that it would be strange to claim that there could never be reason to think again, no matter how unlikely that seems today. If such a reason is advanced then think again we must.

This, then, is the role that everyday judgements of evil may play in constructivist justification. They effectively constitute the judgements of political right and wrong in which we are most confident, enabling our critical reflection to get started. Thus, they are properly regarded as pointers towards an adequate account of principles of political justice. They identify the paradigmatic instances of moral judgement that justified principles must either account for, or provide us with compelling reasons for revising or rejecting.

2. Conceptions of evil and the content of constructivist principles

The second argument of this chapter focuses on the role conceptions of evil might play in constructivism. Conceptions of evil could be regarded as attempts to outline the content of constructivist principles of political justice. Principles of justice at the most basic level make claims to identify a clear account of how people should not be treated, a clear account of basic standards which any social or political order should meet. Failure to meet these standards is a mark of injustice and of unjust political organisation. To the extent that conceptions of evil are usually taken to identify a set of cross-cultural wrongs that should never be visited by human beings or human institutions on other persons, then constructivism may have a place for these conceptions. They do not often do so but, when we find that contemporary political theorists have explicitly turned to the notion of evil, it is for precisely this purpose, to aid in the identification of the content of the most basic principles of justice. Let us illustrate this with several examples.

In *The Atrocity Paradigm*, Claudia Card argues for a conception of evil as 'foreseeable intolerable harms produced by culpable wrongdoing'.[22] 'Conduct is morally bad when it is culpable and wrong. It becomes evil when it also foreseeably deprives others of basics needed for their lives or deaths to be tolerable and decent.'[23] What the conception of evil aims at is to identify 'what no one should be made to suffer, no matter what it does for anyone else'.[24] In a manner that recalls Rawls's account of primary goods, Card lays out a list of basic harms as 'the things that everyone can be presumed to want to avoid, whatever else they may want' and they include, for example, severe and unremitting pain, lack of access to safe food, water and air, extreme and prolonged isolation or restrictions on motility and deprivation of basics of self-respect and human dignity.[25] Card has effectively produced a list of basic and impartial human interests and will regard as justified any principles or institutions that prevent these evil things from systematically happening to human beings.

Rawls also makes explicit use of the idea of the distinctively evil. At various times he identifies evil men who exhibit a love of injustice (in distinction from unjust men who do wrong in the pursuit of material gain and bad men who do wrong because they enjoy social acclaim and power over others),[26] evil acts such as the dropping of the atomic bomb on Hiroshima[27] and evil institutions such as slavery.[28] In *The Law of Peoples* Rawls draws on the last two notions to outline a minimal account of 'necessary conditions of any system of social co-operation', 'a necessary, though not sufficient, standard for the decency of domestic political and social institutions' in any society.[29] He outlines these as a list of human rights protecting a right to life (subsistence and security), a right to liberty (including freedom from slavery and some degree of liberty of conscience), a right to personal property and to the formal equality of natural justice.[30] These rights are necessary to combat the 'great evils of human history – unjust war and oppression, religious persecution and the denial of liberty of conscience, starvation and poverty, not to mention genocide and mass murder'.[31] In Rawls's conception of evil, these great evils are the consequence of political injustices which undermine the principles of human rights. 'Once political injustice has been eliminated . . . these great evils will eventually disappear.'[32] Again, a conception of evil is advanced as part of the process of identifying the content of principles which must be observed by all political orders.

Finally, Stuart Hampshire argues that political theory responds to the great and perennial evils of human life. In a list very similar to Rawls's, Hampshire identifies these perennial evils as 'physical suffering, the destructions and mutilations of war, poverty and starvation, enslavement and humiliation'.[33] The argument is that such evils have a special status, quite apart from our other moral conceptions. While most of our moral ideas reflect the deep level of pluralism and diversity that is a central characteristic of human life, 'such evils, unlike visions of a better social order, are not culture dependent'.[34] They are the 'savage and obvious evils, which scarcely vary from culture to culture or from age to age ... these primary evils stay constant and undeniable as evils to be at all costs averted'.[35] Again, the notion of evil is being used as an aid to the identification of the most basic principles of justice.

So, taking these exemplars seriously, it is clear that there is a second role for a notion of evil in constructivism. Conceptions of evil can be regarded as attempts to fill out the content of basic principles of justice. For the constructivist, each conception seems to stake a claim to lay out the core of those things that are wrong everywhere rather than simply regarded as wrong in this or that polity. This is exactly what a conception of evil is trying to do, account for that category of especially wrong things that have a special status. Now, each conception need not itself be constructivist but the constructivist nonetheless is free to treat each as generating a list of cross-cultural wrongs to be taken seriously and weighed with others in the balance of reasons subjected to critical reflection. Conceptions of evil are claims to have identified particularly weighty reasons.

Let us be careful, however. The claim expounded by this argument is not that constructivist accounts require a notion of evil or that a notion of evil is necessary to ground objective principles of political morality. The claim is rather that conceptions of evil are themselves attempts to explain and understand the sort of thing that political constructivism is focused on and, as such, they should be taken seriously by constructivists. Indeed, there are many accounts, such as that offered by Brian Barry, of basic human interests that underpin basic and universal principles of justice that do not explicitly draw on any notion of evil.[36] These must be weighed in the balance with those which do, none automatically privileged above any other.

3. The concept of evil and the importance of the distinctively wrong

Constructivism, as we have seen, can find a role for judgements of evil and conceptions of evil, but is it necessary that it does so? It can legitimately be asked why we should bother going to the effort of finding room for evil at all, especially as it certainly seems possible to do without evil in these first two roles. Here we turn to the third role, a role for the very idea of evil as a concept. As a concept, evil stakes out a category of the distinctively wrong or unjust, the idea of a 'threshold' within injustice. The idea of such a threshold marks an important distinction between ordinary injustices and those of a qualitatively different sort. Evil is not just an intensifier describing acts that are just very, very wrong, but describes a set of acts that are wrong in a different way. The argument here is that something like the concept of evil must play this role if an account of thin universalism is going to be possible. It will become clear that even in positions that advance a basic normative universalism about justice, such as Sen's, the failure to recognise or acknowledge the importance of such a threshold leads to significant problems. Even a position, like Nussbaum's, which recognises the importance of the idea of a threshold, faces these problems if it fails to take on board the lesson that the concept of evil teaches, that the important threshold marks the low-end distinction between living a tolerable life and suffering intolerably.

To illustrate this role for the concept of evil let us turn to Amartya Sen's argument in *The Idea of Justice*.[37] This is a powerful statement in which Sen criticises what he calls the 'transcendental institutional' approach in favour of 'realization-focused comparison'.[38] The transcendental approach, which he identifies with Rawls and much of mainstream political philosophy, is characterised by its focus on an account of perfectly just institutions. Once the transcendentalist has identified the institutions that embody 'spotless justice' they are satisfied that little else needs to be done – a society shaped by just institutions will be a just society.[39] Sen argues that this approach is misguided and that a comparative approach to justice has much more going for it. He argues that combating injustice is better served by focusing on comparing real-world options as they present themselves than by attempting to identify the 'optimum' set of institutions, and that the temptation to 'overdetermination' in transcendental reasoning about justice will undermine legitimate pluralism. Consider what is involved in making a judgement between a Picasso and a Dali. It is no help in making this choice to be told that the most perfect painting is the *Mona Lisa*. Knowing what the ideal is will certainly not be sufficient to determine our choice between the two paintings and it may not actually be any help at all. Likewise, weighing up the comparative merits of the real political options we face cannot simply be done by reference to the best imaginable option since each real option will vary from the ideal along several different dimensions and be far more attentive to real world considerations.[40] The comparative approach requires impartial reasoned scrutiny of various pairwise comparisons but does not require a blueprint of the perfectly just society.

It is far from clear whether expecting the activity of thinking about justice to justify a single right answer about principles of justice is a realistic expectation at all. Sen argues that the transcendental approach attempts to overdetermine the outcome of reasonable reflection. He illustrates this with a story about three children in dispute about who should get a flute they are quarrelling over.[41] Each child suggests the reason why they should have the flute and Sen asks us to try to judge between them. Anne claims that she should be given the flute as she is the only one who can play it. She argues that it would be an injustice to deny the flute to the only child who could use it. Bob points out that he is the only child too poor to have any toys of his own while the other children have plenty of toys already. Denying him the flute would then reinforce existing inequality. Carla protests that she has worked hard for months making the flute and that this entitles her to it. Sen's point is that if you heard only the argument of any one of these children you might find it convincing. Having heard them all, deciding between the principles they advance is no easy task as all seem reasonable and impartial principles. There may be genuinely reasonable but competing considerations of justice that underpin a 'plurality of unbiased principles'.[42] This is a position that transcendental institutionalism cannot understand as it is entirely focused on determining the optimum principle (or consistent set of principles) using some device resembling Rawls's original position.[43] The comparative approach advanced by Sen is able to understand the balancing of competing reasons that we would expect to find in any situation where a real choice between real alternatives is to be made. It also recognises that real human social interactions with the problems that they throw up may not be receptive to the total solutions offered by perfect principles from ideal theory. The comparative approach expects partial solutions to many problems, in part due to the plurality of reasons that will bear on any situation.[44] It accepts that real choice is always between better and worse options and very rarely about the best option imaginable.

There are good reasons to be concerned with accounts of justice that aim to determine the ideal principles of the optimum society, and with the way this might impact on openness to pluralism.[45] These reasons, however, should not be compelling enough to lead us to accept Sen's comparative approach without significant reform. Approaching Sen with the concept of evil in mind enables us to understand clearly why this is. The apparent strength of arguments designed to highlight the persistence of a plurality of reasonable principles and the futility of attempts to identify determinate solutions is bolstered by the choice of subject matter. If faced with a question about the proper distribution of flutes, it will certainly be reasonable to expect there to be competing reasons that legitimately bear on our choice of distributive principle and no obvious single best way to balance these reasons. This will be the case with the distribution of most goods. It is less likely, however, that such indeterminacy is reasonable in the distribution of very important goods. Consider goods like primary education, a fair trial or personal security. While people can advance reasons for educating their boy children but not their girl children, or for treating the prosecution of people of one skin colour or class differently from another, or even for extending state protection of personal security to one community while withdrawing it from another, this does not mean that these are good reasons. Now, of course, a comparative approach such as Sen's has the resources available to make impartial decisions in these cases but a focus on such basic interests will demand pretty determinate principles of distribution and admit less pluralism. At this point it is worth considering the various conceptions of evil that were advanced by Card, Rawls and Hampshire above. As we noted, each was effectively identifying the basic and fundamental interests of human beings, or at least the basic and fundamental wrongs that can be done to them. When considering how to respond to (or whether to commit) the great evils of slavery, genocide, war and oppression, rather than how to distribute flutes, we can be fairly certain that there will be very few justifiable responses. If the worry is about stifling pluralism generally, then recognising that these conceptions of evil demand determinate and principled responses to prevent evil will do little to limit the range of issues on which a broad plurality of responses is reasonable. Suggesting, however, that plural responses are appropriate for even these evils is to get overly attached to the idea of pluralism and extend it to issues where it ought not be welcome.

We must be clear about this third role for evil. What is distinctive about the concept of evil is that it identifies a minimum threshold, a limit to the treatment of human beings at the bad end of a scale of injustice. It has little to say about the possible, and entirely reasonable, variation in non-evil practice above that threshold. A notion of evil leaves extensive room for pluralism. At the same time it makes a claim that below a certain threshold of treatment there should be less room for pluralism, if any at all. Sen, though, does not like the idea of a threshold and we can see this in his several returns to the example of choosing a painting. One moral of this tale is that even if 'the best' is knowable it is not helpful when it comes to making comparative choices. The idea of the best is a threshold idea. It identifies a state of affairs that is qualitatively different from any imperfect state and should be aimed for. Sen's focus appears to be on rejecting this idea that there is a threshold at the top end of a scale of justice. In focusing on rejecting this upper threshold, however, he neglects the far more important idea of a lower threshold and that is the idea picked out by the concept of evil.[46]

In turning to the various conceptions of evil suggested by Card, Rawls and Hampshire to highlight arguments that some goods or ways of being treated are more basic than others and should be dealt with differently, we are using evil in its second role to highlight its third role as a concept that names the idea of a distinct lower threshold for injustice. This is the key thought for considering evil from the point of view of a constructivist, the importance of this idea of a lower threshold. The argument here is clearly not that Sen sanctions evil and injustice; this would be absurd. The argument, however, is that, in rejecting the notion of a lower-end threshold, Sen's approach does endanger the idea of a thin universalism. It does so in two ways. Firstly, in not adopting the lower threshold Sen runs the risk of developing a political theory that imposes very thick obligations on all of us. He outlines an account of the realisation of the capability of human beings to do things they value as an important criterion for moral judgement.[47] In conjunction with the comparative methodology which asks us to judge the better option in the various pairwise choices we are faced with, this will require a lot of everybody. Faced with a situation in which you are asked to judge between a world where capabilities are realised a little more or a little less clearly, we must choose the more developed option. Each time we are faced with these options we must make this choice. This is true no matter how developed the capabilities are in the first place. All we have is various comparative judgements without a threshold which signals that basic obligations are met. Without this low-end threshold to limit what we owe to all others, Sen's approach endangers the thinness of thin universalism. Secondly, even if there is a common list of human capabilities to aspire to, without the idea of a threshold embodied by the concept of evil, then it is difficult to understand whether we could develop the notion of a universal standard of treatment for human beings. On a comparative approach there is no built-in limit at either end of the scale of justice, just more or less realised capabilities. Different actors in different societies make varied comparative judgements and so develop and realise capabilities at different rates and in different ways in different populations. Adopting this approach we need not – perhaps with Sen's basic methodology we cannot – set a universal standard for the treatment of human beings. If we were to have the notion of a lower threshold for treatment in place, we would be enabled to make the important judgement that each society exceeds the threshold and a basic universal standard is identified and met. Without the idea of a threshold in place, the universalism of a thin universalism is also endangered. So, the concept of a threshold supports both the thinness and the universalism of thin universalism.

Martha Nussbaum, a fellow advocate of a capabilities approach, argues against Sen that a threshold is necessary if this approach is to identify and sustain just constitutional principles.[48] Despite this recognition, the idea of evil still has critical purchase on her account. Nussbaum gives us a clear statement of the list of ten central human capabilities including among other things bodily integrity, bodily heath, play and control over environment.[49] She argues that we need to lay out an 'idea of a threshold level of each capability' and that an important goal of political organisation should be getting citizens above this capability threshold.[50] This is a necessary condition for justice and the minimum threshold level is to be met by nation states, the world community and humanity generally.[51] It is clear that Nussbaum has understood the important role that the idea of a threshold can play in a theory of justice. She expressly adopts it as a means of identifying the universal standard of treatment that is owed to all people and to make room for a pluralism of attitudes once that threshold is achieved.

The basis of the capability threshold she identifies is a conception of the dignity of the human being. She argues that this dignity manifests itself in a life characterised by 'truly human functioning' and that only such a life is worthy of that dignity. Drawing on both Marx's and Aristotle's notions of how human nature is to be conceived, Nussbaum regards the capabilities to be 'prerequisites for living a live that is fully human rather than subhuman', a human rather than a 'merely animal' life.[52] Above the threshold human beings shape their own lives in worthy ways, below it they may go on living but it is an undignified life. In fact, Nussbaum actually identifies two thresholds, the upper one we have discussed and a much lower threshold marked out by 'very severe forms of mental disability, or senile dementia' below which a 'person is not really a human being at all'. She goes on to make it clear that she is much less interested in the lower boundary than she is in the 'higher threshold' and she concentrates on this.[53]

Nussbaum may be right about what justice is; that a society that does not guarantee the capabilities 'at some appropriate threshold level, falls short of being a fully just society'.[54] The concept of evil, however, does not ask us to focus on the 'fully just society'. Nor, indeed, does it ask us to focus on Nussbaum's lower threshold concerned with those in whom the capabilities are (very nearly) absent altogether. Instead, it requires us to pay attention to the wide space between these two limits acknowledged by Nussbaum. This is the space in which human beings are living lives that we would ordinarily regard neither as fully just, nor entirely empty. We certainly would not regard them as subhuman. She acknowledges this space when she argues that a situation where not all capabilities reach her higher threshold may be 'both unjust and tragic . . . even if in other respects things are going well'.[55] What evil as an idea, and the various conceptions of evil that we have introduced, do is to highlight the importance of a threshold within the space left by Nussbaum's analysis. This threshold marks the distinction between ordinary lives, in which not every capability may be developed, and intolerable lives marked by the experience of the great evils laid out above. This threshold does not mark out the 'fully just' but what we might call the 'just enough', where in many respects 'things are going well'. While we might agree with Nussbaum that it would be better if everybody reached her higher threshold, the existence of this higher threshold does nothing to undermine the importance of the lower threshold highlighted by our idea of evil. Nussbaum apparently ignores this lower threshold and, in doing so, effectively ignores the distinction between what is unjust and what is evil. Or even more strongly, she ignores the distinction between what is less than fully just and what is evil. As a result she sets the bar very high, imposing obligations on every society to become 'fully just'. While Nussbaum may regard the thickness of these universal obligations as a virtue, the lower threshold of a thinner universalism has a clear virtue, too. Something important is achieved if no one is forced to live an intolerable life as the victim of evil, and this achievement is not threatened if some people are not able to develop fully the broad range of capabilities. The concept of evil retains its clear role, even when more stringent thresholds are aspired to.

CONCLUSION

We have explored three distinct roles for evil. Firstly, within constructivist justification, there is good reason to start thinking about justice and injustice on the basis of the judgements in which we are more confident. We are generally pretty confident about the wrongness of the things that we are prepared to label as evil so these judgements of evil recommend themselves as a starting point for constructivist justification. Secondly, we should regard the various conceptions of evil as attempts to map out the core of basic principles of justice, the rejection of which is wrong everywhere. Finally, and more generally, the idea of evil focuses our attention on the boundary between bare acceptability and what is intolerable, and marks this down as an important threshold of moral concern. While this makes the case for constructivists to engage with the idea of evil it has also made a case for universalist thinkers more generally to do the same. Thinking about evil would benefit more than just the constructivists.

In fulfilling the third role, the concept of evil faces in two directions at once. In one direction it addresses those sceptics about evil who deny that the term has meaning beyond the fears and beliefs of particular groups.[56] It invites the sceptic to focus on the idea of a distinction between ordinary injustice which is rooted in particular contexts and an idea of intolerable evils which are wrong more generally, a distinction which the sceptic neglects. In doing so, the idea of evil draws attention to itself as a potential resource for universalist argument. Also, in regarding this distinction as morally important in its own right (marking, as it seems to, a basic distinction in the lives of real people) the idea of evil appears to be partly constitutive of political morality rather than a mere instrument in the hands of the ideologist. In the other direction it addresses forms of universalism that fail to recognise the importance of this basic moral distinction, the threshold between the intolerably wrong and other things we judge just or unjust. Here we picked out for discussion Sen, as he denies the importance of any threshold of justice in favour of a thoroughgoing comparativism, and Nussbaum, who acknowledges the threshold between the unjust and the fully just but ignores the more basic threshold picked out by evil. Both, therefore, undermine the idea of a thin universalism that identifies the most basic principles of justice protecting the basic interests of persons. The notion of evil is effectively a reference to that thin universalism, identifying both the idea of a distinct sort of injustice that underpins it and generating several attempts to lay down the content of basic universal principles of justice.

In the final analysis, is the idea of evil *necessary* to constructivism and to our moral thinking? The answer is no, but *the idea of the lower threshold is necessary.* The lower threshold identifies a recognisable boundary, on one side of which fall political conceptions and consequences that are not to be tolerated while, on the other side, space is marked out for a plurality of accounts of what a just political conception might look like. This is the boundary that any attempt to justify thin universalist principles needs to focus on. Given its importance, we need to be clear when thinking and speaking about this lower threshold and, given that we already use the term 'evil' to refer to it, the most straightforward thing to do may be to retain the term and to cash in on its undoubted rhetorical force. So, rather than 'dispose of the concept of evil' as Cole recommends,[57] we must consider taking the basic thought behind the everyday use of evil very seriously indeed.

Notes

1 The sort of constructivist positions referred to here are those advanced by John Rawls in *A Theory of Justice: revised edition* (Oxford: Oxford University Press, 1999 [originally 1971]) and *Political Liberalism* (New York: Columbia University Press, 1996 [originally 1993]) and by Onora O'Neill in *Towards Justice and Virtue: A Constructive Account of Practical Reasoning* (Cambridge: Cambridge University Press, 1996), analysed in my *Political Constructivism* (London: Routledge, 2007) and introduced in my 'Constructivism' in M. Bevir (ed.), *Encyclopedia of Political Theory* (London: Sage, 2010), pp. 297–301.

2 Not all contemporary authors who accept a secular understanding of evil adopt this sceptical approach, instead accepting that such an understanding may be genuinely enlightening. See, for very different examples, Russ Shafer-Landau's *Whatever Happened to Good and Evil?* (Oxford: Oxford University Press, 2004), Claudia Card's *The Atrocity Paradigm: A Theory of Evil* (Oxford: Oxford University Press, 2002), Eve Garrard's 'Evil as an Explanatory Concept', *The Monist*, 85: 2, 2002, pp. 320–36 and Hillel Steiner's 'Calibrating Evil', *The Monist*, 85: 2, 2002, pp. 183–93.

3 Richard J. Bernstein, *The Abuse of Evil: The Corruption of Politics and Religion since 9/11* (Cambridge: Polity, 2005), p. 1.

4 Bernstein, *The Abuse of Evil*, p. 97.

5 Bernstein, *The Abuse of Evil*, pp. 92–3.

6 Phillip Cole, *The Myth of Evil* (Edinburgh: Edinburgh University Press, 2006).

7 Cole, *The Myth of Evil*, pp. 89–90.

8 Cole, *The Myth of Evil*, p. 23.

9 Cole, *The Myth of Evil*, p. 235 and pp. 2, 21.

10 In addition to the references in note 1 above, constructivism is explored in, for example, R. Milo, 'Contractarian Constructivism', *The Journal of Philosophy*, 92, 1995, pp. 181–204, T. M. Scanlon, 'Contractualism and Utilitarianism', in A. Sen and B. Williams (eds), *Utilitarianism and Beyond* (Cambridge: Cambridge University Press, 1982), pp. 103–28, G. A. Cohen, *Rescuing Justice and Equality* (Cambridge, MA: Harvard University Press, 2008), C. MacKinnon, *Liberalism and the Defence of Political Constructivism* (Basingstoke: Palgrave, 2002) and in T. K. Seung, *Intuition and Construction: The Foundations of Normative Theory* (New Haven: Yale University Press, 1993).

11 The constructivist account of practical reasoning, and the objectivity and authority of reasons in particular, is explored in Roberts, *Political Constructivism*, chapter 5.

12 The term 'fact of pluralism' is taken from Rawls, *Political Liberalism*, p. 36.

13 The idea of a thin universalism is explored from several points of view in B. Haddock, P. Roberts and P. Sutch (eds), *Principles and Political Order: The Challenge of Diversity* (London: Routledge, 2006).

14 For the distinction between primary and secondary constructivism see Roberts, *Political Constructivism*, chapter 6.

15 See Rawls, *A Theory of Justice*, pp. 40–6.

16 R. Milo, 'Contractarian Constructivism', p. 203. See also his 'Skepticism and Moral Justification', *The Monist*, 76, 1993, pp. 379–93; p. 390.

17 Rawls, *A Theory of Justice*, pp. 579, 19.

18 T. M. Scanlon, 'Moral Theory: Understanding and Disagreement', *Philosophy and Phenomenological Research*, 55, 1995, pp. 343–56; p. 346.

19 Rawls, *The Law of Peoples with "The Idea of Public Reason Revisited"* (Cambridge, MA: Harvard University Press, 1999), pp. 6–7 and *Political Liberalism*, p. 8.

20 Rawls, *Political Liberalism*, p. 8.

21 Rawls, *Political Liberalism*, p. 152n.

22 Card, *The Atrocity Paradigm*, p. 3.

23 Card, *The Atrocity Paradigm*, p. 102. See also p. 16.

24 Card, *The Atrocity Paradigm*, p. 17.

25 Card, *The Atrocity Paradigm*, p. 63. Although I have suggested a link between the basic harms and primary goods, Card is at pains to point out that, while the primary goods are mainly instrumentally valuable, the basic harms need not be regarded as mainly instrumentally harmful. See Rawls, *A Theory of Justice*, pp. 54–5, 78–81, for an account of primary goods.

26 Rawls, *A Theory of Justice*, pp. 385–6. A similar account of evil persons is advanced in Ernesto Garcia, 'A Kantian Theory of Evil', *The Monist*, 85: 2, 2002, pp. 194–209.

27 John Rawls, 'Fifty Years after Hiroshima', in S. Freeman (ed.), *John Rawls: Collected Papers* (Cambridge MA: Harvard University Press, 1999), pp. 565–72; p. 570.

28 Rawls, *The Law of Peoples*, p. 126.

29 Rawls, *The Law of Peoples*, pp. 68, 80.

30 Rawls, *The Law of Peoples*, p. 65.

31 Rawls, *The Law of Peoples*, pp. 6–7. See also p. 126 where he adds slavery to the list.

32 Rawls, *The Law of Peoples*, p. 126.

33 Stuart Hampshire, *Justice is Conflict* (London: Duckworth, 1999), p. 9.

34 Hampshire, *Justice is Conflict*, p. 9.

35 Hampshire, *Justice is Conflict*, p. 47.

36 In a typically blunt passage of *Culture and Equality: An Egalitarian Critique of Multiculturalism* (Cambridge: Polity, 2001), p. 285, Barry tries to identify the basic interests of every human being by contrasting them with what every human would prefer to avoid. It is, he argues, 'better to be alive than dead, . . . free than to be a slave, . . . healthy than sick, . . . adequately nourished than malnourished, . . . drink pure water than contaminated water, . . . have effective sanitation rather than live over an open sewer, . . . to have a roof over your head than to sleep in the street, . . . to be well educated than to be illiterate.' Taken together, Barry argues, these 'make up the preconditions . . . for what we may describe as a minimally decent human life.'

37 A. Sen, *The Idea of Justice* (London: Allen Lane, 2009).

38 Sen, *The Idea of Justice*, p. 7.

39 Sen, *The Idea of Justice*, p. 99 and pp. 5–6.

40 Sen, *The Idea of Justice*, pp. 101, 16.

41 Sen, *The Idea of Justice*, pp. 12–15.

42 Sen, *The Idea of Justice*, p. 57.

43 Rawls, *A Theory of Justice*, pp. 15–19.

44 Sen, *The Idea of Justice*, pp. 399–400.

45 I broach some of these reasons in *Political Constructivism*, pp. 144–5.

46 Indeed, the transcendental approach that Sen is so keen to reject need not be focused on picking out the optimum society. It is just as likely to have

been put to use in identifying the limits on societies at the bottom end, the limits identified by conceptions of evil.

47 Sen, *The Idea of Justice*, p. 231.
48 Martha Nussbaum, *Women and Human Development: The Capabilities Approach* (Cambridge: Cambridge University Press, 2000), p. 12 and *Frontiers of Justice: Disability, Nationality, Species Membership* (Cambridge MA: Harvard University Press, 2006), p. 70.
49 Nussbaum, *Frontiers of Justice*, pp. 76–8 and *Women and Human Development*, pp. 78–80.
50 Nussbaum, *Frontiers of Justice*, p. 71.
51 Nussbaum, *Frontiers of Justice*, p. 291. In *Women and Human Development* (p. 5) she argues that her account identifies principles 'that should be respected and implemented by the governments of all nations, as a bare minimum of what respect for human dignity requires'.
52 Nussbaum, *Frontiers of Justice*, p. 278 and *Women and Human Development*, p. 72.
53 Nussbaum, *Women and Human Development*, p. 73.
54 Nussbaum, *Frontiers of Justice*, p. 75.
55 Nussbaum, *Women and Human Development*, p. 71.
56 Not all sceptics about evil need be sceptics about moral universalism generally. Universalists may also be sceptical of the idea of evil and, in an obvious sense, the arguments put to Sen and Nussbaum are aimed at these.
57 Cole, *The Myth of Evil*, p. 235.

Chapter 4

SYSTEMIC EVIL AND THE LIMITS OF PLURALISM

Bruce Haddock

Contemporary political theory has never been comfortable with the idea of evil. Indeed, the gradual, sporadic, but nevertheless incomplete secularisation of political discourse since the Renaissance has made the conceptualisation of absolute value deeply problematic. One response, dominant in the liberal tradition, is simply to deny that politics is the realm of absolute value at all. The pragmatic adjustment of competing interests in a scheme of social co-operation invites, at the very least, a moderation of tone. And increasing empirical awareness of the diversity of different schemes of (merely political) co-operation has made us (rightly) guarded in the language we use to defend specific positions. Modern liberals are unlikely to go to the stake for politics in any of its guises. Politics is not that important. We shouldn't get too excited about the give and take, and sometimes unseemly compromise, that characterises the banal politics of everyday life.

And yet atrocity remains to shock us – sometimes, indeed, to render us truly speechless. We mutter to ourselves, in all innocence, 'how could anyone do that?' Modern (predominantly secular) political theory ceases to be very helpful when confronted with extreme experiences. It is not surprising that an earlier religious language is sometimes seen to have far richer resources in such cases, even for thinkers whose cast of mind is otherwise thoroughly secular. It doesn't usually help much to characterise political opponents as 'evil' in an unqualified sense. We scarcely know, in fact, what we might be claiming. But there is no doubt that some actions strike us as intolerable, unacceptable, no matter how they might be justified in instrumental terms.

No doubt political theorists have much to learn from theology in their efforts to characterise the limits of experience. But, as John Milbank has shown in this volume, theological accounts of evil are themselves fraught with controversy. And metaphorical use of religious language goes only so far in rendering the limits of experience intelligible. It is an open question whether (secular) political theory has the resources to meet these challenges.[1] In a disenchanted world, however, we are bound to try to extend political understandings in order to bridge the very real divisions within and between communities on fundamental questions of value. Thinking about extreme cases challenges us, theoretically and practically.

Extreme cases are not restricted to headline-grabbing public events. Norms and values are the most ordinary things to us all, and we sometimes find ourselves having to extend the scope of conventional understandings in response to experience. Ways and means must be found to manage vulnerability and uncertainty. Lines must be drawn and publicly defended, even in cultures where the relevant public is a very small elite. Such discussions are largely couched in instrumental terms, not least because fundamental values are likely to be shared. When they are not, a different discussion ensues. Whether or not we should dispose of the chronically dependent may not be an issue that can be effectively handled in narrowly instrumental terms. In this chapter I am not concerned with detailed cases, difficult and interesting though they are, but rather with our characterisation of what might be styled the limits of community. The issue is evident even in stable liberal polities, where discussions of the limits of pluralism have been bedevilled by a failure to specify reasonable terms of association. What is taken to be 'reasonable' in any given context is notoriously parochial. The more attention we give to the term 'reasonable' itself, the more culturally specific we seem to get. What we owe to each other, in Scanlon's felicitous phrase, very often reduces to a discussion of individual responsibility.[2] The 'we' in the phrase is silently set aside, as if it goes without saying that responsibility is ultimately exercised individually. This serves us very well in predominantly individualist cultures. And I have to say that I have no objection to it on philosophical grounds. But it plainly limits the relevance of what we have to say.

If we want to establish an objective basis for ethics, as I do, at least at the margins, we clearly need to look elsewhere. A notion of 'reasonableness' helps to frame our discussions only where there is a deep cultural consensus about the meaning of the term. For the purposes of this discussion I am prepared to accept that the consensus is cultural rather than philosophical.

What happens if we look at the other end of the spectrum, at the things that can go so very badly wrong rather than the things we value or might ideally aspire to? Hampshire, Glover and others have pointed to very broad, cross-cultural (and, indeed, cross-philosophical, if I may be forgiven a very ugly phrase) agreement on the great evils that disfigure human life.[3] Hans Jonas, whose view of the world was formed in response to Auschwitz, puts the point succinctly. 'The perception of the *malum* is infinitely easier to us than the perception of the *bonum*; it is more direct, more compelling, less given to differences of opinion and taste, and, most of all, obtruding itself without our looking for it.'[4] Rawls, too, who was not prone to hyperbole, insists that if anything is evil, slavery must be; and he refers to the 'manic evil' of the Holocaust without the need for further discussion or justification.[5] We do not often come face to face with Holocaust deniers, but the experience is a bit like finding yourself beyond the realm of conversation (and, if Aristotle is right, that is a serious condition to be in). What can we say to people who deny that there are any limits to individual or organised conduct? I am not making a philosophical point here, but asking you to reflect on the philosophical significance of an aspect of our experience. What does (apparent) agreement about the very great evils tell us? Our language suggests that this is not simply a matter of being wrong.

In this chapter I will say very little about evil deeds. I want to restrict myself to discussion of the 'basic structure of society', in something like the broad Rawlsian sense. My focus will be on conceptions of political order that either promote or condone evil. I take for granted that human flourishing comes in a rich variety of guises, some weird and wonderful, others decidedly dull. But there are limits. Values frame human flourishing but the values we encounter are plainly contingent. What is not contingent (or so I want to claim) is that human beings cannot flourish in any and every context. If we can identify necessary conditions for human flourishing, and also contexts in which those conditions are wilfully denied, we will at least have highlighted matters that need exceptional justification. To drop a nuclear bomb on a city just because you can would be deeply troubling, even in a context of just war. Agreement on very great evils tells us something about the limits of justification. The context here is our ordinary, untutored, moral sensibility.

It is worth recalling here that Kant, routinely derided in some quarters as the worst kind of abstract moralist, actually begins his *Groundwork of the Metaphysics of Morals* at exactly this point.[6] In Section I he takes for granted that untutored moral sensibility is entirely on the right lines. The 'categorical imperative' models what he assumes goes on in ordinary moral thinking, whether we are aware of it or not. Philosophical reflection on morality can start nowhere else. Philosophers, however, can easily go astray, and Kant focuses his criticism specifically on consequentialist moral theories. If Kant is preaching moral lessons, it is only to philosophers who have confused themselves and others. It may well be, and this is entirely beyond my present purpose, that Kant's preoccupation with the philosophical sources of moral error obscures in some measure his respect for ordinary moral sense. But ordinary moral sense is manifestly what he takes himself to be modelling.

It is also instructive that Kant, who was notoriously suspicious of received wisdom, felt unable to dispense with a concept of evil, despite his reservations about the dominant treatment of the concept within the theological tradition. The thought that nothing in our experience 'could be considered good without limitation except a good will', involved, as a corollary, that an evil will might be regarded as a threat to anything we might value.[7] Kant's most extensive discussion of the issue in *Religion within the Boundaries of Mere Reason* is instructive because he focuses not on evil acts or decisions, but on what he calls 'a natural propensity of the human being to evil'.[8] Here he draws on the notion of 'original sin', but shifts the focus of attention. We might all be said to have a natural inclination to pursue our interests, yet that in itself is neither good nor evil, simply a statement of sources of motivation. What worries him is that pursuing our inclinations might be raised to a principle of action, effectively treating self-love as a moral maxim. This is the standing temptation that must always be guarded against. He treats it as an irreducible snare ('a radical innate evil in human nature') that demands forethought on our part whenever we are faced with a moral dilemma.[9] All this, thinks Kant, is evident in our basic moral intuitions, the good no less than the evil. The intriguing point from the perspective of this volume is that he had recourse to a concept that would have had awkward theological connotations for most of his readers. Evil as a standing condition is a threat to the possibility of a decent human life. It is all-pervasive, and hence radical, in Kant's terms, something that we must confront in our most ordinary deeds. His concern is that, in the wrong philosophical hands, it can compromise our basic capacity to do the decent thing.

Rawls and the modern Kantians, of course, develop Kant's point in rather different terms. Their focus, however, is always on structural features rather than on specific acts. Where Kant stresses the defects in our conceptions of moral thinking that might prevent us from acting well, no matter what we might want, the Rawlsians highlight the structure of society and the basic primary goods, necessary conditions for leading any kind of fulfilling life. In this chapter I broadly adopt a Rawlsian perspective. To focus on the 'basic structure of society' is not to equate evil with injustice, though evil is, of course, unjust. What needs to be identified is something more basic (foundational, if you will) that prevents human beings from leading a worthwhile life (in all the many forms that that can be attained). It may even be possible to breathe fresh life into a notion of natural justice, despite the well-documented difficulties that the term glosses over.

What we need to characterise is a limit beyond which a fully human life is unthinkable. Ideas of this kind are, of course, commonplace in moral realist thinking. Standard versions of moral realism, however, are too thick (at least in my view) to accommodate the genuine diversity of forms of human flourishing. As soon as we specify details of a good life, we find ourselves involved in rich social description that will capture specific forms of flourishing and not others. Evil opens up wider possibilities. In this chapter I suggest that it functions as a limiting condition, a negative version of an 'ideal' type that cannot be countenanced, anywhere, at any time.

This is the stuff of nightmares, and nightmarish literature is a very good place to find it. My favourite example here is Kafka's *The Trial*.[10] The plot is straightforward and will be familiar to most readers. Josef K. finds himself accused of a non-specific crime. He tries (unsuccessfully) to find out what he is alleged to have done. In the process he discovers that the legal system under which he is arraigned is a mystery even to its officers. There are no clear procedures to follow, no experts to guide him through the arcane structures and conventions. Functionaries are no clearer about how to pursue a grievance than poor K. himself. He is passed from one level of competence to another, only to find that positions in the hierarchy seem to depend on personal qualities and connections that have nothing to do with the law. But neither is anything as straightforward as self-interest a key to the erratic behaviour of individuals. What seems to be at issue is a desperate struggle to survive, on the part of both K. and the characters he encounters. It is a context that makes the ordinary pursuit of objectives impossible.

Kafka is clear from the outset that K.'s position makes no sense at all. He announces in the first sentence that 'somebody must have made a false accusation against Josef K., for he was arrested one morning without having done anything wrong'.[11] He assumes that he will be able to sort out matters. There is no doubt about his innocence according to conventional standards. His enquiries, however, reveal a world in which truth is irrelevant. Accusations are indicative of something but not guilt. K. learns to mistrust everyone around him. What modern theorists describe as social capital simply drains away. K. finally discovers that, in these circumstances, it is not possible to do anything. His final execution strikes as a moment of release from an unliveable world.

Hannah Arendt, in a wonderfully perceptive essay, summarises *The Trial* succinctly. 'It is the story of K., a man who is accused without knowing what he has done, tried according to laws which he cannot discern, and finally executed without having been able to find out what all this is really about.'[12] Throughout, Kafka's tone is matter-of-fact. But the point of the story is precisely that facts don't count. K.'s innocence is neither here nor there. It is no more relevant to try to prove innocence than to justify a guilty verdict. If this is how things stand, what is to be done? Kafka's answer, nothing. We endure or not, as the case may be. If Josef K. learns anything, it is that he, along with everyone else, is personally irrelevant.

Political interpretation of great works of literature is often foolhardy, and I make no claims as an original reader of Kafka. What interests me is simply the portrayal of the limits of social organisation. Arendt treats it is a portent of the nightmare that Europe would endure in the 1930s but she is clear that it is much more than that. It is deeply unsettling at a psychological level. Much is missed if we read it as a portrayal of totalitarian society *avant la lettre*. There are very few institutional details and nothing as directly shocking as organised terror. What we are presented with, instead, is a very ordinary world that happens to make no sense. The framework is bureaucratic but arbitrariness seems to be the rule. People turn up for work, go through the motions of getting things done, and nothing happens. The appropriate individual response is paranoia. We may wonder, of course, how far any actual society resembles Kafka's picture but that is beside the point. Kafka was drawing upon experience of the declining years of the Austro-Hungarian Empire, not describing it. Commentators like Arendt can use it as a measure of the quietly sinister side of totalitarianism. For the purposes of my argument, terror is too obvious. We know it is wrong. In *The Origins of Totalitarianism* Arendt makes an important distinction between the authoritarianism of Fascist Italy and celebration of power for its own sake in Nazi Germany.[13] Kafka helps us to see that it is not just abuse of power that makes the Nazi model so chilling. We understand perfectly well that power is sometimes abused in the pursuit of given ends. What is so chilling in Arendt's account is that Nazi Germany makes sense only as an endless exercise in systematic demoralisation. The allusion to system here sounds like a contradiction in terms, and so it is. The point is that it is untenable.

Theory can use Kafka's model as an instance of political perversion, much as Aristotle distinguished between healthy and degenerate forms of constitution. Indeed, Kafka may present us with the specifically degenerate form of a mass-based polity. It is certainly difficult to understand individuality in the context Kafka offers us. What would it mean to bear responsibility in such a system? How could co-operative engagement with strangers be envisaged? How would we seek redress if things went wrong? These are basic issues that have to be confronted in any conceivable society of any size. The temptation in Kafka's world is to stay in bed. You can't *do* anything.

All this is food for thought but the tired dichotomies that have addressed (something like) this dilemma do not help us in conditions of deep pluralism. A distinction between 'civilization' and 'barbarism', framed as it has been in so many different ways in the history of political thought, is simply no help at all if the position we favour can be portrayed as a culturally specific preference. Kafka invites us to ask ourselves a different question. He has presented us with a model context in which human flourishing is inconceivable. Much more than political philosophy is involved here. Economists and sociologists (I contend) would be able to argue that much more than politics goes wrong in Kafka's world. Knowing how bad things can get, we can ask what would need to be in place for human beings to flourish even minimally. This takes us back to traditional ground, but with dramatically reduced expectations.

So, how can theory respond to Kafka's challenge? Some of the resources of the natural law tradition can help us, though in radically revised form. In earlier exploratory work I have tried to use the idea of a 'weak foundation' as a necessary, but not sufficient, condition for human flourishing, very much along the lines of Michael Oakeshott's reading of minimum conditions for civil association in his interpretation of Hobbes.[14] To invoke Hobbes for my purposes is a remedy beset with a host of obvious difficulties from the perspective of liberal theory. Whatever the problem, absolute sovereignty cannot be the solution, for very good Lockean reasons. I want to separate the idea of necessary conditions of civility from the wider Hobbesean context, focusing instead on the idea of law as a necessary condition for co-operation among strangers. I want to stress procedures and practices, rather than goals and objectives (good, bad, indifferent or evil).

The terms of reference of *The Trial* take us straight to the idea of legal order. Josef K. found he could not make headway because laws and procedures seemed to be entirely arbitrary. He was confronting what looked like a legal problem (he was, after all, obliged to present himself to the courts), only to find that the root of his difficulty was simply being Josef K. It would be stretching understanding to call what was being played out as legal practice, even in the broadest understanding of the term. We can appropriately ask ourselves what needs to be put back in place.

The resources of the natural law tradition can help us here, though in radically revised form. Interesting work along these lines has been done by Nigel Simmonds in his recent book, *Law as a Moral Idea*.[15] The centrepiece of his argument is a contrast between 'evil regimes and the rule of law'.[16] His specific concern is to challenge the separation of law and morals in legal positivist theory, focusing specifically on Hart's reworking of that position.[17] Hart (you will remember) was engaged through a great deal of his career in controversy with Lon Fuller, whose defence of 'a minimum content of a substantive natural law' struck many analytical philosophers as a last desperate effort to defend a thoroughly outmoded position.[18] Simmonds defends Fuller's argument in more or less its original form.

Fuller's is a developmental theory that highlights basic features of legal reasoning. He takes for granted that interesting legal judgements are much more than the application of rules. They are attempts to develop the logic of legality in problematic situations. Fuller talks about an 'impulse towards legality' or an 'aspiration toward perfection in legality'.[19] He takes for granted that, in difficult cases, we may not be sure precisely what legality requires. We have an implicit model in our minds that helps us to refine the application of formal criteria to substantive cases. Note that we are not simply applying rules but deepening our understanding of them in practice. Any hint of arbitrary decision here is entirely out of place. Even executive discretion must be guided by principles of legality.

What might these principles of legality amount to? Crucially for my argument, Fuller develops his own position through an account of the way law-making can go very badly wrong. He pictures a zealous monarch, Rex, who initially seeks to remedy the obvious shortcomings of established practice by wiping the slate clean and concocting a completely new legal system. Anomalies, of course, arise. Rex tries to respond to each case in turn, and ends up creating chaos and confusion that neither he, nor his subjects, can understand. Where system fails, Rex has recourse to secrecy. But subjects find that life under unknown rules is no more convenient for them than rules that make no sense. Rex is an ingenious fellow. Undeterred, he tries case-by-case decisions, a proliferation of amendments, new codes with the full force of sovereign authority but all to no avail. The imperfections of the practical world always reassert themselves.

Fuller highlights 'eight distinct routes to disaster'.[20] These are, briefly: (i) 'failure to achieve rules at all'; (ii) 'a failure to publicise' rules; (iii) 'abuse of retroactive legislation'; (iv) 'failure to make rules understandable'; (v) the 'enactment of contradictory rules' or (vi) 'rules that require conduct beyond the powers of the affected party'; (vii) 'introducing such frequent changes in the rules that the subject cannot orient his action by them'; and (viii) a 'failure of congruence between the rules as announced and their actual administration'.[21] All these conditions are in place in the plight of Josef K. And, arguably, and to different degrees, they were in place in Nazi Germany, Stalin's Soviet Union, and Ceaușescu's Romania. Above and beyond the obvious abuse of power in these contexts and many others, individuals are prevented from organising their lives in very ordinary ways. Where the exercise of power is not legally structured, we are left with the (more or less benign) decisions of particular individuals who happen to be able to mobilise sufficient resources for the moment. Trying to second-guess arbitrary decisions is a demoralising experience. In a literal sense, we don't know where to turn. At best, we adopt survival strategies. At worst, like Josef K., we simply resign ourselves to our fate.

Regimes we call evil practise illegality by design rather than by accident. In Hannah Arendt's seminal account in *The Origins of Totalitarianism*, the destruction of stable expectations, for anyone, anywhere, in a (so-called) hierarchy is a key strategy in the erosion of practical independence in totalitarian states. The basic capacity of individuals to initiate activities is undermined. Arendt's account is, of course, highly contentious. Whatever the merit of her detailed depiction of the rise and consolidation of totalitarian regimes, she enables us to focus on the things we take for granted in our ordinary pursuits. This is much more than a defence of political freedom in a conventional sense. It is a fundamental feature of a recognisably human life that we try things out, respond to situations as best we can in shifting co-operation with friends and strangers in a dimly understood context of institutions and practices. A corollary of doing anything at all is that we make mistakes. We accordingly may need to seek redress or ask forgiveness. These are simple consequences of the fact that we (necessarily) lack perfect knowledge. Rules, practices and laws are (more or less effective) means of managing radical uncertainty. To deny people the ordinary procedures of social life as a matter of policy is to strike at their capacity to lead a fulfilling (but very ordinary) life. Evil (with all its difficult connotations) serves as a term to describe political wrongdoing on this scale.

When Arendt used the phrase 'banality of evil' in her Eichmann book, she got herself into all sorts of trouble with her critics.[22] Her point, of course, was that systematic evil on the scale of the Holocaust involved the active co-operation of thousands of people, very few of whom could be described as evil. Like Eichmann, but with rather more justification, they could claim that they were only doing their jobs. This is evasion of responsibility on a massive scale. Indeed, her point in *The Origins of Totalitarianism* is precisely that totalitarian strategy is designed to make it impossible for people to assume responsibility. A regime of terror, directed at arbitrary individuals as well as at declared enemies of the state, is difficult to resist, especially where you take your life in your hands if you trust strangers. Personal survival might depend upon shutting up, effectively condoning what you know to be wrong.

Arendt's point, however, is that exercising responsibility is precisely what being human involves. Nobody *has* to do anything. The price to pay if we refuse to do certain jobs is largely economic, especially for functionaries who might see themselves as mere cogs in a social machine. A regime that makes everyday discretion a serious matter is plainly attacking basic conditions for flourishing of any kind.[23]

Banality of evil may be an ill-advised phrase but, in an important sense, the good life is also banal. We should remember that Hobbes justifies *Leviathan* as a means of securing the commonplace features of our daily lives.[24] His politics shuns glorious visions of the good life, and focuses instead on basic co-operative resources without which life would be unsustainable. The stress on fear as a motive for co-operation is obvious in the text, and perfectly intelligible in light of the dire circumstances he was addressing. But he also dwells on the inescapable ordinariness of our most basic desires. We may disagree about very many of the good things in life, if we have the luxury of worrying about such things. But no one could dispute the overriding importance 'of such things as are necessary to commodious living', whatever else they might make of their situation.[25] In the classic paragraph of chapter 13 Hobbes focuses on the ordinary things we are likely to take for granted in reasonably stable circumstances ('. . . no place for industry; because the fruit thereof is uncertain: and consequently no culture of the earth etc.').[26] Without social co-operation on a predictable basis, all manner of ordinary tasks are rendered deeply difficult. Economic (no less than political) survival is threatened, along with the trust and fellowship that people savour in quiet moments. Policy and practice, that make very ordinary tasks monumental, strike at our capacity to lead social lives. Basic conditions for flourishing are not in the least obscure. Hobbes's point is that we should all be able to recognise them, no matter how we might construe the larger purposes in our lives.

Arendt's claim is that modern Leviathans have means of control at their disposal that rule out the Hobbesian solution as a reasonable response to the problem of radical uncertainty. What she sees as a distinctively twentieth-century phenomenon is the mobilisation of a whole society through ideological logic, based on a reading of history or nature, that detaches political language from the ordinary business of deciding what to do next in shifting circumstances. Terror adds another dimension, isolating individuals from one another such that they cannot trust their own judgements. And when reflective confidence is undermined, ideological commitment is available to rescue us from the agony of indecision. We are saved from paralysis only if we endorse (at least tacitly) a rhetoric that flies in the face of common sense.

Arendt's language repays careful consideration. In her view, totalitarian domination strives to 'eliminate precisely the capacity of man to act'.[27] That most basic of human experiences, wondering how to respond to a tangled moral situation, is portrayed as a wanton indulgence. Our moral dilemma may be unlike any other in its detailed circumstances but we can try to work our way through it by marshalling all the resources available to us. The totalitarian regime deplores such moral scruple. We are exhorted to follow ideological logic, not moral conscience. At the very least, we should do as we are told, despite the fact that our dilemma strikes us as personal and unique. The underlying maxim is effectively 'don't think for yourself'.

This is much more than a denial of personal responsibility. It challenges some of our most basic assumptions about vulnerability and uncertainty. As social animals, awareness of mutual interdependence has in some sense always been with us. We know what it is to need help, comfort, support, advice and so on. Our various projects depend upon different micro-schemes of social co-operation, and we make our own judgements about the complex relations between our activities. Totalitarian domination, however, undermines social trust. Isolated, lonely and fearful individuals are much easier to manipulate than overlapping groups in civil society. In Arendt's reading, mass societies with high mobility are very likely to uproot people psychologically, leaving them without the ordinary sources of social support. The totalitarian regime fills the void but at an alarming cost. Thinking and conversation are open-ended activities; we don't know where a thread or theme will take us. But they both depend upon high levels of trust. Conversation is deeply and dangerously self-revealing. It actually highlights our (all too human) vulnerability. We may inadvertently hurt one another, regret an insensitive form of words. In the ordinary way of things, we apologise, we ask for forgiveness. But how do we carry on if personal forgiveness is no longer something we can freely give?

This is not the place to pursue a full account of Arendt's (highly controversial) theory of ideology.[28] Terms of reference have changed significantly since the early post-1945 period, and distinctions between open and closed societies look much more problematic. What she highlights, however, is the impossibility of leading a fully human life in totalitarian conditions. She links thinking and freedom together, and neither is possible if personal judgement and responsibility are denied. We are distinguished as creatures by a 'great capacity ... to start something new'.[29] Nothing could be more threatening to the totalitarian world view.

Arendt's point, of course, is not simply that we have good grounds for preferring certain political regimes to others. She knows that human beings can manage their affairs effectively in all manner of ways. Relative political values are unlikely to be the most significant in a life lived well. But the totalitarian model prevents us from leading a *properly* human life. Even our experience of 'the materially and sensually given world depends', she suggests, upon each of us 'being in contact with other men, upon our *common* sense which regulates and controls all other senses and without which each of us would be enclosed' in our 'own particularity of sense data which in themselves are unreliable and treacherous'.[30] Our capacity to make ourselves at home in the world depends upon our plurality, and that plurality is denied in the totalitarian vision.

Politics as a practice, which necessarily presupposes at least some stable assumptions, keeps the worst at bay but it cannot be any and every politics. For Arendt, a recognition of plurality is a necessary condition of a defensible politics. She treats plurality as a natural feature of the human condition, yet it is vulnerable to malice and neglect in modern mass-based polities.[31] Plurality demands procedures; and procedures need institutional support.

This takes us back, by a circuitous route, to Fuller's 'eight desiderata' for a viable legal system. In a nutshell, he insists that we need published, prospective rules, intelligible to agents, internally coherent, feasible, reasonably stable, that are respected by officials. He treats these as purely formal requirements, neutral with respect to substantive laws and objectives.[32] Agents are left to pursue their various goals, as Arendt insists they should be, and to bear responsibility for their actions and choices. Note that the desiderata themselves are not at all controversial. I think we can properly describe them as banal. But they leave human beings free to go about their business in a context of substantive rules that enable them to fashion their lives in reasonable awareness of the consequences of their actions.

Arendt is not usually regarded as a foundational thinker but she actually defends minimum conditions that would have to be satisfied in any sustainable polity, taking ordinary human capacities into account. And the defence she offers is philosophical, not ideological, compatible with a host of different circumstantial perspectives. I am not suggesting that she would necessarily endorse Fuller's desiderata but they are compatible with her endorsement of a procedural politics in *The Human Condition*. To be sure, her critics have argued that her Aristotelian citizens are so detached from mundane concerns that they have little in substantive terms to talk about. Fuller offers conditions that they would have to discuss, whatever they wanted to do collectively.

On this reading, absence of rules is a political evil of a rather subtle kind. It does not strike us in the same way as atrocities but we can see that its impact is demoralising. Without rules, co-operation with strangers is impossible. In the extreme cases Arendt focuses on in *The Origins of Totalitarianism*, whole populations are denied a capacity to act independently. In both horrific and quiet forms, what we are faced with is wilful denial of human agency.[33] It does not follow that agency should never be denied. Judicial punishment is a serious matter but justified in appropriate circumstances. We punish people for what they do, not simply for being Josef K. (a Jew, black, Roma, gay or whatever).

What I offer here is not a theory of evil (I'm not sure what that would look like) but a characterisation of limits we should not knowingly cross, no matter what we want. It has close affinities with standard arguments in political philosophy. Mill's 'harm' principle also sets limits though, in practice, they look too intrusive, too difficult to apply consistently to cases. A concept of evil leaves us with limits but very broad ones, compatible with the deep pluralism of the modern world.

My own feeling, though I don't have the space to develop the idea properly here, is that a concept of evil, for limited purposes, can replace the curious fiction of a state of nature as a limiting condition for any conceivable polity. In Hobbes's classic account, a state of nature is a standing hypothetical threat, a condition in which 'commodious living', no matter how conceived, is actually impossible. To prefer a state of nature to civil society is to set oneself beyond co-operative discussion. Put bluntly, we can disagree about all manner of things but not about the co-operative basis of a worthwhile human life.

A concept of evil does similar work for us. It is no longer simply a question of deep disagreement, or even disgust. No serious person could endorse the pervasive, and utterly unpredictable, vulnerability that Kafka so vividly depicts. It is not a fully human life, though episodes in recorded history come close enough to it to put us on our guard. The point is very simple. Interesting disagreement about the relative merits of various schemes of social co-operation presupposes that co-operation of some kind is inescapable. Once that point is established, all manner of ordinary considerations come into play. Co-operation might commit us to consensual agreement as a regulative ideal, at least in spheres where it can be reasonably attained. There is plenty of scope for considering exceptions to that rule, driven by concerns about security or relative advantage, but they would have to be defended. We can hardly get into practical conversation at all if consensual agreement is ruled out from the outset as a relevant normative criterion.

The pervasive influence of Hobbes is still evident in this recasting of contractual argument. It reminds us, though, that there is a good deal more to *Leviathan* than the first half of the book. The fact that Hobbes dwells so extensively on the Kingdom of Darkness in the concluding sections must be taken seriously.[34] For a man who took a deeply sceptical view of moral argument, warning us at every turn not to get carried away by passions and personal conviction, he has some very dark things to say about the Church of Rome. He identifies the domain of the Church with the 'principality of Beelzebub over daemons', where genuine worship is reduced to 'conjuration or enchantment', the evidence of the senses overturned, bread and wine miraculously transformed, all in an attempt to buttress the dubious authority of what should properly be regarded as a teaching institution.[35]

It is not surprising that Hobbes should hold these positions but we must ask ourselves why he chose to devote time and effort to the detailed refutation of arguments that he could hardly take seriously. What he highlights again and again is the presumption of speaking with authority on the basis of conviction alone. The (claimed) civil authority of the Church of Rome, he argues, is pure fancy, manifestly 'grounded in two errors'.[36] The Bishop of Rome claims that his 'kingdom is not of this world' and that he is 'Christ's vicar' on earth.[37] In a literal sense, however, these are things we cannot know but only take on trust if we are so minded. And this, for Hobbes, leaves us without any hope of reasonable agreement because it is simply a fact that we may (or may not) be moved by someone else's conviction. We may have prudential grounds for going along with a conviction we don't share but there is no possibility of reasonable agreement. In Hobbes's account, claims to civil authority made on behalf of the Church undermine the prudential consensus that drives his civil philosophy. And the Church of Rome's assumption of universal jurisdiction effectively sets it in a (potential) state of war with all established political orders.

Hobbes's outrage at the Church of Rome operates at a number of levels. The fact that he takes issue with doctrine is not, in itself, philosophically interesting though his attempts to marshal theological and scriptural argument are deeply revealing. What is crucial, however, is his insistence that the pretensions of the Church are incompatible with a robust civil philosophy. Absurdity can be discounted, but not claims to inspiration. A special kind of understanding, revealed to a select few, enshrined in an institutional structure that guarantees rectitude, cannot be a basis for consensual agreement.

We should be clear here that Hobbes's expectations about consensus are modest. He knows that individuals are partial and passionate, blinkered in everything they say and do. This is inescapable, though it will not affect all our thinking in equal degree. It is simply the case that preferences are assessed from a personal perspective, hence the scope for agreement on all manner of substantive issues is strictly limited. But we can factor that point into our thinking, and then move on. It is precisely because he recognises the partiality of preferences that Hobbes invokes Leviathan in the first place.

Partiality is everywhere but the Church of Rome is a special case for Hobbes. It claims authority and universal jurisdiction without appealing to demonstrable grounds. Fanatical individuals are equally unguarded and can, of course, be awkward partners in collaborative projects. The Church, however, invokes standing authority, no matter what is being discussed. Hobbes's basic position presupposes a distinction between things we can, in principle, agree on and other matters where disagreement is inevitable. The fanatic blurs the distinction; the Church, worryingly, as a matter of institutional principle.

My concern here is not to defend Hobbes's case against Rome, rather to highlight his clear conception of the limits of a defensible civil philosophy. He accepts diversity in judgement as a fact of moral and political life, and strives to adapt institutions to the vagaries of ordinary experience. Nothing is served by supposing that all would be well if only human beings could somehow transcend their condition. Moral realism along these lines is, in fact, available in Christian doctrine but its merits are lost if we extend institutional judgement beyond strictly demarcated spheres. Hobbes wants to create security and predictability through politics but that is precisely what is lost if we equate truth with inspiration.

Hobbes takes our mundane experience very seriously indeed. It is based on a boring predictability that is actually a necessary condition for sustained co-operation. What the image of a state of nature shows, beyond all doubt for Hobbes, is that without stability and predictability, nothing can be taken for granted, even life itself.

Kafka's depiction of K. vividly illustrates a very similar point. The poor man could take nothing at face value. The more he tried to resolve his desperate dilemma, the deeper his confusion became. What had he done? Where had he gone wrong? No one can tell him.

Dystopian images of this kind are not depictions of actual societies though they do give us a horrifying picture of what life might be like when things go very badly wrong. For any regime to use arbitrariness as a systematic strategy in political control is to invoke an institutional contradiction in terms. Institutions require rules. And, in Hobbes's view, bad rules are better than no rules. Without rules of some kind, human beings simply cannot live effectively, whether we adopt a model of state of nature or totalitarian dystopia to explain why that might be so. In a literal sense, any such regime is inhuman, contravening the myriad ordinary assumptions that human beings make in order to keep going. Anything that comes remotely close to that should serve as a warning to us. The term evil does not seem to be too strong to capture the enormity of that experience.

Notes

1 See John Milbank, *Theology and Social Theory: Beyond Secular Reason* (Oxford: Blackwell, 1990); and Creston Davis, John Milbank and Slovoj Zizek, eds, *Theology and the Political: The New Debate* (Durham, NC: Duke University Press, 2005).

2 See T. M. Scanlon, *What We Owe to Each Other* (Cambridge, MA: Harvard University Press, 1998).

3 See Stuart Hampshire, *Justice is Conflict* (Princeton: Princeton University Press, 2001); and Jonathan Glover, *Humanity: A Moral History of the Twentieth Century* (London: Jonathan Cape, 1999).

4 Cited in Richard J. Bernstein, *Radical Evil: A Philosophical Interrogation* (Cambridge: Polity, 2002).

5 John Rawls, *Political Liberalism* (New York: Columbia University Press, 1993).

6 See Immanuel Kant, '*Groundwork of the Metaphysics of Morals*', appearing as a chapter in his *Practical Philosophy*, ed. Mary J. Gregor (Cambridge: Cambridge University Press, 1996), pp. 41–108.

7 Kant, '*Groundwork of the Metaphysics of Morals*', p. 49.

8 Immanuel Kant, *Religion within the Boundaries of Mere Reason*, ed. Allen Wood and George di Giovanni (Cambridge: Cambridge University Press, 1998), p. 53.

  9 Kant, *Religion within the Boundaries of Mere Reason*, p. 56.

10 Franz Kafka, *The Trial*, trans. Idris Parry (London: Penguin, 1994).

11 Kafka, *The Trial*, p. 1.

12 Hannah Arendt, 'Franz Kafka, Appreciated Anew', in her *Reflections on Literature and Culture*, ed. Susannah Young-ah Gottlieb (Stanford: Stanford University Press, 2007), p. 95.

13 See Hannah Arendt, *The Origins of Totalitarianism* (London: George Allen and Unwin, 3rd edn, 1967).

14 See Bruce Haddock, 'Liberalism and Contingency', in Mark Evans, ed., *The Edinburgh Companion to Contemporary Liberalism* (Edinburgh: Edinburgh University Press, 2001), pp. 162–71; Bruce Haddock, 'Practical Reason and Identity', in Bruce Haddock and Peter Sutch, eds, *Multiculturalism, Identity and Rights* (London: Routledge, 2003), pp. 10–24; Bruce Haddock, 'Thin Universalism as Weak Foundationalism', in Bruce Haddock, Peri Roberts and Peter Sutch, eds, *Principles and Political Order: The Challenge of Diversity* (London: Routledge, 2006), pp. 60–75; and Michael Oakeshott, *Hobbes on Civil Association* (Oxford: Blackwell, 1975).

15 See Nigel Simmonds, *Law as a Moral Idea* (Oxford: Oxford University Press, 2007).

16 Simmonds, *Law as a Moral Idea*, p. 69.

17 See H. L. A. Hart, *The Concept of Law* (Oxford: Clarendon Press, 1961).

18 Lon L. Fuller, *The Morality of Law* (New Haven: Yale University Press, 1969, revised edition), p. 184.

19 Fuller, *The Morality of Law*, p. 41.

20 Fuller, *The Morality of Law*, p. 39.

21 Fuller, *The Morality of Law*, p. 39.

22 See Hannah Arendt, *Eichmann in Jerusalem: A Report on the Banality of Evil* (London: Penguin, 2006).

23 See Hannah Arendt, *Responsibility and Judgment* (New York: Schocken Books, 2003).

24 See Thomas Hobbes, *Leviathan*, ed. Richard Tuck (Cambridge: Cambridge University Press, 1991), chapter 13, p. 89.

25 Hobbes, *Leviathan*, p. 90.

26 Hobbes, *Leviathan*, p. 89.

27 Hannah Arendt, *The Origins of Totalitarianism*, p. 467.

28 See Margaret Canovan, *Hannah Arendt: A Reinterpretation of her Political Thought* (Cambridge: Cambridge University Press, 1992).

29 Hannah Arendt, *The Origins of Totalitarianism*, p. 473.

30 Arendt, *The Origins of Totalitarianism*, pp. 475–6.

31 See Hannah Arendt, *The Human Condition* (Chicago: University of Chicago Press, 1999).

32 See Lon L. Fuller, *The Morality of Law*, p. 153.

33 See Arne Johan Vetlesen, *Evil and Human Agency: Understanding Collective Evildoing* (Cambridge: Cambridge University Press, 2005).
34 See Thomas Hobbes, *Leviathan*, pp. 417–82.
35 Hobbes, *Leviathan*, pp. 417, 412, 341.
36 Hobbes, *Leviathan*, p. 354.
37 Hobbes, *Leviathan*, p. 354.

Chapter 5

UNREASONABLE OR EVIL?

Kerstin Budde

MODERN THEODICIES

In her book *Evil in Modern Thought*, Susan Neiman argues that the root of the *problem* of evil can be found in the fact that the world is not as it ought to be.[1] Around us, we see needless suffering, callous and thoughtless cruelties, monstrous atrocities, unjust punishments and so much more which makes us cry out: This ought not to have happened! Once we utter this cry, Neiman thinks that we are 'stepping onto a path that leads straight to the problem of evil'.[2] That is, once we admit that reality is not as it ought to be, that it contains numerous evils which are inflicted upon (innocent)[3] people, we are faced with how we should react and respond to this world.

Should we despair at the imperfection of our world and resign ourselves to a hopeless situation where the innocent suffer and our social world is ridden by numerous evils? Or is there a way out? Is there a way to explain and account for the evil in our world?

Here the problem of evil becomes a problem of intelligibility.[4] We want to know and understand why the world is structured as it is; we need to find reasons of why it does not measure up to the way it ought to be. The implicit belief here is that the world is, indeed, intelligible, that we can make it intelligible, that it is not obscure to our reasoning capacities. If we had to admit that the world is not intelligible, then in both theoretical and practical terms we would be lost. How could we orient our thinking and acting in the world if the world was obscure to reason, that is, if we had no way of grasping and understanding it.[5] Thus, Neiman states that: 'Belief that there may be reason in the world is a condition of the possibility of our being able to go on in it.'[6] The confrontation of a world that is not as it ought to be leads us to ask why the world is structured as it is. We try to comprehend how evil can happen, even though it ought not to happen. But our goal is not just comprehension. The motivation to understand is rooted in our need to orient thinking and acting. We try to understand what has gone wrong so that we might put it right.

Facing the problem of evil in this sense then implies not just the quest for understanding evil in the world but the quest for a better future. This is what Neiman calls theodicy in the broad sense.

> Theodicy, in the broad sense, is any way of giving meaning to evil that helps us face despair. Theodicies place evils within structures that allow us to go on in the world. Ideally, they should reconcile us to the past evils while providing direction in preventing future ones.[7]

Neiman is emphatic that the problem of evil and the attempt to provide theodicies in the broad sense are the heart of the history of philosophy but also that those attempts are not confined to history. Instead she argues that the problem of evil is so persuasive to our situation in the world that modern political philosophy also cannot but engage in it (though they might not name it as the 'problem of evil'). In particular, Neiman also states that Rawls, perhaps despite himself, was deeply concerned with the problem of evil.[8] This paper will attempt to show that Neiman is right to say that Rawls addresses the problem of evil and provides us with a theodicy, and will develop an account of (political) evil on that basis. Finally, I will highlight the usefulness and the dangers of such an account.

RAWLS AND THE PROBLEM OF EVIL

Rawls ends the introduction to the paperback edition of *Political Liberalism* with the following statement,

> The wars of this century with their extreme violence and increasing destructiveness, culminating in the manic evil of the Holocaust, raise in an acute way the question whether political relations must be governed by power and coercion alone. If a reasonably just society that subordinates power to its aims is not possible and people are largely amoral, if not incurably cynical and self-centred,

one might ask with Kant whether it is worthwhile for human beings to live on the earth?[9]

This statement, perhaps like no other in Rawls's work, shows the centrality of the problem of evil in his work. It echoes old questions of classical theodicy whether humanity deserves to be created or whether the world would be better off without humans given that we do so much evil.[10] However, more importantly, it also betrays the initial dismay at a world that admits of so much evil and the equally strong belief that this is not how the world ought to be and that to be able to continue to act in the world we must find a way of understanding and changing the present condition.

Rawls's programme for change is his account of a realistic Utopia, most extensively developed in the *Law of Peoples*. He states two motivating ideas for the *Law of Peoples* and its idea of a realistic Utopia. The first is that,

> the great evils of human history – unjust war and oppression, religious persecution and the denial of liberty of conscience, starvation and poverty, not to mention genocide and mass murder – follow from political injustice, with its own cruelties and callousness.[11]

The second idea is closely connected. Rawls argues that 'once the gravest forms of political injustice are eliminated by following just (or at least decent) social policies and establishing just (or at least decent) basic institutions, these great evils will eventually disappear.[12] Here we can see clearly aspects of a broad kind of theodicy that Rawls can be said to provide us with. He identifies the great evils in the world – unjust wars, oppression and so on – and provides us with an explanation for their existence: they are the result of political injustice. We are given thus a framework through which to comprehend the great evils that afflict us: They are not God's punishment for our sins, they are not entrenched in the very nature of the world, but human made. Furthermore there is one rather specific cause of the greatest evils, namely political injustice. And once we have this framework in place that identifies the cause of great evils in the world, we also have guidelines for creating a future without these evils. If political injustice is the root of all great evils, then we have to eradicate political injustice, and the world will become as it ought to be – without great evils. And Rawls, of course, famously claims that we can eradicate injustice by establishing a just political society, at home in the form of a constitutional democracy that exemplifies a form of political liberalism, and abroad by uniting under a reasonable law of peoples with other liberal and decent peoples.

Rawls terms this blueprint for the eradication of great evils a realistic Utopia. He thereby confronts one of the key questions of the problem of evil: Might it not be the case that even if we can pinpoint the root of all evil, we are still too corrupted, unwilling or unable to change anything? No progress of the human race can be made, it might be said. Rawls here adopts Kant's idea of a reasonable faith. Kant had argued against Mendelssohn that moral progress can be detected in the world.[13] Furthermore, Kant argues that even if no progress could be detected, unless the opposite is proven, we would still be justified – indeed even morally obliged – to assume that progress of the human race is possible.[14] Thus Rawls attempts to show at length in his works how a just political system, domestically in the form of political liberalism and internationally in form of a society of liberal and decent peoples, is possible. He defines the task as follows,

> political philosophy assumes the role Kant gave to philosophy generally: the defense of reasonable faith (III: 2.2). As I said then, in our case this becomes the defense of reasonable faith in the possibility of a just constitutional regime.[15]

This reasonable faith involves the belief in a fundamentally moral nature of human beings. Human beings are capable of being moral, they have a sense of justice and a conception of the good, and they are capable of being reasonable and of following the principle of reciprocity.

> We must start with the assumption that a reasonably just political society is possible, and for it to be possible, human beings must have a moral nature, not of course a perfect such nature, yet one that can understand, act on, and be sufficiently moved by a reasonable political conception of right and justice to support a society guided by its ideals and principles.[16]

Furthermore it involves the belief that the natural and social conditions are such that we can, if we try, achieve such a just national and international order.[17]

The reasonable faith that Rawls advocates and defends in his later works also leads to a reconciliation with our social world. Reconciliation is one of the aims of theodicies conceived in the broad sense.[18] Reconciliation is achieved by showing that the world gives us no reason for despair because it contains neither incomprehensible nor unchangeable evils. By providing an explanation for evil in the world and at the same time the hope to change it, we can again live and act in the world. Consider the following statement that Rawls makes at the very end of the *Law of Peoples*,

> While realization is, of course, not unimportant, I believe that the very possibility of such a social order itself can reconcile us to the social world . . . For so long as we believe for good reasons that a self-sustaining and reasonably just political and social order both at home and abroad is possible, we can reasonably hope that we or others will someday, somewhere, achieve it; and we can then do something toward this achievement.[19]

Furthermore, Rawls later adopted a Hegelian view of the role of political philosophy as concerned with reconciliation.[20] In *Justice as Fairness: A Restatement*, Rawls defines this task as follows,

> political philosophy may try to calm our frustration and rage against our society and its history by showing us the way in which its institutions, when properly understood from a philosophical point of view, are rational, and developed over time as they did to attain their present, rational form.[21]

In the *Law of Peoples* Rawls summarises his view on reconciliation by saying that 'To be reconciled to a social world, one must be able to see it as both reasonable and rational.'[22]

Rawls is trying to fulfil this role of political philosophy by showing us that, implicit in the culture and institutions of our constitutional democracies, we can find the political ideas and concepts from which we can construct a political conception of justice and forge an overlapping consensus. Already within our institutions through a long history – think of Rawls's frequent discussions of the role of the Reformation – we find implicit the ideas and concepts which will enable us to construct a just political system. Even facts that might contribute to strife and conflict,

Rawls argues, are, in fact, rational. Thus, in the *Law of Peoples*, Rawls asks whether we should be reconciled to the fact of pluralism. And he answers his own question as follows,

> To show that reasonable pluralism is not to be regretted, we must show that, given the socially feasible alternatives, the existence of reasonable pluralism allows a society of greater political justice and liberty. To argue this cogently would be to reconcile us to our contemporary political and social condition. [23]

Although Rawls does nothing here to argue the case, it is clear that he in fact thinks this is possible.[24] Reasonable pluralism leads us to adopt the ideas of political liberalism and the idea of a society of liberal and decent peoples. This would, Rawls suggests, eradicate all the great evils in the world, leading to greater justice. Thus, we can view reasonable pluralism as rational and a world that contains it as a world that is as good as it can be. Hence, by showing that our world, our institutions, besides containing evil, also contain those elements that are reasonable – that is those elements of the world that are as they should be – Rawls can reconcile us to our world and give us hope.

I would conclude then, that Rawls can, indeed, be seen as being deeply concerned about the problem of evil and as providing us with a theodicy in the broad sense as Neiman defines. To recapitulate the key points: Rawls provides a framework and explanation for the great evils in the world: they are the result of unjust institutions. He provides us with a theoretical blueprint towards a future world which is without those evils, that is, a blueprint for a just political order at home and abroad, and argues forcefully that we can at least hope to attain it one day. He thereby reconciles us to our social world in two ways. Firstly, reasonable faith in a just political order fences off despair and gives moral direction to our action here and now and for the future. Secondly, identifying and explaining those elements in our social world which are already rational or reasonable and showing how they are or can be the grounds for a just world order can reconcile us to our present condition in reassuring us that, although evil is present at the moment, so are goodness and rationality. The world is already partly as it ought to be. The world is intelligible to us and it is (at least partly) reasonable and rational.

EVIL OR UNREASONABLE?

In the previous section I have analysed how far Rawls can be said to provide us with a theodicy in the broad sense as Neiman has defined it. I argued that there is, indeed, good and consistent textual evidence that warrants such a reading. Thus, from now on, I want to presume that Rawls is, indeed, providing us with a theodicy and to continue to ask what implications his particular theodicy has for the nature of evil. That an account of the nature of evil must be connected to a particular theodicy seems obvious.[25] If the aim is to explain evil, to make a world that contains evil intelligible, and to suggest ways to eradicate that evil, some account of the nature of evil seems to be necessary. If I cannot pinpoint what makes certain persons, actions, institutions or states of affairs evil, I can hardly understand or explain their evilness. Furthermore without an account of what makes persons, actions, institutions or states of affairs evil, we cannot aim to avoid evil in the future. Thus, if I identify the cause and root of evil in the sinfulness and godlessness of humans, then it seems logical that sinful and godless actions, persons, institutions are evil and, to avoid evil, we have to become faithful and morally righteous. If the root of all evil is social inequality, which leads to envy and destructive self-love, then it seems that all actions or institutions which create or further social inequality are evil and to eradicate evil we need to establish social equality. I shall then assume that any theodicy will tell us at least something about the nature and cause of evil in the world.

Turning then to Rawls's theodicy, we can ask what exactly his account of the cause and nature of evil is. Given that Rawls never explicitly sets out to provide a theodicy, this might involve some reconstruction but, as I argue below, his argument has some clear implications with regard to the cause and nature of evil.

The most obvious starting point for Rawls's account of evil can be found in his motivation for putting forward a realistic Utopia. As quoted above,[26] Rawls states there the belief that, firstly, all great evils follow from unjust institutions and that, secondly, once just institutions replace unjust institutions, all great evils will eventually disappear.[27] Thus, we might reasonably say that Rawls identifies political injustice as cause for the great evils. The opposite, just political institutions, do not cause any great evils and, importantly, he assumes that great evils are not created by any other source. If political injustice causes great evil exclusively, then something about political injustice must account for the nature of great evils. But to say political injustice causes evil, and political justice eradicates evil, does not yet tell us much. We need an account of what makes a political institution just or unjust to get a substantial grasp on the cause and nature of great evil.

Now I would suggest that what makes a political institution just on Rawls's account is that it fulfils the criteria of reasonableness and reciprocity: that is, any political institution that is designed and governed by principles that all could reasonably accept in a position of mutual equality.[28] Those principles are fair and, thus, on Rawls's account of 'Justice as fairness', just. To be able to find and agree on such just principles, people themselves must be 'reasonable'. This reasonableness includes 'the willingness to propose and honor fair terms of cooperation, and . . . the willingness to recognize the burdens of judgment and to accept their consequences'.[29] Furthermore reasonable people affirm reasonable comprehensive doctrines which recognise the burdens of judgement and which support a democratic society[30] and accept the democratic freedoms.[31] Thus just institutions are those that embody reasonable principles of justice, which reasonable people can accept as fair terms of co-operation between them. A just society is one which endorses and maintains just institutions because they are supported by reasonable people who hold reasonable comprehensive doctrines. The key to political justice is then reasonableness. If we are all reasonable and thus accept reasonable principles of justice we will have just institutions. And as just institutions will eradicate all the great evil in the world, we can now say that reasonableness is the key to eradicating great evil.

Now if what I sketched here is right, and reasonableness is the ingredient which secures political justice and banishes great evil on Rawls's account, then unreasonableness must do the opposite: it is the ingredient that causes political injustice and thus causes the great evils in this world. To support this claim let us look at some of the statements that Rawls makes about unreasonable doctrines or unreasonable people:

Unreasonable people
- are unwilling to 'propose principles and standards as fair terms of cooperation and to abide by them'[32]
- 'plan to engage in cooperative schemes but are unwilling to honor, or even to propose, except as a necessary public pretense, any

general principles or standards for specifying fair terms of cooperation. They are ready to violate such terms as suits their interests when circumstances allow'[33]

• will think it reasonable'to use political power, should they possess it, to repress comprehensive views that are not unreasonable, though different from their own'[34]

Unreasonable doctrines

• 'reject one or more democratic freedoms'[35]
• cannot support a democratic society[36]
• assert that religious or philosophical truth override political reasonableness[37]
• 'are a threat to democratic institutions, since it is impossible for them to abide by a constitutional regime except as a *modus vivendi*. Their existence sets a limit to the aim of fully realizing a reasonable democratic society with its ideal of public reason and the idea of legitimate law'[38]
• exemplify the existence of'unreason'[39]
• must be contained'like war and disease – so that they do not overturn political justice'[40]

Examples of unreasonable doctrines are: fundamentalist religious doctrines; doctrine of the divine right of monarchs; the various forms of aristocracy; and the many instances of autocracy and dictatorship.[41]

Looking at these statements, we can draw the following conclusion: unreasonableness in persons and in doctrines prevents or endangers the establishment of just institutions and they positively aim to establish institutions which reject the ideas of reciprocity, fair co-operation and tolerance – on Rawls's definition, those people and doctrines will bring about only unjust institutions. Unreasonableness is the cause of unjust institutions and unjust institutions cause the great evils. And we might say that what causes evil is evil itself. Thus, a religious person might say sin does not only cause evil but actually is evil in itself; similarly, a Rousseauian might say social inequality does not just cause evil but is evil in itself. If we accept the hypothesis that what causes evil is itself evil, then the analysis so far would suggest that unreasonableness as the cause of great evils is itself evil. And, indeed, I want to suggest that reading Rawls as providing us with theodicy in the broad sense, and tracing back the implication that has for the nature of evil itself, commit us to assume that unreasonableness is the essence of great evils. The nature of (great) evil is unreasonableness.

IS THE UNREASONABLE EVIL?

I have started from Neiman's assumption that Rawls is engaged in theodicy defined in a broad sense. In the first section I have shown that there is very good textual evidence to suggest that one can read Rawls's project that way. I have then in the second section tried to trace one implication of viewing Rawls's argument as a theodicy, namely the implied cause and nature of evil itself. Tracing backwards from Rawls's statement that political injustice causes all great evils and political justice will eventually cure us from all great evils, I have shown that this belief in effect – within the framework of Rawls's argument – implies that reasonableness causes justice and eradicates evil and that, on the flipside of it, unreasonableness causes injustice and evil and is thus itself evil. The root cause of evil is unreasonableness.

Now this seems quite a stark statement. Ordinarily, when we accuse someone of being unreasonable, we do not necessarily think they are evil. Unreasonableness seems like a common feature of ordinary people: sometimes we are all unreasonable. Evil seems to indicate more than just unreasonableness. To be evil is to be wicked, vile, a monster, doing wrong and hurtful actions for the fun of it.[42] Does it not totally devalue the concept of evil if we identify it with unreasonableness? And, indeed, when Rawls talks about his paradigmatic example of evil, Nazism and the Holocaust, he seems to imply that evil has a demonic character: thus, he speaks of the 'manic evil of the Holocaust'[43] and the demonic possibility that the Holocaust exemplifies.[44, 45] The key point here may be the malicious intention of murder and cruelty. When Rawls describes the 'particular evil of Nazism' he draws attention to their deliberative and premeditated intent always to cow their enemies by brutality and terror and to rule them by force; to exterminate or enslave the enemy people.[46] We expect this kind of description when we talk of evil persons or doctrines. If we believe that evil can be equated only with such demonic and monstrous personalities or acts, then to call the unreasonable evil is clearly false. But is this more traditional description of evil actually an adequate or exhaustive description of evil? And does it fit well into Rawls's overall account?

Hannah Arendt in her book *Eichmann in Jerusalem* notes the comforting factor of thinking that evilness requires monstrousness,[47] because then it can be construed as the utterly alien and extraordinary. What Arendt argued in her account of the Eichmann trial was something different. She pointed out the ordinariness and normality of this man who had done such great evil. He was more like us than like some kind of demonic monster.[48] Evil was not demonic or monstrous but, as she provocatively claimed, banal.[49] Furthermore, when Arendt describes Eichmann, she attributes to him something which I think we might call with Rawls 'unreasonableness'. She says,

> The longer one listened to him, the more obvious it became that his inability to speak was closely connected with an inability to think, namely, to *think* from the standpoint of somebody else.[50]

Eichmann's inability to think about what other people would think or accept as right or reasonable, marks him out as someone who will not be able or willing to offer others terms of social co-operation that they could reasonably be expected to accept. In addition, this inability to see or comprehend the standpoint of others, made him unable to see or comprehend the wrongs he did. Eichmann did not have a bad conscience when he did his evil acts because he did not think he was doing anything wrong.[51] The wilful intent to do wrong was missing, and on a classical understanding of wrong and evil acts, the intent to do wrong was seen as the key ingredient.[52] Thus, to call the unreasonable evil might not be so outlandish after all. And the unreasonable doctrines that Rawls describes share many similarities with the kind of evil that Arendt describes. When Rawls asks whether fundamentalist religious or secular doctrines could be reconciled to the social world that political liberalism envisages, he denies that possibility. He argues that, for those fundamentalist doctrines, 'the social world envisaged by political liberalism is a nightmare of social fragmentation and false doctrines, if not positively evil'.[53] Thus, Rawls himself argues that those doctrines that prevent the establishment of just institutions, thus the eradication of evil, do so not out of malicious or demonic intent. Instead, they think they are doing the right thing to oppose a liberal society and to impose their fundamentalist doctrine on others. Again, the characteristic feature of them is their unreasonableness not their monstrous and sadistic character.[54] Those fundamentalist doctrines, however, are the cause of great injustices and, thus, great evils. Here again, we have come back to the initial thesis: the cause and nature of evilness are essentially unreasonableness. This I argue fits better with Rawls's overall account: To eradicate evil, that is, to establish a just society, all unreasonable doctrines need to be contained or destroyed – not just all sadistic or demonic doctrines.

I have so far argued that political injustice causes the great evils. Furthermore, because political injustice is caused by unreasonableness (either of persons or of comprehensive doctrines) unreasonableness is the root cause of evil and, thus, evil itself. Although this seems to me a logical conclusion, one could, of course, question this assumption. Thus, it would be possible, I think, to say that, although injustice causes all the great evils and injustice itself is caused single-handedly by unreasonableness, this in itself does not imply that unreasonableness itself is evil. Thus, one would have to maintain that evil is caused by something which is not in itself evil. I think, however, we would then expect an explanation of how the cause of evil falls short of being evil itself and more importantly how exactly evil is created, that is, what property exactly transforms what is not yet evil into something evil? Perhaps one such explanation could be that it is the amount of suffering created by acts (unreasonable or otherwise) that transform those acts into evil ones. That would mean the act as such is not evil in itself. It is only if those acts have specific consequences that we retrospectively call them evil. But the same act in different circumstances might not create great suffering and, thus, not be evil on that account. If two people press a button they believe will turn Australia into a nuclear wasteland but in only one case is the button real, then the person pushing the fake button will not have committed an evil act as no great suffering occurs. This account of evil runs counter to many of our intuitions which would still deem the act evil.[55] Similarly, we would not call all causing of great suffering necessarily evil. War inevitably causes great suffering. Yet, those who believe that some wars could be justified, would not call such wars evil.[56] I think Rawls's remarks that, unreasonable doctrines exemplify 'unreason' and should be contained like war and disease, would support my thesis that he is committed to view the unreasonable as evil in itself.

Even if we think that there is a link between what causes evil and what is evil itself, however, we might ask how strong this link really is. Is it only unreasonableness that causes evil, and thus is evil? Is evilness exhaustively captured by unreasonableness? So we might say that while we are happy to acknowledge that unreasonableness is partly the cause of evil and, thus, itself partly evil, something must be added to unreasonableness for it to become fully 'evil'. Thus, we might say that unreasonableness is a necessary but not sufficient cause of evilness. This relates back to the debate whether evilness is a matter of degree of wrongness or whether evilness must, in addition to having wrong-making features, also have a qualitatively different feature to call it evil.[57] On this view evil is not just something very, very wrong, and to equate evil with the end-point of our ordinary scale of wrongness is to misconceive the distinctiveness of evil. So we might say with respect to Rawls's theory that unreasonableness is bad and wrong, and evil acts are of course in a sense bad and wrong, thus evil acts are also unreasonable. But for acts, persons or doctrines to be called evil something qualitatively different must be added, say the enjoyment of the evil one does, or a particularly dehumanising cruelty. Rawls might on occasion even seem to take this route, when he talks of the demonic nature of Nazism as the prime example of evil. However, if Rawls really thought so, then nearly all of the great evils he identifies would not count as evil. Unjust wars, poverty, religious oppression for most of the cases do not necessarily happen because of monstrous and demonic intentions. The additional requirement of evil intention or monstrous personality would make evilness too narrow a category and could not really account for all the great evils in the world.[58]

Yet another question regarding the strength of the link between unreasonableness and evil is whether any amount of unreasonableness causes evil and thus is evil. Thus, we might ask whether any small amount of unreasonableness constitutes evilness or whether only fully or thoroughly unreasonable people, actions or comprehensive doctrines are really evil? Anything below that might be bad or wrong but not evil. This would place evil on a continuum of wrongdoing which understands it not as something qualitatively different from normal wrongs but as quantitatively different. I think this might be a promising route to take and I also think there is evidence that Rawls is committed to it. Consider his argument that to eradicate all great evils we need to eradicate political injustice. Rawls had identified political justice with his conception of liberal justice put forward in *Political Liberalism*. Now this idea of justice is based on the idea of reasonableness and supports only a constitutional democracy. It would then seem that any other form of regime is unjust and would cause great evils in the world.

Rawls goes on to argue, however, that, if we have a federation of liberal and decent regimes, all great evils will be eradicated. How can that be? Decent regimes are not liberal democracies, thus they are not fully just. How can they help to eradicate the great evils? I think the answer lies in Rawls's argument that, while decent societies are not fully reasonable and just, they are also not fully unreasonable or unjust.[59] Their acceptance of human rights and a common good conception of justice prevent them from being fully unreasonable.[60] Thus, he states when discussing decent peoples,

> The question might arise here as to why religious or philosophical doctrines that deny full and equal liberty of conscience are not unreasonable. I do not say that they are reasonable, but rather that they are not fully reasonable; one should allow, I think, a space between the fully unreasonable and the fully reasonable.[61]

Furthermore decent societies do accept a reasonable law of peoples. Within the context of a law of peoples, decent societies accept equality and reciprocity and are prepared to offer, accept and abide by fair terms of co-operation, even if internally in the treatment of their own citizens they lack reasonableness. Thus, decent peoples are fully reasonable on the international level and not wholly unreasonable on the domestic level, as they accept basic human rights and have a common good conception of justice. An example of a fully unreasonable people would be what Rawls terms an outlaw state. A criterion for outlaw states is that they are not willing to propose, accept and abide by fair terms of co-operation on the international level: they think war an acceptable or desirable means to further their self-interest[62] and they are fully unreasonable at the domestic level, too: they deny even basic human rights to their citizens.[63] Outlaw states are the only ones that warrant military intervention. We might say that it is the fact of their being fully unreasonable that explains and justifies this drastic measure. Burdened societies, on the other hand, being prevented by adverse circumstances from being decent or liberal, are not subject to military intervention. They are not unreasonable but unlucky or disadvantaged[64] and thus deserve our help. Furthermore, burdened societies deserve help even if human rights abuses occur in them[65] and even if the human rights abuses and the human suffering might, in effect, be the same in burdened societies as in outlaw states.[66] The point to make here is that burdened societies are not fully unreasonable in the sense that they are unwilling to abide by fair terms of co-operation but, rather, burdened societies are, through no fault of their own, unable to do so. Outlaw states, on the other hand, are able to do so but unwilling.

Thus, we might want to say that what is fully unreasonable (be it persons, actions or institutions) causes great evil and is evil in itself. If we understand by fully unreasonable the systematic and flat refusal to accept any norms of reciprocity or any attempt to offer or act according to reasonable terms of co-operation that others could reasonably accept, then I think this might capture what we perceive as evil about acts, persons or institutions.

Even if we might have qualms about labelling a person evil if they are unreasonable, I want to suggest finally that this account of evil might, in fact, be particularly apt to describe *political evil*. It is a fact of the human condition that human beings are both needy and vulnerable and not co-ordinated by instinct. Human beings have to create organisations and structures that provide for their needs and co-ordinate their living together peacefully. Any political doctrine or institution which is fully unreasonable jeopardises this fundamental goal of political organisation. By being fully unreasonable, those doctrines lack the idea of social co-operation, and instead aim to impose order and co-operation through force.[67] For their own (selfish) interests, fully unreasonable regimes exploit the fact that human beings are needy and dependent on co-operation.[68] In the game of co-operation, they are only takers, never givers: they deny the idea of reciprocity on which peaceful social co-operation is built. And, as the political creates the conditions for our living together, fully unreasonable institutions and doctrines threaten the possibility of human beings living in this world peacefully and with dignity. That is what makes unreasonableness on the political level such a great evil, and perhaps even the greatest evil.

CONCLUSION

Is an account that classifies the unreasonable, even if only the fully unreasonable, as evil a useful account? We might ask whether it does not fail to mark out and name strongly the particular wrong that evil acts are, that it might easily lead us to classify as evil acts which are not, and that it might lend itself to the demonisation of others.[69] In a few concluding remarks I want to spell out in which sense I think that an account of evil in terms of unreasonableness is useful and in which sense it might be dangerous. It is useful in terms of enabling us to understand evil not as something totally other or demonic but something that all human beings are capable of: sometimes we are all unreasonable though not many people are consistently fully unreasonable. Understanding evil in terms of a continuum of a characteristic helps to prevent us from demonising people in one sense: we cannot say that evil people (acts, doctrines) are totally unlike us (or the doctrines we accept) thus, there is no room for smug self-righteousness.[70] There is also the danger, however, of demonising people or doctrines in another respect. Just because unreasonableness is, to a certain extent, such an integral feature of most people (and doctrines) sometimes, it might be easy to label people and doctrines, which are indeed unreasonable but not fully so, as evil. Thus, one might be tempted to call every state that is not a liberal democracy unreasonable and therefore potentially evil. The question here is one of judgement. When is a doctrine fully unreasonable and when merely partially so? This highlights a general difficulty with gradual accounts of evil. If evil is the end of a continuum (here of unreasonableness) then where do we draw the line on this continuum between the evil and the non-evil (the fully unreasonable and the partially unreasonable). The danger here lies in the fact that, to suit one's own (political) purposes, it might be easy to classify as evil that which is not evil. Thus, it might be tempting to label as fully unreasonable those doctrines, institutions or persons that simply do not accept as reasonable all policies, arguments and institutions that we deem reasonable. But I think, firstly, that this danger is not exclusive to the gradual account, as history has proved that it is also fairly easy to portray as 'demonic' and 'monstrous' doctrines, acts or peoples that have no inherent demonic characteristics. Secondly, I think it might misconceive the leeway for judgement that this account leaves. Full unreasonableness lies at the outer end of the continuum; as I said, we best understand it as the flat refusal to accept any norms of reciprocity or any attempt to offer or act according to reasonable terms of co-operation that others could reasonably accept. As such, any attempt to label acts, peoples, doctrines or persons as evil which are, in fact, not fully unreasonable but open – even if to a limited extent – to offer reasons others could accept should be easy to spot. This is especially so if we accept the requirement of publicity for political discourse. If those persons and peoples who hold opposing views and doctrines have the possibility of presenting their reasons for public scrutiny, labelling them as fully unreasonable should be difficult if they are not, in fact, fully unreasonable. Of course, the danger that we delude ourselves and others still remains but that is a general danger of individual and political life.

Any account of evil brings with it the danger of misuse. But the concept of evil fulfils a need we have to name properly the phenomena we encounter.[71] Evil is more than just what is bad, wrong, unfortunate or unlucky. It is the starkest term for disapprobation we have, naming those things that we find most dangerous, most troubling and incomprehensible in the realm of human action. I have tried to show how a Rawlsian account of (political) evil as unreasonableness can account for that sentiment and fulfil our need to identify and name evil where we find it. As such, it should also help us to refute the application of that concept where it is not warranted.

Notes

1 Susan Neiman, *Evil in Modern Thought: An Alternative History of Philosophy* (Princeton: Princeton University Press, 2004), p. 322.
2 Neiman, *Evil in Modern Thought*, p. 5.
3 It is a question on its own whether only underserved harm is called evil or whether all harm whether deserved or undeserved should count as evil. Geoffrey Scarre, *After Evil: Responding to Wrongdoing* (Aldershot: Ashgate, 2004), p. 7. I leave the question here open.
4 Neiman, *Evil in Modern Thought*, p. 7.
5 Neiman, *Evil in Modern Thought*, p. 7.
6 Neiman, *Evil in Modern Thought*, p. 324.
7 Neiman, *Evil in Modern Thought*, p. 239.
8 Neiman, *Evil in Modern Thought*, p. 314.
9 John Rawls, *Political Liberalism* (New York: Columbia University Press, 1996), p. lxii; see also John Rawls, *The Law of Peoples* (Cambridge, MA: Harvard University Press, 1999), p. 128.
10 Peter de Marneffe, 'The Problem of Evil, the Social Contract, and the History of Ethics', *Pacific Philosophical Quarterly*, 82, 2001, pp. 11–25; p. 11.
11 Rawls, *The Law of Peoples*, pp. 6–7.
12 Rawls, *The Law of Peoples*, p. 7.
13 Immanuel Kant, 'On the common saying: That may be correct in theory, but it is of no use in practice', in M. Gregor (ed.), *Practical Philosophy* (Cambridge: Cambridge University Press, 1999), p. 8: 307–9.
14 Kant, 'On the common saying', p. 8: 309.
15 Rawls, *Political Liberalism*, p. 172.

16 Rawls, *Political Liberalism*, p. lxii.
17 Rawls, *The Law of Peoples*, p. 7. John Rawls, *Lectures on the History of Moral Philosophy*, B. Herman (ed.) (Cambridge, MA: Harvard University Press, 2000), p. 321.
18 Neiman, *Evil in Modern Thought*, p. 239.
19 Rawls, *The Law of Peoples*, p. 128.
20 Neiman, *Evil in Modern Thought*, p. 313.
21 Rawls, *Justice as Fairness: A Restatement*, E. Kelly (ed.) (Cambridge, MA: Harvard University Press, 2001), p. 3.
22 Rawls, *The Law of Peoples*, pp. 126–7.
23 Rawls, *The Law of Peoples*, p. 12.
24 Rawls, *The Law of Peoples*, pp. 126–7.
25 Neiman herself is not interested in the property or definitions of evil, and she suggests that there might not be an intrinsic property of evil (*Evil in Modern Thought*, p. 9). Rather, she is interested in tracing what the changes in the understanding of the problem of evil reveal about the understanding of ourselves and our world. While being reticent to give a definition of evil is understandable, I think it cannot be denied that, to provide a theodicy (which Neiman is arguably not) one would have to say something about the nature and property of evil.
26 Rawls, *The Law of Peoples*, pp. 6–7, 126.
27 It might at first seem puzzling how Rawls can claim that the great evil of starvation can be caused by unjust institutions. Rawls follows here Sen's argument that famines are caused by faults within the political and social structure (Rawls, *The Law of Peoples*, pp. 9, 109), and thus also a result of political injustice.
28 Rawls himself points out in the passage quoted about his motivation for a realistic Utopia that the idea of political justice he is referring to is the same as in *Political Liberalism*, and he also points to several pages in the paper 'The Idea of Public Reason Revisited' reprinted in the *Law of Peoples* (Rawls, *The Law of Peoples*, pp. 7, 7n.9). I believe the reference to *Political Liberalism* and to those pages supports my suggestion that 'reasonableness' is key to the idea of political justice (see especially Rawls, *The Law of Peoples*, pp. 136–7, 140–1). For the interconnection of the idea of reasonableness with reciprocity see Rawls, *Political Liberalism*, pp. 49–50 and Rawls, *The Law of Peoples*, p. 14.
29 Rawls, *Political Liberalism*, p. 48n.1.
30 Rawls, *The Law of Peoples*, p. 173.
31 Rawls, *Political Liberalism*, pp. 63–4.
32 Rawls, *Political Liberalism*, p. 49.
33 Rawls, *Political Liberalism*, p. 50.
34 Rawls, *Political Liberalism*, p. 60.

35 Rawls, *Political Liberalism*, pp. 63–4.

36 Rawls, *The Law of Peoples*, p. 173.

37 Rawls, *The Law of Peoples*, p. 178.

38 Rawls, *The Law of Peoples*, p. 179.

39 Rawls, *Political Liberalism*, p. 65.

40 Rawls, *Political Liberalism*, pp. 63–4.

41 Rawls, *The Law of Peoples*, p. 173.

42 See Marcus G. Singer, 'The Concept of Evil', *Philosophy*, 79: 2, 2004, pp. 185–214; pp. 196–7 for an account of evil which puts emphasis on evil intention.

43 Rawls, *Political Liberalism*, p. lxii.

44 Rawls, *The Law of Peoples*, p. 21

45 In *A Theory of Justice* Rawls sketches the distinction between the unjust, bad and evil man, as part of a full theory of the good yet to come. Again, here, the intention to do wrong and the enjoyment of the wrong act seem crucial. He says: 'What moves the evil man is the love of injustice: he delights in the impotence and humiliation of those subject to him and he relishes being recognized by them as the wilful author of their degradation.' (John Rawls, *A Theory of Justice,* revised edn (Oxford: Oxford University Press, 1999), p. 386). Rawls never proceeded to offer a full theory of the good which would explain theses distinctions in more detail. I have tried to argue that his later theory commits him to a wider definition of evil.

46 Rawls, *The Law of Peoples*, p. 99.

47 Hannah Arendt, *Eichmann in Jerusalem* (New York: Penguin, 2006), p. 276.

48 Arendt, *Eichmann in Jerusalem*, p. 276.

49 Arendt, *Eichmann in Jerusalem*, p. 252.

50 Arendt, *Eichmann in Jerusalem*, p. 49.

51 Arendt, *Eichmann in Jerusalem*, pp. 267–7.

52 Arendt, *Eichmann in Jerusalem*, p. 277.

53 Rawls, *The Law of Peoples*, pp. 126–7.

54 Or consider Rawls's later discussion of the evilness of Hiroshima and the fire-bombing of Japanese cities in his paper 'Fifty Years after Hiroshima', in S. Freeman (ed.) *John Rawls: Collected Papers* (Cambridge, MA: Harvard University Press, 2001), pp. 565–72, especially 569–70. The evilness of the bombing and the order to bomb could not be explained by a sadistic enjoyment of seeing civilians suffer (not even by the fact that civilians suffered, as Rawls is ready to admit that causing the suffering of civilians might under certain circumstances be justified). The reasons that make the bombings evil, according to Rawls (limited means-ends reasoning, assigning American lives more value than Japanese lives, intimidating the Russians) are more signs of unreasonableness than of wickedness.

55 Daniel M. Haybron, 'Moral Monsters and Saints', *The Monist*, 85: 2, 2002, pp. 263–4.
56 Eve Garrard, 'Evil as an Explanatory Concept', *The Monist*, 85: 2, 2002, p. 327.
57 Ibid. p. 321; Haybron, 'Moral Monsters and Saints', p. 262.
58 See Scarre, *After Evil*, pp. 5–7. Quite another question – which is beyond the bounds of this paper to pursue – is what causes human beings to be unreasonable? Is it something inherent in their nature or is it due to social circumstances (Paul Formosa, 'The Problems with Evil', *Contemporary Political Theory*, 7, 2008, pp. 401–2)?
59 Rawls, *The Law of Peoples*, pp. 67, 74, 83–4.
60 Rawls, *The Law of Peoples*, pp. 74–5, 83–4.
61 Rawls, *The Law of Peoples*, p. 74.
62 Rawls, *The Law of Peoples*, p. 90.
63 Rawls, *The Law of Peoples*, pp. 81, 90n.1, 93n.3.
64 Rawls, *The Law of Peoples*, p. 106.
65 Rawls, *The Law of Peoples*, pp. 108–9.
66 Thus, in a burdened society, people might starve to death because the society does not have the technological means to provide for food reserves in case of need while, in an outlaw state, people might starve to death because the dictatorship callously refuses the distribution of food reserves.
67 Rawls, *The Law of Peoples*, p. 65.
68 Here I understand under selfish interest both personal gain and aggrandisement or the advancement of an ideology or religion.
69 On the dangers of demonisation, see Haybron 'Moral Monsters and Saints', p. 261, and Formosa 'The Problems with Evil', p. 398.
70 Formosa, 'The Problems with Evil', pp. 401–2.
71 Neiman, *Evil in Modern Thought*, p. xv; Formosa, 'The Problems with Evil', p. 410.

Chapter 6

EVIL IN CONTEMPORARY INTERNATIONAL POLITICAL THEORY: ACTS THAT SHOCK THE CONSCIENCE OF MANKIND

Peter Sutch

If there is one branch of contemporary political theory that has many concrete examples of 'evil' as its subject matter, it is international political theory. Indeed, the word has made a spectacular return to international political discourse since 9/11. In this chapter I suggest a novel approach to theorising 'evil' in international political theory. It is an approach that diverges from much of the established (and very useful) commentary that has explored the concept as it emerges in the rhetoric of political leaders on both sides of the war on terror. I think that dealing with evil in that context has limited political utility and suggest that we turn our attention to the broader institutional construction of, and response to, evil in international society. As a sub-discipline, that has traditionally had war as its principal focus normative International Relations (IR), theorists have had to deal not just with the prospect of armed conflict between states but with genocide, war crimes and crimes against humanity, including the killing of civilians, institutionalised rape and torture and the grotesque human suffering that follows conflict-created famine and refugee flows. At the extreme end of this suffering is a phrase that has enormous significance in international politics. That phrase is found in the claim that there are 'acts that shock the conscience of mankind'. This phrase has been used time and time again (sometimes with the more politically correct 'humankind' as its referent) to evoke great evil of such unimaginable proportions that it precipitates new forms of legal, political or military sanction.

In what follows I explore the claim that the ideas associated with this phrase play a key role in the normative development of international society. Such development is found primarily in the field of humanitarian law but has evolved to play a more controversial role in international human rights law and international criminal law and an even more controversial role in the political debates surrounding humanitarian intervention or the preventive use of force in response to the war on terror. Although I intend to show that the historical development of international society is driven, in part, through our responses to 'acts that shock', I am not going to suggest that there is a discernible 'lowest common denominator' kind of morality, that universally we know 'real evil' when we see it. Although the idea of 'acts that shock' is tremendously evocative, this would be too simplistic an interpretation of a complex legal and social phenomenon. The word 'evil' has a long history in the history of IR scholarship. In much of the contemporary literature, the association of the re-emergence of the term in political discourse with the eruption of the war on terror has signalled increased interest in its meaning but also increased scepticism towards its use and conceptual worth.[1] For some critics the circumstances we face underpin a 'lesser evil ethics' as we are forced to choose between bad and worse.[2] For others 'the designation of one's adversaries as evil and the associated assumption that all actions taken in response to it are inherently good is not only practically dangerous but morally hazardous'.[3] The connection between 'acts that shock' and the category 'evil' is made regularly in the literature but very little work has been done on fleshing out its meaning. In part this is because, as Ervin Staub notes 'evil is not a scientific concept with an agreed meaning, but the idea of evil is part of a broadly shared human cultural heritage'.[4] Much contemporary analysis emphasises the vagueness of the concept while urging the reader not to underestimate its importance.[5] While the argument in this chapter seeks to firm up the terms of the debate by exploring evil in terms of the socio-legal concepts that inform the phrase 'acts that shock', it cannot fully overcome these concerns. 'Evil', as a word, has a strong currency in political and popular rhetoric but it is also a word that has many problems. As Jarna Petman argues, more often than not the use of evil in international politics is 'a hegemonic argument . . . an attempt to represent one's particular interests as cosmopolitan, one's values as universal, one's reign as community'.[6] The use of the category to describe international terrorism, genocide, or the crimes against humanity detailed in the Rome Statute adds little to the detailed legal construction of those crimes, and using evil to describe those acts not explicitly provided for or subject to international controversy is legally, politically and morally problematic.[7] It also suggests that the perception of evil is different from other political judgements.[8] Typically the international community navigates around such controversy by purposely leaving the meaning of vital, but contestable, ideas ambiguous. This is the pattern observable in the evolution of international human rights (note the vague preamble to the Universal Declaration of Human Rights [UDHR]) and it is the pattern we find in the development of 'acts that shock'. As with human rights, however, the greater the normative burden that 'acts that shock' is asked to shoulder, the more urgent the matter of normative justification becomes.

Narrowing our focus from evil as a concept in itself to 'acts that shock' is, of course, going to miss some very important ideas and analysis. It does give us, however, the opportunity to engage in political interpretation of how the international community purports to come to know evil and to think about its normative potential as a driver of institutional development. 'Acts that shock' is very much a normative category. It exists at the fringes of positive law but has a significant impact on both the development of public international law and on the rulings and opinions of international courts. Beyond the law, it has been used as a moral bludgeon to urge a greater humanitarianism in international affairs and to explain the development of concepts such as 'the responsibility to protect', human security and humanitarian military intervention. The phrase appears in international legal and political discourse regularly from 1899 to the present day. It has been used in the important treaties and declarations that seem to provide the normative trajectory of international society. Its reappearance is normatively significant in the sense that it has become indelibly associated with the progressive development of legal and political institutions which have at their core the protection of individuals from severe harm.

The phrase itself is tremendously evocative. It implies (at least in its more contemporary formulation) universality. More than this, it implies a universal and immediate reaction to evil; a shared, reflex reaction. Importantly, however, the phrase is most commonly found in legal and political documents. These treaties and declarations are not reflex, natural reactions. They are laboriously debated and drafted. They are institutionally interpreted within a framework that is pluralist in its nature and frequently subject to the hegemonic influence of the politically and economically powerful. This should not concern us too much. Norms have always developed in socially complex ways. This chapter seeks to contribute to an understanding of how agents come to know evil (or that which shocks the collective conscience of humanity). The purpose of trying to understand this process is to develop a basis for reflecting on the confidence we can have in the idea of evil as associated with 'acts that shock' because it is on the back of these claims that policy prescriptions for more assertive international institutions and actions rest.

A central claim in this chapter is that in order to understand 'acts that shock' we need to develop a social epistemology. The idea of a social epistemology explores the collective and social/political ways in which we come to know – in this case – evil. The purpose of exploring the institutional responses of the international community to 'acts that shock' has two elements. First, I think we gain more from thinking about the way evil is used in this formal way than if we engage with the contemporary political rhetoric that seems to fuel both terrorism and the war on terror. Much of the literature cited above draws inspiration from the return of the category 'evil' to the political discourse of contemporary international politics. But it is no surprise that the general views expressed by scholars searching for meaning in that discourse are highly critical of the unreflective and extremely partial way the concept is employed.[9] We gain more simply because the social construction of 'acts that shock' is a discursive and deliberative process. Looking at the social processes of how we come to know evil is not simply a matter of describing the conference proceedings, examining the outcome documents they produce, or exploring the judicial interpretation of their application (although these are inevitably important parts of that process). This brings us to our second and core theoretical point. There is a healthy debate concerning social epistemology emerging in international political theory. The central issue is the extent to which we can have confidence in the institutional/normative 'progress' of international society. In this chapter this debate manifests itself as the question 'should we create more assertive policies and institutions to respond to "acts that shock"?'

The idea of a social epistemology is firmly embedded in the constructivist tradition in IR theory. The phrase is found in the work of scholars such as Emanuel Adler but Adler is describing a project typical of many social constructivists and International Society (English School) theorists.[10] In a fascinating development Alan Buchanan has recently developed a neo-Kantian cosmopolitan argument about the legitimacy of global governance institutions that also explicitly relies on what he labels 'social moral epistemology'.[11] This approach is less well estab-

THE MARTENS CLAUSE, ACTS THAT SHOCK AND THE EVOLUTION OF INTERNATIONAL LEGAL PRINCIPLES

Perhaps the most celebrated instance of the phrase 'acts that shock' is in the preamble to the Universal Declaration of Human Rights. That document is built atop the recognition that 'disregard and contempt for human rights have resulted in barbarous acts which have outraged the conscience of mankind'.[21] The idea of a public conscience that is a universal moral compass has a much longer history, however.[22] In modern thought expressions of this idea, including that found in the UDHR, are regarded as expressions of the 'Martens clause' which is found in the preamble to the 1899 Hague convention with respect to laws and customs of war on land (Hague II). The clause, inserted by the Russian delegate to the conference (Friedrich Martens or Fyodor Fyodorovich Martens), reads:

> Until a more complete code of the laws of war is issued, the High Contracting Parties think it right to declare that in cases not included in the Regulations adopted by them, populations and belligerents remain under the protection and empire of the principles of international law, as they result from the usages established between civilized nations, from the laws of humanity, and the requirements of the public conscience.[23]

The Martens clause has been subject to a considerable amount of debate in legal circles. While there is significant dispute (in scholarly and juridical argument) about the normative import or precise meaning of the clause, it has become a permanent feature of humanitarian law and of public international law more generally.[24] We find the phrase (in various forms) in all Hague law (which principally regulates the specific means of war) and Geneva law (which protects victims of warfare) which together constitute the primary instruments of international humanitarian law (IHL).[25] We find the phrase in specific IHL treaties that ban particular weapons or modes of killing and injuring that are either indiscriminate or induce abhorrence because of the way they kill or maim. Here, for example, we see the ideas associated with 'acts that shock' come in to play in respect of bacteriological or chemical weapons or in treaty or case law dealing with sea and land mines.[26] The clause has also been debated by jurists in authoritative forums such as the Nuremburg tribunals, the International Court of Justice (ICJ or World Court) and in the International Criminal Tribunal for the Former Yugoslavia (ICTY).[27] Over time, International Humanitarian law (IHL) and international human rights law (IHRL) became more integrated under the auspices of the Martens clause as its principles became applicable both in peace and war and in internal as well as international conflicts (key here are the rulings of the ICJ in the *Corfu Channel Case* and in several rulings at the ICTY.[28] Further developments include the development of a category of crimes against humanity which spans and directly builds upon IHL and IHRL,[29] and the development of International Criminal Law where, according to the Rome Statute of the ICC, 'mindful that during this century millions of children, women and men have been victims of unimaginable atrocities that deeply shock the conscience of humanity', parties have sought to establish individual criminal liability to such acts.[30] We also find its meaning and import debated by the representatives of states in the General Assembly or before international courts and tribunals,[31] relied upon by agents of international organisations, and we even find it embedded in the military manuals of states such as the United Kingdom, the United States, and Germany.[32]

Despite (or perhaps because of) such widespread usage there is no agreement on the precise meaning and normative import of the Martens clause. There is, however, a clear sense that the idea of an 'humanity' capable of being shocked by the infliction of severe harm on persons plays a significant role in the development of the international legal order. This shock may lie in a reaction to vast acts of violence, such as genocide, or to the development of new technologies that bring indiscriminate or grotesque suffering and death. Among the contending claims, we find some very important legal interpretations of the Martens clause that underpin the political invocation of 'acts that shock'. The first is the idea that the norms associated with the clause underwrite what Meron calls 'the humanization of international law'.[33] Central to this idea is the claim that the response to 'acts that shock' has, since the UDHR, brought IHL under the broad wing of IHRL.[34] This does not mean that the law of armed conflict is 'trumped' by IHRL. Rather, the progressive development of IHL is now guided by human rights standards.[35] A second vital claim is that the gradual legal development of 'principles of humanity and of the public conscience' (an alternate version of the Martens clause) is creating new normative hierarchies in public international law. Here we find claims concerning the development of a hierarchy of fundamental human rights and of the evolution of peremptory norms of international law (norms that have superior status and are universally binding with no possibility of derogation). Here we must grasp the essential nature of obligations *erga omnes*, 'owed to the whole international community, with the practical consequence that the right to react to any violation of the norm is not confined to the state or states directly injured',[36] and the genesis of peremptory norms *jus cogens* where certain rights begin to eclipse the traditional rights of sovereignty.[37] Even though there is a solid consensus on the elements of the history of 'acts that shock', every step is contestable and subject to multiple interpretations and, once in the thick of the detail, we begin to see the tentative, even fragile, development of a community of practice that reaches beyond the law. A complete exposition of the normative import of the Martens clause for public international law is beyond the scope of this chapter. It is important, however, to get a clear sense of the contours of the principal debates so as to begin to grasp the normative potential of 'acts that shock' for international political theory.

The original intention of Friedrich Martens, the Russian delegate to the Hague Peace Conference and after whom the clause is named, was not to develop a normative principle at the heart of humanitarian law. As Cassese shows, it was a diplomatic ploy designed to meet the concerns of the great powers in respect of provisions relating to the legal status of citizens of occupied countries taking up arms (as partisans) against the occupying powers.[38] Nevertheless there is a consensus view that the Martens clause has enjoyed an evolving importance in IHL and in general public international law more broadly.[39] To get a sense of what 'acts that shock' actually means it is enlightening to look at the construction of the clause and its constituent parts and at the range of general interpretations that exist in the scholarly literature and in the practice of international actors. The Martens clause has taken several forms over its long life. The broad contours of 'acts that shock' are nevertheless clearly linked to the various expressions of the clause as it appears in law. I am not claiming that a positivist legal interpretation of 'acts that shock' has a monopoly on meaning.[40] I do think, however, that exploring the reiterative interpretation of the clause in practice gives us a sense of the ways in which its meaning and import are socially constructed and disputed. This process is itself an examination of the social construction of knowledge, an exploration of the 'socially sanctioned' interpretation of norms.[41]

When exploring the Martens clause, legal scholars tend to treat considerations of 'humanity' and the idea of the 'public conscience' as distinct elements.[42] The idea of humanity, as expressed here, is given a narrow, but still important, construction. It is narrow in the sense that it reaffirms the principle in IHL that acts of war that are not necessary for the attainment of definite military advantage are unlawful.[43] It is important because the clause in not a simple matter of treaty law. It is significant that the clause is most often found in the preamble to key documents rather than in the main body of the text of most of the instruments that repeat it. The Martens clause is taken to be part of customary international law and is therefore of universal scope. It serves to remind all actors (whether party to the treaty or not) that there are some standards that are binding regardless of whether a state has become party to a particular treaty or has reservations against some elements of treaty law.[44] Even in the case of the Geneva conventions, where there is no lengthy preamble and where the clause is found in the body of the text, there is general agreement that the clause functions to remind parties of their obligations under customary international law.[45] The importance of this is clear as Ticehurst, quoting the International Law Commission demonstrates:

> [the Martens clause] ... provides that even in cases not covered by specific international agreements, civilians and combatants remain under the protection and authority of the principles of international law derived from established custom, from the principles of humanity and the dictates of public conscience.[46]

The interpretation given to the 'dictates of public conscience' is even more interesting because there is some dispute over the source of 'public conscience'. For some it has its roots in *opinio juris*, for others it is broader and can be found in the vox populi or public opinion more generally.[47] *Opinio juris* is an essential element of customary international law which is constituted by *usus* (state practice) and the vital normative element (*opinio*), the belief that such action is required by international law. If the public conscience were to be determined by the (admittedly rather tricky) exploration of *opinio juris* it would not really add anything to existing customary international law and would thus continue to ground the concept in the consent of states. At the other end of the scale is the thought that public conscience reflects natural law and, as such, represents universally binding moral rules. The displacement of natural law by legal positivism has meant that contemporary public international law is quite hostile to the idea of natural law; nevertheless, some scholars maintain that the Martens clause has preserved its influence.[48] A third view here (and one that coexists with the first interpretation) is that public opinion influences the development of international law (including customary law) 'when governments are moved by public opinion to regard certain developing norms as already declaratory of customary law or as *jus nascendi*'. According to Meron 'this was precisely how the Rome Conference on the Establishment of an International Criminal Court formulated certain crimes in its proposed statute'.[49]

The various interpretations of the elements of the Martens clause lead to similar contestations over the meaning of the clause as a whole. Most scholars follow a similar pattern to Cassese's position which divides the key claims into three broad camps. The first is broadly interpretative and uses the clause either to establish the importance of existing customary law (to rule out the argument that whatever is not regulated by treaty is permitted) or to require that, where doubt concerning the interpretation of principles of IHL arise, demands of humanity and of the public conscience should inform the interpretation. The second camp is far more radical and argues that the elements of the clause establish new sources of international law – that principles of humanity and the public conscience stand beside treaty and custom as the basis of legal norms. The third argues that the clause has 'motivated and inspired' the development of IHL.[50] There is real disagreement in scholarly reflection and judicial application, with each interpretation finding some support in the opinions, rulings and *obiter dicta* that stem from international courts. This disagreement concerns the extent to which 'acts that shock' establishes a moral principle at the heart of positive law.

Rather than revisit the analysis of judicial decisions found in the work of Cassese and others cited above, I want to explore the sense in which the influence of 'acts that shock' has inspired international society to develop a broad consensus on a core set of community values that have a higher status than most public international law. There is a sense in which the weight of public opinion forged in response to 'acts that shock' first yielded legal instruments designed to deal with specific acts and, gradually, led to the development of general principles capable of standing above state consent and of driving international institutional reform. Veuthey shows that,

> Public conscience, or perhaps it would be more accurate to say 'public revulsion', has been the driving force behind every codi- fication of international humanitarian law over the last 150 years. Rather than the proactive inscription of lofty ideals, the major humanitarian and human rights instruments in use today are mainly the products of the painful lessons learned from the col- lective tragedies and humanitarian disasters of modern history. Indeed the list of humanitarian catastrophes of the late 19th and 20th centuries mirrors the timeline for the adoption of these instruments.[51]

Veuthey goes on to give just this list. Lowlights include: the terrible predicament of the wounded at the battle of Solferino in 1859 (first Geneva Convention 1864); the suffering of civilians under occupation and in camps in World War II (1949 Geneva conventions): the indis- criminate use of conventional weapons in Vietnam (Convention on Certain Conventional Weapons 1980); the hazard to civilian popula- tions caused by the use of landmines (Ottowa 1997); as well as ethnic cleansing in the Former Yugoslav Republic and Rwanda (International Criminal Tribunal and International Criminal Tribunal for Rwanda).[52] In all of these cases, a combination of lobbying by non-governmental organisations (NGOs) and civil society groups and the work of states and international organisations can be seen to generate the response to 'acts that shock'. There appears to be a reliance on this contested and morally indeterminate idea as part of a shared process of responding to great political challenges where we lack the moral and institutional resource to cope. Under the influence of human rights, however, there has been a step-change in the way this process worked. As early as 1950, human rights principles were being used to flesh out the meaning of the Marten's clause.[53] Now, however, human rights principles are being used to assert the peremptory nature of norms closely associated with 'acts that shock'. Meron argues that,

> under the influence of the concepts of human rights, of obligations erga omnes ... and of peremptory norms, international law has

embarked on a limited transition from bilateral legal relations to a system based on community interests and objective normative relationships.[54]

It is the development of this hierarchy of norms that suggests to some the subversion of the state-consent model of international law and its replacement with a hierarchy of universally binding, human rights-based norms.

While the categories of norms *erga omnes* and *jus cogens* have been recognised in courts, treaties and the declaratory statements of key actors and scholars, the idea that we have an uncontroversial hierarchy of norms is still hotly disputed. There is general consensus that reference to such norms has been largely (although not solely) doctrinal and rhetorical.[55] Nevertheless, the way these categories respond to 'community interests' and issues of global public policy, core values such as 'basic human rights', and pressing challenges such as environmental change where international society can ill-afford to wait for consensual instruments to develop, gives the political theorist, interested in the development of justice rather than law in itself, significant pause for thought. Obligations *erga omnes* were first identified by the International Court of Justice in dictums in the *Barcelona Traction* case in 1970. Such obligations are owed to the international community as a whole. This means that states not harmed by the wrongful act can pursue their legitimate interest in the protection of the rights involved. Such obligations generally aim at regulating action within the borders of a state (where no other state is harmed) and so the importance of the norms themselves validates the legal interest of unaffected states.[56] Similarly, the category of *jus cogens*, recognised in article 53 of the Vienna Convention on the Law of Treaties, develops that idea that there are certain peremptory norms from which there can be no derogation. While the notion arose initially as a constraint on freedom of contract, the more usual contemporary contention is that there are matters of global public policy or vital community values (often expressed in the style of the Martens clause or basic human rights) that are so fundamental to the system that the law could not survive without them. There are two main ways in which this latter sense of *jus cogens* has been interpreted. Alexander Orakhelashvili draws the distinction between systemic and substantive norms where systemic norms are inherent in the character of the international legal order. Thus, such principles would be those such as *pacta sunt servanda*, recognition and consent.[57] The more radical interpretation, however, places the emphasis on the centrality of certain substantive norms, such as the prohibition on the use of force, self-determination and fundamental human rights.[58] The crucial issue here, of course, is the extent to which international law has moved beyond a voluntarist model of legal obligation in deference to what Charney terms universal law.[59] The evolution of peremptory norms has led some scholars to claim that certain 'acts that shock' demand international responses that trump the desires or consent of states. Such responses, argue liberal cosmopolitans, such as Buchanan, may demand an overruling of the mechanisms of consent-based international politics. Examples of such action include bypassing the Security Council to embark on unilateral humanitarian military action, or overriding established interpretations of the United Nations Charter principles on the use of force, or establishing the universal and compulsory jurisdiction of the International Criminal Court.[60] The key question thus becomes: are we confident enough in our institutionalised response to 'acts that shock' to support such radical prescriptions?

The short answer to this question is that there is still considerable room for debate. It is certainly not the case that the progressive development of international law leads inexorably to the cosmopolitan conclusions. We do see some striking examples of superior norms in action. The overruling of Rwandan reservations to the Racial Discrimination Convention and the Genocide Convention, on the grounds that the rights and obligations contained in those conventions were *erga omnes*, is a case in point.[61] We also see some important dissenting opinions which, while not influencing the judgment of the court, have an important impact on the development of law. Here the views of Judges Weeramantry and Shahabuddeen in the *Nuclear Weapons Advisory Opinion*, that the threat or use of nuclear weapons could not satisfy the requirements of the Martens clause, are especially important.[62] Yet we also see the persistent abuse of human rights that are readily acknowledged as *jus cogens* such as the prohibition on torture and *refoulement*,[63] ongoing controversy concerning humanitarian military intervention in the UN and passivity in the face of gross human suffering. As Shelton argues,

> The most significant positive aspect of this trend toward normative hierarchy is its reaffirmation of the link between law and ethics, in

which law is one means to achieve the fundamental values of an international society. It remains to be determined, however, who will identify the fundamental values and by what process.[64]

Ultimately this recognition brings us back to politics.

THE POLITICS OF 'ACTS THAT SHOCK THE CONSCIENCE OF MANKIND': EPISTEMIC UNCERTAINTY AND INSTITUTIONAL REFORM

The final question I want to pursue here is whether we 'know' evil clearly enough to override the pluralist structure of international society. It should be clear now that the idea of a social epistemology of evil has real content, a more tangible existence than that found at the root of much contemporary political rhetoric. It should be equally clear that, while there has been a substantial move towards filling out the content of 'acts that shock' with serious human rights abuses, the extent to which that drives a cosmopolitan reform agenda is unclear. Here, returning to the work of the political theorists we examined in the first sections of this chapter enables us to see the political potential of 'acts that shock'. In looking at 'acts that shock' in the legal context, it became clear that there is no unified sense of what such acts are or what institutional response they demand. In contemporary international political theory the debate similarly divides into radical and conservative camps. Both camps recognise the vital importance of human rights to the normative and institutional structure of international society but they have different views on the desirable pace of legal and institutional reform. Here, however, the debate is not just about the proper construction of the legal meaning of the Marten's clause. Rather it is about the processes by which we come to know what evil is in this socially constructed sense. In other words, the debate is about social moral epistemology and how much confidence we can have in our knowledge of evil. Are we confident enough to abandon the pluralist framework of international society and replace it with a human rights-based account of legal and political legitimacy?

On the progressive side of the debate, Buchanan argues that this is precisely what we should do. Buchanan points out that the debate goes well beyond procedural concerns towards more substantive issues. What he means is that we are not looking at questions such as

'Is the World Court procedurally justified in using the Martens clause to over-rule a reservation to a human rights treaty?' Instead, we are asking whether our current institutions live up to our moral obligations to respect human rights. The core of Buchanan's argument is that a systematic application of human rights principles is warranted and that this demands far-reaching reforms in the legal and political institutions of global affairs.[65] Such reforms include a radical overhaul of the United Nations Security Council (or, failing that, the establishment of a coalition of reasonably democratic states) to enable the just pursuit of humanitarian and human rights goals (including humanitarian military intervention, preventive self-defence and democratisation).[66] The idea is that such reforms put the protection of human rights at the centre of decision-making rather than the self-interested and strategic bargaining that current institutions encourage. Key to this claim is the further claim that it is possible to accommodate the 'facts of moral disagreement and uncertainty' through institutional reforms that can enhance the confidence we can have in the ways in which international legal and political order discovers and responds to these norms.[67] The challenge from more conservative theorists, such as Walzer, Reus-Smit and Adler, is that a social order that protects pluralism is essential to ensure that the social construction of the normative order continues to draw on the conscience of all mankind rather than a specific subset of them.[68]

The idea of epistemic uncertainty is the key to thinking about this debate. The more uncertain we are about 'acts that shock', the more reason we have for adopting an institutional structure that preserves the political space for peoples to determine their political and social futures in accordance with their own (internally and externally contested) account of moral legitimacy. To do otherwise is normatively risky. Buchanan refers to this risk when he describes the 'parochialism objection' to human rights-based reform. This refers to the concern 'that human rights are expressions of either an arbitrarily limited set of values or an arbitrary ranking of values' and that the powerful can assert a self-interested account of these values and norms.[69] Nevertheless we know that certain acts shock the conscience of mankind and that those acts can be described in terms of serious human rights abuses and crimes against humanity. The exposition of 'acts that shock' given here dovetails with Buchanan's account of the modern conception of human rights grounded in the legal and political development of human rights norms. There is a clear risk, or a great moral hazard, in not living up to these standards. It is undoubtedly the case that more conservative scholars (such as Adler, Walzer and Reus-Smit) have grown increasingly ambitious on the back of the development of a global human rights culture. But the reason they advocate a more pluralist approach is less to do with what we know 'shocks' the human conscience than with the desire to preserve the epistemic quality of international society so that the future development of this category is safeguarded. Once again the real argument is about the politics of social moral epistemology.

Buchanan argues forcefully that the progressive development of human rights norms have made them the central constitutive norms of international society.[70] The core of the modern conception of human rights is not disputed.[71] Buchanan maintains, however, the institutional framework through which the empirical or factual requirements of human rights are specified lacks the confidence of international actors.[72] They lack 'epistemic legitimacy' because they are subject to the self-interested behaviour of hegemonic actors and encourage strategic bargaining rather than human rights-based decision-making.[73] This, rather than any scepticism regarding the core human rights norms, informs the reliance on the conservative norms of non-intervention that often serve to frustrate human rights-oriented policy initiatives. In a powerfully argued article, Buchanan, writing with Robert Keohane, offers a 'cosmopolitan institutional proposal' that is designed to overcome these epistemic concerns.[74] The ideal solution, they argue, is to reform the United Nations Security Council, dropping the veto privilege for the five permanent members (P5) on issues relating to the protection of human rights under chapter VII of the United Nations charter (and therefore requiring the use of force) and augmenting the Council with some accountability mechanisms.[75] Recognising the challenges of reforming the UNSC, however, the most feasible effective reform is presented as the development of a supplementary body (a coalition of reasonably democratic states) capable of taking the lead when the UNSC cannot or will not act.[76] This builds on and supplements Buchanan's key insight that institutional legitimacy is a central part of moral legitimacy and forms the core of his account of social moral epistemology. Overcoming a lack of confidence in the ability of international institutions to deliver on human rights should encourage global actors to transcend the conservative and narrowly drawn legal norms governing self-defence, intervention and even forcible democratisation and to put human rights in their rightful place at the core of reformed international legal order. More radically still it should, Buchanan argues, move us away from a state consent-based model of international law to one firmly grounded on the systematic application of human rights principles to all areas of law.[77]

The reaction of Reus-Smit to the proposed dismantling of the 'equalitarian regime' in favour of a 'rehierarchisation' of international politics spells out the alternative point of view clearly.[78] His work sharply criticises Buchanan's argument and, in part, this is because the constructivist approach to social and institutional reasoning has a distinct view of the epistemic qualities of institutions. Reus-Smit's account of the constitutive and complex nature of reason requires us genuinely to defer to the outcomes of institutionalised reasoning.[79] Buchanan and Keohane make it clear in the very first paragraph of 'the legitimacy of global governance institutions' that they are more interested in the morally normative than in any question of sociological legitimacy.[80] Yet as Reus-Smit, and many others who concentrate on the politics of international law have demonstrated, the way that agents constitute the legal order, debating the merits of various interpretations of the law and of the merits of human rights-driven reform, is an essential part of any social moral epistemology and one that must be preserved. One of Reus-Smit's key criticisms of the liberal argument in favour of establishing a hierarchical international politics concerns the lack of sociological legitimacy such an order faces.

> By definition legitimacy is a social phenomenon, it depends on the judgment of others . . . Theorists such as Fukuyama and Buchanan and Keohane might decide that democratic coalition is legitimate a priori, but if international society determines otherwise, then their judgment is moot.[81]

The desire to preserve the equalitarian regime is not, however, simply down to the fact that recalcitrant (or nervous) states refuse to move to a human rights-based order. The need to preserve the political space for genuine debate on what shocks the conscience of mankind and how to respond is also taken up fully in the work of Walzer and Adler. Walzer's ideal global constitution sacrifices (to a degree) the ability to enforce human violations in order to preserve the global pluralism of what Adler calls the 'epistemic community'.[82] This position is not statist or 'communitarian' in the usual sense. Adler demonstrates that communities of practice cut across state boundaries and mediate between states, individuals, and human agency on one hand, and social structures and systems, on the other. It is within communities of practice that collective meanings emerge, discourses become established, identities are fixed, learning takes place, new political agendas arise and the institutions and practices of global governance grow.[83]

It is recognition of the importance of this element of social epistemology that militates against the establishment of a transcendental or hierarchical institutional order. The combination of the fact of political disagreement about the virtues of a robust response to 'acts that shock' combined with the normative importance of preserving access to the community of practice that will continue this debate gives us reason to 'wait for a larger transformation of social epistemology, practice and organization'.[84]

CONCLUDING REMARKS

The arguments presented in this chapter may seem a little circuitous in the face of a conclusion that suggests that we must wait and see what the international community makes of the opportunity to respond to 'acts that shock'. The present argument has two principal themes, however. The first is that a socio-political understanding of evil in international affairs can be grounded in the evolving practice of international society in its response to 'acts that shock'. This gives the concept substance in its consideration of humanitarian and human rights principles and epistemic legitimacy in that it is drawn from the interaction of international actors in the normative development of the legal and political order. It is sufficiently substantial to enable us to resist and critique the partiality of the use of the word 'evil' in much political rhetoric. The second theme offers reasons to take seriously the social processes by which we come to know such evil and counsels against an overly hasty push to institutions that shut down the avenues of participation in the social construction of evil. The temptation to institutionalise a robust response to these hideous harms is entirely understandable but there is clearly a need to recognise that there is still moral uncertainty – not so much about the moral qualities of those acts that shock the conscience of humanity but of the moral

and legal elements of an appropriate institutional response to those
acts.

Notes

1 P. Cole, *The Myth of Evil* (Edinburgh: Edinburgh University Press, 2006), pp.
   1–3; R. J. Bernstein, *Radical Evil: A Philosophical Interrogation* (Cambridge:
   Polity, 2002), p. 226; R. Jeffery, *Evil and International Relations: Human
   Suffering in an Age of Terror* (Basingstoke: Palgrave Macmillan, 2008), p. 157.
2 M. Ignatieff, *The Lesser Evil: Political Ethics in an Age of Terror* (Edinburgh:
   Edinburgh University Press, 2005), p. 5.
3 Jeffery, *Evil*, p. 158.
4 E. Staub, *The Roots of Evil: The Origins of Genocide and Other Group Violence*
   (Cambridge: Cambridge University Press, 1989), p. 25.
5 Bernstein, *Radical Evil*, p. 226; Jeffery, *Evil*, p. 158.
6 J. Petman, 'Evil in International Law', *International Law Forum*, 5, 2003, p.
   236.
7 A. M. Weisburd, 'International Law and the Problem of Evil', *Vanderbilt
   Journal of Transnational Law*, 34: 2, 2001, pp. 227–81.
8 Petman, 'Evil in International Law', p. 240.
9 Jeffery, *Evil*, p. 157.
10 E. Adler, *Communitarian International Relations: The Epistemic Foundations of
   International Relations* (London and New York: Routledge, 2005), p. 3.
11 A. Buchanan, *Human Rights, Legitimacy and the Use of Force* (Oxford: Oxford
   University Press, 2010), p. 6.
12 See, for example, C. Beitz, *The Idea of Human Rights* (Oxford: Oxford
   University Press, 2009), p. 108.
13 Buchanan, *Human Rights*, p. 253.
14 A. Buchanan and R. O. Keohane, 'The Preventive Use of Force: A
   Cosmopolitan Institutional Proposal', *Ethics and International Affairs*, 18: 1,
   2004, p. 20.
15 C. Reus-Smit, 'Liberal Hierarchy and the License to Use Force', *Review
   of International Studies*, 31, 2005, p. 73; M. Walzer, *Arguing About War*
   (New Haven and London: Yale University Press, 2004), p. 188; Adler,
   Communitarian IR, pp. 14–15.
16 M. Walzer, *Just and Unjust Wars: A Moral Argument with Historical
   Illustrations*, 3rd edn (New York: Basic Books, 2000), p. 107. Walzer, *Arguing
   About War*, p. 69.
17 M. Walzer, *Thick and Thin: Moral Argument at Home and Abroad* (Notre
   Dame: University of Notre Dame Press, 1994), p. 16; Walzer, *Arguing about
   War*, pp. 171–92.
18 Walzer's preferred term is reiterative universalism. M. Walzer, 'Nation

and Universe', in B. Haddock, P. Roberts and P. Sutch (eds), *Principles and Political Order: The Challenge of Diversity* (Oxford: Routledge, 2006), pp. 10–41.

19 Beitz, *The Idea of Human Rights*, p. 14.

20 Buchanan, *Human Rights*, p. 51.

21 The Universal Declaration of Human Rights, G.A. res. 217A (III), UN Doc A/810 at 71 (1948).

22 For the prehistory see M. Veuthey, 'Public Conscience in International Humanitarian Action', *Refugee Survey Quarterly*, 22: 4, 2003, pp. 198–201.

23 The Laws and Customs of War on Land (Hague II), 29 July 1899 at http://avalon.law.yale.edu/19th_century/hague02.asp accessed 27/1/2011.

24 T. Meron, 'The Martens Clause, Principles of Humanity, and Dictates of Public Conscience', *American Journal of International Law*, 94: 1, 2000, pp. 78–89; V. V. Pustogarov, 'The Martens Clause in International Law', *Journal of the History of International Law*, 1, 1999, 125–35; A. Cassese, 'The Martens Clause: Half a Loaf or Simply Pie in the Sky?', *European Journal of International Law*, 11: 1, 2000, pp. 187–216; R. Ticehurst, 'The Martens Clause and the Laws of Armed Conflict', *International Review of the Red Cross*, 37, 1997, pp. 125–34.

25 V. Chetail, 'The Contribution of the International Court of Justice to International Humanitarian Law', *International Review of the Red Cross*, 85, 2003, pp. 235–69, p. 238; Meron, 'The Martens Clause', p. 78.

26 Meron, 'The Martens Clause', p. 84; Chetail, 'Contribution', p. 243; Veuthey, 'Public Conscience', p. 613.

27 Cassese, 'The Martens Clause', pp. 202–8; Chetail, 'Contribution', p. 235; Meron, 'The Martens Clause', pp. 79–87.

28 Cassese, 'The Martens Clause', p. 205; Chetail, 'Contribution', pp. 235, 243, 253.

29 M. Freeman, 'International Law and Armed Conflict: Clarifying the Interplay between Human Rights and Humanitarian Protections', *Journal of Humanitarian Assistance* 24, 2000, http://jha.ac/2000/07/24/international-law-and-internal-armed-conflicts-clarifying-the-interplay-between-human-rights-and-humanitarian-protections/ accessed 7/4/2011.

30 A. Cassese, *International Criminal Law* (Oxford: Oxford University Press, 2003), p. 7.

31 Cassese, 'The Martens Clause', p. 210. Ticehurst, 'The Martens Clause', pp. 130–1.

32 Meron, 'The Martens Clause', p. 83, p. 78.

33 T. Meron, *The Humanization of International Law* (The Hague: Martinus Nijhoff, 2006).

34 Meron, 'The Martens Clause', p. 88; Cassese, 'The Martens Clause', p. 212.

35 Chetail, 'Contribution', p. 241; Meron, *Humanization*, p. 9.

36 H. Thirlway, 'The Sources of International Law', in M. Evans (ed.), *International Law*, 2nd edn (Oxford: Oxford University Press 2006), p. 142.

37 Pustogarov,'The Martens Clause'; p. 134. Chetail,'Contribution', p. 338.

38 Cassese,'The Martens Clause', p. 198; also Ticehurst,'The Martens Clause', p. 125.

39 Cassese,'The Martens Clause', p. 188; Meron,'The Martens Clause', p. 89; Chetail,'Contribution', p. 240.

40 On this see R. Vernon, 'What is a Crime Against Humanity?', *Journal of Political Philosophy*, 10: 3, 2002, pp. 231–49, p. 235.

41 C. Reus-Smit, *The Politics of International Law* (Cambridge: Cambridge University Press, 2004), pp. 36–44.

42 Meron,'The Martens Clause', pp. 82–4. Pustogarov,'The Martens Clause', p. 131; Chetail,'Contribution', p. 258.

43 Ticehurst,'The Martens Clause', p. 129.

44 Cassese,'The Martens Clause', p. 192.

45 Meron,'The Martens Clause', p. 80.

46 Ticehurst,'The Martens Clause', pp. 128–9. On the impact of this on case law see Meron,'The Martens Clause', pp. 82–3.

47 Meron,'The Martens Clause', p. 83.

48 Ticehurst,'The Martens Clause', p. 133.

49 Meron,'The Martens Clause', p. 83.

50 Cassese,'The Martens Clause', pp. 189–90.

51 Veuthey,'Public Conscience', p. 202.

52 Veuthey,'Public Conscience', pp. 203–4.

53 Cassese,'The Martens Clause', p. 207.

54 Meron, *Humanization,* pp. 187, 256.

55 Meron, *Humanization,* p. 262; D. Shelton, 'Normative Hierarchy in International Law', *American Journal of International Law*, 100: 2, 2006, pp. 291–323, p. 318.

56 Shelton,'Normative Hierarchy', p. 318; Meron, *Humanization,* p. 259.

57 A. Orakhelashvili, *Peremptory Norms in International Law* (Oxford: Oxford University Press, 2006), pp. 44–5.

58 Orakhelashvili, *Peremptory Norms*, pp. 50–66.

59 J. Charney,'Universal International Law', *American Journal of International Law*, 87 (1993), pp. 529–43.

60 See my discussion of Buchanan (below).

61 Shelton,'Normative Hierarchy', pp. 306–7.

62 See Meron,'The Martens Clause', p. 86; Cassese, 'The Martens Clause', p. 192; Ticehurst, 'The Martens Clause', pp. 126–33; Chetail, 'Contribution', pp. 239–41.

63 Report of the Eminent Jurists Panel on Terrorism, counter-terrorism and

human rights, *Assessing Damage: Urging Action,* at http://ejp. icj.org/IMG/ EJP-Report.pdf accessed 27/1/2011.

64 Shelton, 'Normative Hierarchy', p. 323.

65 See Buchanan, *Human Rights,* p. 71; also A. Buchanan, *Justice, Legitimacy and Self-Determination: Moral Foundations for International Law* (Oxford: Oxford University Press, 2004) *passim.*

66 Buchanan and Keohane, 'The Preventive Use of Force', p. 20; Buchanan, *Justice,* pp. 434–9.

67 Buchanan, *Human Rights,* p. 116.

68 Adler, *Communitarian IR,* pp. 3–5; Reus-Smit 'Liberal Hierarchy', p. 8; Walzer, *Arguing About War,* p. 188.

69 Buchanan, *Human Rights,* p. 76.

70 Buchanan, *Human Rights,* p. 71.

71 This is Buchanan's account of the 'modest objectivist view' of human rights. Buchanan, *Human Rights,* p. 86.

72 Buchanan, *Human Rights,* pp. 82–8.

73 Buchanan, *Human Rights,* p. 97.

74 Buchanan and Keohane, 'The Preventive Use of Force', pp. 1–22.

75 Buchanan and Keohane, 'The Preventive Use of Force', pp. 15–16.

76 Buchanan and Keohane, 'The Preventive Use of Force', p. 20.

77 Buchanan, *Justice,* pp. 427–74; Buchanan, *Human Rights,* pp. 250–96.

78 Reus-Smit, 'Liberal Hierarchy', pp. 71–92.

79 Reus-Smit, *The Politics of International Law,* p. 30.

80 Buchanan, *Human Rights,* p. 106.

81 Reus-Smit, 'Liberal Hierarchy', p. 85.

82 Walzer, *Arguing About War,* pp. 189–90; Adler, *Communitarian IR,* pp. 16–17.

83 Adler, *Communitarian IR,* p. 15.

84 Adler, *Communitarian IR,* p. 27.

Chapter 7

DOING EVIL JUSTLY? THE MORALITY OF JUSTIFIABLE ABOMINATION

Mark Evans

[I]f you are confronted with two evils, thus the argument runs, it is your duty to opt for the lesser one whereas it is irresponsible to refuse to choose altogether ... The weakness of the argument has always been that those who choose the lesser evil forget very quickly that they chose evil.

Hannah Arendt[1]

At the end of a war, when peace is not concluded, it would not be inappropriate for a people to appoint a day of atonement after the festival of thanksgiving. Heaven would be invoked in the name of the state to forgive the human race for the great sin of which it continues to be guilty, since it will not accommodate itself to a lawful constitution in international relations.

Immanuel Kant[2]

INTRODUCTION

When faced with a choice between courses of action both or all of which have significant attendant costs or drawbacks – a scenario to which politics is, by its nature, especially prone – we are wont to call the choice on which we settle 'the lesser of two evils' (or the 'least evil' if the options were more numerous). We employ this phrase when we believe our choice has incurred the least cost compared with the alternatives and, to that extent, it is proffered in justification of the choice made. But it is also an acknowledgement that there is a cost which we should not forget: the choice is not, or has not led to, an unalloyed good. In politics, especially, a 'lesser-of-two-evils' decision will typically impose burdens on some people which they might possibly not have had to bear under one of the alternatives. (The latter, being 'greater evils', would have imposed comparatively greater burdens but on other people, for example.) Thus, the phrase also typically conveys regret that no cost-free option was available: ideally, there should be no such loss attendant on the choice but, alas, things were not ideal.

Now, unwelcome though these may be, it is often an exaggeration to call the negative outcomes 'evils' in any literal sense, and hence the saying tends to be merely figurative. On at least some such occasions, no particular moral problem arises from choosing the 'least worst' course of action: the costs are just not that great. I conjecture that the phrase's figurative usage standardly facilitates the belief that, if we do the best thing possible in lesser-of-two-evils scenarios, then we are justified in doing it and *therefore* are not at any moral fault for the negative consequences, for any alternative action on our part would have been (even) worse in its outcome. We may regret that we couldn't have done *better* but we can be secure in our conviction that we have done our *best*.

But does this 'standard' account of justificatory exculpation still apply when the lesser of two evils really is an evil whose costs are way beyond the merely unwelcome? Many would say yes: awful though the consequences have been, the best possible course of action, again, has nevertheless been taken which means that it is therefore justified and that one cannot be blamed, or otherwise held to be at fault, for having taken it. The end justifies the means, they might familiarly claim: the agent's conscience can be clear in its own rectitude, and the justifiability of what they have done cleanses their hands.

This straightforward form of means/end reasoning has, of course, prompted plenty of controversy, and some would urge that the problem of dirty hands simply cannot be washed away so easily as it assumes. And yet the standard account remains a favoured response in this kind of case. Its appeal can be seen in the riposte, 'so, you would rather I had done the greater evil?' Indeed, the 'figurative' account of 'lesser of two evils' is likely to reappear even here to dissolve the distinction between the present types of case, for it can readily seem reasonable to conclude that, terrible in costs though some action might be, if one was nevertheless justified in doing it, by conceptual definition it cannot therefore be really 'evil' at all, for that is a quality which attaches only to (the most extreme varieties of) the unjustifiable.

In this chapter I challenge the standard account – not, obviously, on the grounds that it is wrong to think that the lesser of two evils should, *ceteris paribus*, be the one chosen but for the reason that it is wrong to assume: (a) that justified evil-doing is a conceptual impossibility; (b) that justified evil-doing wipes the slate clean as far as what we might call the moral liability of justified evildoers is concerned. The lesser of two evils sometimes really is an evil, and sometimes a very great evil. And, whereas the forgetfulness of which Arendt speaks seems on the standard account to be perfectly natural, indeed justifiable, I argue that it is a serious dereliction of responsibility: all evildoers, and hence justified evildoers, have seriously defaulted with respect to morality. Justified evil-doing is vastly different from unjustified evil-doing but I shall claim that even the former carries with it something akin to a responsibility of *atonement* for the breaches of morality it has entailed.

If this position immediately strikes one as overly harsh on those who have justifiably done the lesser of two evils, then my response is that this is a tough consequence of morality in a tragically non-ideal world (and presumably not as tough as it is for any victims of the justified evil). To the charge that it nevertheless looks very counter-intuitive, I shall show how it actually makes better intuitive sense than does the standard account of the perplexities in the morality of war that just-war theory (hereafter: JWT) attempts to codify. That being said, the position has important transformative effects on what JWT is traditionally thought to require of just combatants.

THE EVIL OF WAR

What 'evil' actually means is, of course, a disputed matter of the kind that could fuel the very debate between the positions just sketched. I would not rule out the possibility that it is an essentially contested concept in a broadly Lukesian sense of being inherently liable to rival interpretation.[3] The fact that it remains contested, 'essentially' or not, may be partly due to the kind of scholarly neglect that prompted the present volume into being. Certainly, Arendt's judgement that 'the problem of evil will be the fundamental question of post-war intellectual life in Europe' seems somewhat misplaced in hindsight.[4] It is definitely awry with respect to the overlapping fields of non-theological anglophone moral and political philosophy.[5] The latter's quietude on the matter may have been due to a sense that 'evil' is 'radical' in the early Arendt's sense,[6] incomprehensible to the realm of Rawlsian reasonable citizens and the like, beyond which political philosophy has apparently nothing to say.

To be sure, the concept's permissiveness in how readily it lends itself to the previously observed figurative usage might deter us from treating it to philosophical scrutiny. Its careless deployment in political rhetoric might be held to be good reason why 'evil' has no place in any measured account of political morality. Alternatively, one might think that to call someone or something 'evil' is to imply irredeemable badness, a 'rottenness to the core'. There is no point in trying to explain why this person or thing is so morally reprehensible, not least because there is no point in hoping for compromise with, or reform of, the evildoer. So, the argument continues, the use of 'evil' in politics is, indeed, often 'radical', dramatically demonising one's enemy, making comprehension of them *in principle* impossible. (It may well help to excite public sentiments exaggeratedly in support of such demonization, too, of course.) It is the dangers of such usage – think, for example, of George W. Bush's 'axis of evil' – that might lead some to conclude that 'evil' is not a 'serious' concept for a theory of political morality.

The problem with this conclusion is that there has been so much in human experience that has been appalling, shocking, horrifying that, if we were to drop 'evil' from our stock of moral concepts, we would find ourselves having to replace it with something else to express the heightened senses of revulsion and condemnation that the label of 'evil' can still now do adequately well. What we need is not to jettison or substitute the concept but to give it criteria for its proper application such that its abuse in political discourse, for example, can be seen as just that: *abuse*. This need is highlighted when we recognise that, far from being alien to 'us', the experience of 'evil' is, in a profound sense, a 'human, all-too-human' affair. Consider Arendt's thesis of the banality of evil, which is really a theory of the nature of (some) evildoers. What is truly shocking about Eichmann was that he '*never realised what he was doing* . . . He was not stupid. It was sheer thoughtlessness – something by no means identical with stupidity – that predisposed him to become one of the greatest criminals of that period.'[7] 'Banality' indicates that it is ordinary human beings who perpetrate monstrosities, and we should not be so sanguine about humanity's potentialities by casting evil's perpetrators into a realm of alien, unfathomable non-humanity. Evil is not committed only by monsters; it is also done 'routinely' by banal bureaucrats (people like us) who think themselves merely following another set of orders and procedures. My point is this: if the Holocaust, for example, was not evil, then what was it, morally speaking? And if we agree that 'evil' is appropriate here, we should also accept that it is very much a part of *ordinary* human experience in terms both of who *suffers* it and who *commits* it.

All of this is not to say that conceptualising 'evil' in an appropriate manner is easy, after all. To the extent that it is contestable will obviously become manifest in disputes over 'criteria for its proper application', for example. But even essentially contested concepts are not entirely indiscriminate in this regard: there must be some agreement over what is at issue for the contest to be about the same concept. So we can proceed by trying to characterise some of these shared features to yield a partial concept which captures *something* of what 'evil' denotes, incomplete though it may be in having put to one side its more contested elements.

In proposing what it is about war that makes it evil, then, I am not claiming to be accounting for everything that makes it evil: its evilness may well be heavily overdetermined. But I want to identify one evil characteristic that is highly relevant for this chapter's argument, and it is prompted by Arendt in particular. 'Evil' is embodied in the profoundly inhuman treatment of people as intended by other human beings: the purposeful denial of their humanity as expressed in the deliberate indifference to, and violation of, their basic rights as human beings. This may not be limited to the deliberate extinction of other people's lives, though this is obviously paradigmatic in any conceptualisation of 'evil'. And the fact that 'evil' is what some ('ordinary') human beings do to others is entirely compatible with the judgement that their treatment of others is radically 'inhuman', a term which denotes a normative standard of how human beings ought not to treat each other. 'Evil', we might say, represents a deliberately (even if sometimes, Eichmann-like, thoughtlessly) extreme disregard of that standard.

For Arendt, evil arises 'in connection with a system in which all men have become equally superfluous'.[8] This refers to the specific evil of totalitarianism which she characterises as striving to obliterate the very conditions that make humanity possible: human plurality and individuality, natality and spontaneity. No human (and humane) life can be led under such conditions, and this is what paves the way for the physical destruction of those groups that stand in the way of the totalitarian project that has already destroyed the juridical, moral and individual being of its subjects.[9] But I would like to uncouple the characterisation from totalitarianism to say that, in general, 'evil' is manifest in any deliberate treatment of others' lives as *profoundly* superfluous to the point of expendability. To suffer evil is *really* to suffer but those who cause it do not, at heart, care that they are so dismissively destroying the lives of others.

From these remarks it is not difficult to see one way by which war can be regarded as evil. In both the intended and unintended killings and injuries caused, the organised deployment of lethal force that is 'war' ultimately treats its victims (which include the soldiers sent to fight as well as their victims) as essentially superfluous: that is its ultimate inhumanity. If anything, the ostensibly dispassionate, functional discourse of modern Western warfare heightens the superfluity: soldiers 'are just getting on with their jobs' as if their 'dedicated professionalism' is all that should rightly concern them and us all; military units 'clear areas of resistance' as if they are merely hacking back bushy undergrowth – and then, of course, we have the (rightly) now notorious phrase 'collateral damage'.

I do not deny that the evil of a particular war can be massively *exacerbated* by an immorality of the ends for which people's lives are being so sweepingly disregarded. On the contrary, this bears crucially on the possibility of a just war, and I shall say more about this in the following sections. But I am claiming that the moral character of the ends have no bearing on the moral fact that to wage war – any war – is to do something evil because of the way in which it necessarily (by definition, indeed) treats people's lives as so casually and radically superfluous in the horrors inflicted upon them.

JUST WAR AS THE LESSER OF TWO EVILS

Before I elaborate the idea of a just war in 'lesser-of-two-evils' terms, it must be noted that not all just-war theorists would treat just war as evil in the sense I am describing. James Turner Johnson, for example, argues that the 'classic' just-war tradition is based on

a conception of life in political community oriented to a just and peaceful order, in which the use of armed force is a necessary tool to be used by responsible political authority to protect that just and peaceful order in a world in which serious threats are not only possible but actual . . . To be sure, force is evil when it is employed to attack the justice and peace of a political order oriented toward these goods, but it is precisely to defend against such evil that the use of force may be good. Just war tradition has to do with defining the possible good use of force, not finding exceptional cases when it is possible to use something inherently evil (force) for the purposes of good.[10]

It is not my purpose here to debate the nature of 'classic' just-war thinking but to vindicate the idea of a theory that can treat war as both evil but also, under certain conditions, just. We can note, however, that JWT has always been concerned to restrain the resort to war. It has always resisted its normalisation. And the admonition that even a justified resort to war is to do something evil would seem to be more conducive to that function than Johnson's formulation which seems to say that you are doing good *in* using force as opposed to the 'evil' formulation which says, at most, good is what is aimed for as the result of using force.

The 'lesser evil' characterisation of JWT gains strength when we identify three different dimensions of evil, understood as the treatment of people as inhumanly superfluous. Just-war theorists recognise that such is the nature of war that 'mistakes' are made even by the most well-intentioned of just combatants: deaths and injuries that cannot (properly, at least) be justified by the discrimination and proportionality principles of *jus in bello*. To say that a war should be regulated by the latter is not to claim that we should expect nothing less than perfect adherence to them in practice. War being what it is, regulation will never reach such levels of perfection. The results of such shortfalls are tragic errors – but they are nevertheless regarded, insofar as the war remains just, as 'prices worth paying' for the greater good.

These errors are distinct from the 'regrettable' deaths of 'innocent' non-combatants that are, in fact, justifiable under the discrimination principle, that is, when they have not been deliberately targeted and all due care has been taken to avoid them. JWT will not call these 'mistakes' but they are no less tragic for that: it is hardly 'good' that these deaths have happened. The tragedy of a just war lies in the fact that the action which caused these deaths was a justifiable part of a war which again, if it had not been waged, would have led to worse *overall* consequences (part of the tragedy being that the outcome may well have been better for at least some of the specific victims in that they would not have been killed). The just combatants faced two terrible choices: the choice they made, though better overall in the long run, nevertheless did grievous wrong to certain people.

These two dimensions alone are sufficient to establish the claim that a just war is still an evil but a third dimension of evil may be thought to lie in the deaths even of those unjust combatants who are justifiably killed. Those who are targeted are being treated as 'superfluous' in the sense described previously as well and, no matter what the injustice of their cause, this is not enough (or perhaps, only very rarely is it enough) to dispel altogether the evil of their extermination.[11] JWT may also be sometimes prone to forget that, in a just war, it is not only the combatants of the unjust side who have to be deliberately targeted and killed, and not only the innocent civilians on the unjust side who may be unavoidably slaughtered. Civilians who work in occupations that service war efforts could be legitimately targeted as well and their culpability for the injustice of their war's cause may be vanishingly small. Some might enthusiastically support it, but many may not, or may not even know the full range of issues at stake. They may be forced into what they do or brainwashed into doing what they do ostensibly more freely. (The same can, of course, be true in essence for conscripted combatants, too.)

Even those who lead their people into just wars are sending their own soldiers to their deaths, and may perhaps be exposing their own civilians to attack as well. They may not be treating their own with *quite* the same degree of indifference manifest in the 'superfluity' of war's victims when compared with unjust war leaders – but they are still nevertheless sacrificing them for 'a greater cause' and that, on this analysis, is to visit evil upon *them*.[12] (Is there any more appropriate term for what it is that people are subjected to by dint of any decision to send them, directly or indirectly, into any war?)

So: another way of thinking that war, even a just war, is an evil is that, *pace* Johnson, it is one which must employ evil ends for an ultimately just cause:[13] there is nothing in itself good about killing and maiming people. Very great wrongs are being visited on the casualties of war which deeply problematises the idea that it can be *right* to kill anyone in even a just war.

Now, of course, this last claim may look deeply paradoxical: we might be able to agree that something which is justified may not be 'good' in any 'positive' or 'upbeat' sense, for it could still be very costly and imposes

burdens and misery on people. But to say that something which is justified may not be straightforwardly 'right', when 'right' lacks the 'sunnier'
implications that 'good' might be thought to have, seems bafflingly contradictory. In the next section, I shall present some considerations as to
why it need not be so but we should acknowledge that this conceptual
feature may allow pacifism a way to challenge JWT's moral coherence.
So we pause briefly to consider two pacifist arguments.

First: it might be objected that, even if we can sometimes measure
'amounts' of evil, which is what lesser-of-two-evils judgements obviously assume, in situations of potential *war* (when we are deciding
whether to go to war is really the best thing to do) very often we cannot,
for a variety of possible reasons. The hypothetical nature of the judgements, for example, makes weightings difficult to judge, and the various
considerations being weighed may not anyway even be commensura-
ble. Now, if it is the case that the two evils – to go to war or not to go
to war – really cannot be weighed in a particular instance, for whatever reason, then I believe that JWT would say that war should not be
waged: there has to be a degree of reasonable certainty in the weighting its judgement here requires. This is because its various criteria
for justifying war seem so demanding that it is safe to say that JWT's
'presumptive position', so to speak, is to keep the peace. (Put differently: it is 'going to war', not 'keeping the peace' that has to be justified.)
And if it were true that no weighting for any potential war could ever
be reasonably judged, then we would have a strong case for pacifism.
But this seems to be too sweeping: the weightings are not always so
difficult to ascertain, even though we sometimes have to learn through
bitter historical experience how to make such judgements with any
degree of wisdom. For example, I wonder how many people think that
it would have been better not to fight Nazism, or that non-intervention
in Rwanda in 1994 – the failure by everyone to go to war against the
Interahamwe on behalf of the Tutsis – was the lesser of two evils, or
even too tricky to call.[14]

Second: pacifists might argue that combatants always have a choice
not to go to war (they are not 'forced', in any literal sense: conscripts
might refuse, even if they sacrifice themselves in the process) and even
if terrible things happen because of their pacifism, morality forbids
them from doing evil themselves in taking up arms to kill people. 'Two
wrongs do not make a right', they might say: it is tragically wrong that
they may have reason to fight but morality places them in the tragedy of

not being *justified* in fighting. The prohibition on the evil of killing over-
rides all other considerations. Two lines of argument might be invoked
to substantiate this position.

The first takes a broad, overall consequentialist perspective of its
own and says that, though the outcome of the pacifist attitude may be
dreadful in the short term, resorting to war in this instance as a solution
to the crisis will merely exacerbate the willingness to employ war as
such a means, to the longer-term greater detriment of humanity. Now,
though not inherently implausible, this empirical assumption is hardly
obviously correct either. Failure to respond to aggression with force,
for example, may provide great incentives for some to use aggression
as a normal strategy. And even if a refusal to take up arms reduced the
number of wars, one could only be sure that this was better for humanity in general, longer-term perspective if 'peace' was the only benefit
being counted. What else may be sacrificed for such peace, however,
must surely count (a lesson many drew with respect to the 1930s'
appeasement of the Nazis).

The second is, from the perspective being unfolded here, perhaps
rather more troubling (the reason may become clearer in the next
section). This puts aside the 'global' consequentialist view and focuses
on the idea of there being a personal duty, or personal virtue, that *you*
do not do evil, for what goes on beyond your control, by dint of other
people's deeds, is not your responsibility. It is your own ethical integrity
that counts. Now, my concern is not that I think this kind of argument
(which, as might be gathered, can be developed in distinct ways) is
always going to be difficult to defeat. To my mind, it is in obvious danger
of encouraging a peculiarly narcissistic form of moral bystander.[15] ('I'd
love to rescue you from those genocidal maniacs but my own ethical
purity would be impugned if I did, so I'm sorry . . .' which sounds even
worse than the coward, or the 'indifferentist' who simply hasn't even
bothered to think about it.) But I do not think issues of moral character
have no bearing on the morality of war. It matters much what sort of
person it is that wages just war precisely because it involves the doing
of evil and, when JWT embraces the 'evil' characterisation it needs to
show how it meets this pacifist challenge as part of its project to demonstrate how war can be just at all.

JUSTICE, TRAGEDY AND MORAL PLURALISM

Thus far, I have suggested that the 'lesser evil' characterisation of just war holds that having to use such violence can nevertheless neither be good nor even, in *some* sense right, because the suffering it causes is a very great wrong that reflects the characteristic of evil in war that I drew from Arendt. Where, though, is the justice?

A simple but important point to make in response to this question is that it is the justice of the cause for having gone to war which makes a war just. For JWT, the ultimate goal of a just war is a just peace, and war is justified – by the considerations of *jus ad bellum* – when there is a grave actual or threatened assault on an existing peace or when the peace currently at hand is gravely unjust (which standardly justifies some wars of self-defence or liberation, and humanitarian intervention).[16] This could allow us to say that whatever is done in pursuit of the just cause is informed by, pursued for, that cause. The problem for JWT here, though, is that, via the considerations of *jus in bello*, it says 'whatever is done' in waging a just war is not merely 'informed' by just cause but is also itself just: 'justice in the conduct of war'. The 'evil' characterisation renders vivid what that conduct actually leads to in terms of deaths and suffering but how can that be a matter of doing 'justice' to the victims? In drawing attention to the moral horror of what is done in any war, hasn't this characterisation inadvertently exposed a fundamental flaw in JWT which pacifists highlight?

One strategy in response to this problem is to say that 'justice' is not a single concept. JWT uses at least two clearly distinguishable concepts, and the pacifist critique fails to recognise this. The first concept regards justice as a 'pristine' virtue and it is, very generally stated, what we would expect to find as (partly) constitutive of the ideal world. It is a feature of the world we ideally wish to live in. In other words, this is the concept which informs the 'justice' of the just peace that is a just war's goal, which obviously rejects any notion of violence being justifiable in that ideal scenario ('justice' here, then, is a certain kind of peace).

The second concept of 'justice' does not treat it as a characteristic of the ideal world for which we aim. Instead, it posits justice as a remedial or rectificatory principle for the non-ideal world. It is what we invoke to right a wrong, or at least assist in writing a wrong, and would not therefore be needed if there were no wrong in the first place. It is the sense of 'justice' we find in conceptions of punishment, for example:

just punishments are inflicted on wrongdoers as morally appropriate responses to their wrongdoing which may partly have the function of restoring things to the way they ought to be. Put differently: the first concept treats justice as pure, unalloyed ('good', in the sense previously invoked), in not being a response to a wrong, whereas the second concept treats justice as just such a (morally appropriate) response. To be sure, the two concepts are related in the sense that morally appropriate rectificatory justice is necessarily inspired at some level by the pristine view of the way the world ought to be. But the former becomes no less a matter of justice, in its understanding of the concept, to any extent that it falls short of an unqualified reiteration of pristine justice.

Those who would call the justice in the conduct of war 'rectificatory' might try to draw an analogy with the punishment of criminals. They are harmed when they are punished but we conventionally say that justice has been done: they deserve it. Harm does not cease to be harm when it is deserved and thus evil may not cease to be evil when it is deserved. It is a terrible thing to have to kill soldiers fighting for an unjust cause but that is what justice requires. It is also a terrible thing – certainly, even worse – when innocent civilians are caught up in the fighting and are killed or maimed. But, to go back to the 'criminal' analogy, it is often the case that innocent people – their dependants, say – suffer when criminals are punished (their own standard of living may fall, they suffer emotional deprivation, and so forth).

Yet no one would want to say that, *ceteris paribus*, justice has been done *to* these victims, as opposed to the properly convicted criminal. To be sure, the costs they incur arise from the criminality of the convict on whom they depend but the justice meted out to him, if anything, compounds their burdens (nothing is rectified for them in this regard). Further, the use of this analogy to explain the justice in *jus in bello* feebly fails to capture the enormous horror of what is being done to the victims of war, which also has an impact upon the moral standing of those inflicting war even for a just cause (what a judge justly inflicts upon a criminal is of a totally different order to what just combatants inflict upon their opponents).

Thus, I believe the 'evil' characterisation necessitates the dropping of *justice* in the conduct of war. To employ Jeff McMahan's distinction between 'the deep morality of war' and the 'laws of war',[17] we can talk about *justified* conduct in war, constituted by the aforementioned laws, with the justification informed by the deep morality in two ways: (a)

the (rectificatory) justice of the cause of the war; (b) the moral considerations which shape but do not fully constitute the laws or rules of
conduct (it is a consideration of justice that prompts the rule that one
should not directly target 'innocents' in war but that rule is not itself a
principle of justice).

Now, this conceptual move goes some way towards adapting JWT to
embrace the claim that what is done in war is evil but it does not go far
enough on its own. The simple consequentialist could agree with it by
saying that the 'deep morality' is the goal of a just peace, and the laws of
war's conduct are, when justified, simply the most efficacious practical
(that is, not themselves intrinsically moral) means to achieve the goal.
Fully to capture the claim that just combatants are doing evil when they
pursue the least of the evils available to them, we need to amplify what
it means to say that they find themselves in a tragic situation.

Christopher Gowans says that 'a moral tragedy is a moral conflict
in which moral wrongdoing in the sense of violating a moral responsibility is inescapable, and the action that *all things considered* morally
ought to be done, or may be done, nonetheless has one or more tragic-
making consequences'.[18] [My italics.] Tragedies in this sense arise not
simply when we have cause for regret that what we justifiably do – the
best that we can do – has (serious) consequences for some but when
what we do 'all things considered' nevertheless requires us to violate
some moral obligation or responsibility we have – in this instance, not
to kill or injure.

Simple consequentialism rejects the possibility of tragedy conceptualised thus: when 'all things' are considered, namely what it is that will
produce the best overall outcome, any principle or norm that would
frustrate or preclude the achievement of that outcome (in this instance,
'thou shalt not kill or injure') ceases to be obligatory and hence no
countervailing moral requirement has to be violated. Many have, of
course, found this kind of solution to moral dilemmas attractive: the
postulation of 'tragedies' and the like, they would say, occurs because
of confusion in our moral judgements which require reordering by the
adoption of an overarching moral theory that can sort and order ostensibly clashing moral stipulations. For all its official resistance to simple
consequentialism, I submit that the form of JWT favoured by Johnson
reflects this approach to the various moral judgements which can be
made about war. Removing the 'evil' characterisation of what is done in
war with reference to the overall good that a just war pursues quells, if

not dispels altogether, the deep moral perturbation about killing in war that many feel, a move which many critics of JWT believe renders it far too sanguine about what it is that it justifies (and, more dramatically in some cases, renders it prone to 'ennoble' all that just war entails by sole reference to the justice of its cause).

We preserve those deep reservations about war with the evil characterisation and the recognition that the possibility of moral tragedy indicates that moral values are 'plural and conflicting'. To quote Michael Stocker, a prominent exponent of this meta-ethical thesis:

> there is no need to confuse what is here and now best or right with what is perfectly good or wholly right. Even what is best or right can have features that are and remain bad or wrong. One can be justified in doing an act that ineliminably has a part it would be wrong to do on its own – and more importantly for us, which remains a wrong, albeit a justified wrong, when done in doing what is right.[19]

To do anything in a moral tragedy, moral pluralists will 'consider all things' and may well still be guided by simple consequentialist calculations. But they do not think that each component moral consideration of the tragic situation disappears into this overall perspective. Moral losses and violations, and consequent moral liabilities, remain: what justice requires all things considered violates what justice requires when some things are considered in isolation from the whole. A just war represents perhaps one of the most extreme examples of this moral complexity, where the evil of what is done is not cancelled out by the justice of the cause which necessitated it. To address the problem posed in this chapter's title, then, although one cannot do evil justly it can be done for the sake of justice and, in that way, the undoubted abomination that is war can, under certain strict conditions, be justified. But the moral phenomenon of 'dirty hands' is a real one: the fact that they have been dirtied in the cause of justice does not mean they are clean after all, and this has significant implications for those whose hands they are.

JUS POST BELLUM: ATONING FOR THE LESSER EVIL

The foregoing account of just war undoubtedly has implications for how just combatants feel about what it is that they are doing in going to war, and I have argued that this should remove any taint of vainglory which JWT's critics often accuse it of promoting in the taking up of arms for justice.[20] Just combatants, or at least their leaders,[21] should instead manifest what Stephen de Wijze calls 'tragic remorse' among the attitudes they take to their war.[22] But the critics might suspect that this account has little more than palliative consequences for the consciences of combatants who think themselves just, helping themselves to be at ease with what they are doing by feeling really bad about having to do what they are doing ('we are *really* sorry about this . . .'). In this final section, I want to sketch in general form the much more substantial implications for what just combatants should actually do which are prompted by this account, and which have important revisionary consequences for what JWT is typically thought to entail.

Some just-war theorists have recently argued that JWT needs to adopt a theory of *jus post bellum* (hereafter: JPB), of justice in the ending and aftermath of war on the grounds that the permissions and demands of justice for just combatants with respect to securing a just peace do not come to an end immediately on the formal cessation of hostilities. As I have argued elsewhere,[23] the conceptions of JPB that have been offered have typically been 'restricted' in the sense that they have concentrated on specifying just peace terms and what follows more or less immediately after the war: their implications are relatively short term. I also here add another sense in which they are restricted: their stipulations draw, for their moral foundations, on the justice for which just combatants took up arms in the first place. They specify what justice reasonably requires in the treatment of former enemies once they lay down their arms.

I do not deny that, in some cases, a restricted understanding of JPB's requirements may be appropriate or even the only workable option. But I do not think its restricted form exhausts what JPB might legitimately require in every post-just-war circumstance. I have previously suggested that we sometimes need a conception of JPB that is extended both in terms of the range of concerns and concomitant principles it embraces and of the demands on time and resources it makes of just (ex-)combatants. This is partially because what we might reasonably expect of just ex-combatants in securing the just peace for which they originally went to war might be more extensive than restricted conceptions allow (especially in occupations of defeated unjust aggressors where the just occupiers become directly involved in post-conflict reconstruction of their former enemy). But we should amplify a further reason for seeing JPB in extended terms: having done evil in going to war, albeit necessary and justified with respect to the overall cause, just ex-combatants have incurred significant and potentially demanding moral liabilities in recompense or, more appropriately, atonement.

Why 'more appropriately' atonement, even if we agree that a reason for not preferring 'recompense' here is that it is difficult to think that we can 'compensate', morally and materially, for the suffering of war? (How, for example, can you compensate the dead?). Standardly, one treats atonement as a requirement of those who have done what is comprehensively unjustified. Richard Swinburne argues that, though they are not always all required for it to be satisfactorily demonstrated, atonement comprises four elements: repentance, apology, reparation and penance.[24] I would add a fifth, which is arguably implicit in each, namely, a commitment not to do the atoned-for wrong again. While we would naturally expect each aspect of atonement from a defeated unjust side in a just war (and I am certainly not denying their duties in this regard are very great) these may, indeed, look at first sight distinctly inappropriate requirements to levy on just combatants. Yet, if they have done justified evil, is it necessarily inappropriate to expect of them something which at least partially parallels atonement, as a consequence of the tragic choice they found themselves having to make?

If the just combatants baulk at this idea, we should first remind them of the mistakes that are inevitably made in war, and for which atonement can be conventionally expected. Further, even without the 'evil' characterisation of JWT it must be acknowledged that probably no war in history, and hence no war that just-war theorists are inclined to think was nevertheless justified, properly satisfied all of the criteria JWT sets down. If we must then say that a just war is one that passes a certain threshold of satisfaction of the theory's requirements, we must concede that there will be features of a just war that JWT *itself* identifies as morally flawed, and which again may prompt something at least akin to atonement on the part of the just.

But if we are to take seriously the idea of a just war as the lesser of two evils, the moral liability which prompts atonement must necessarily be incurred regardless of these considerations. Justified evil is not to be punished, so no moral equivalence is being established here between just and unjust combatants but it is to be profoundly regretted in ways which manifest themselves in more than just an abjuration of self-satisfied 'victor's justice'. Thus, JPB's requirements should reflect that regret, the atonement of the justified combatant.

What these requirements may be are doubtless highly contestable and, given the variety in situations to which they might apply, any adequate general statement of it, therefore, is likely to be *highly* generalised and abstract. Briefly, however, I suggest the following. In addition to

(a) JPB requires just combatants to set peace terms which are proportionately determined to make that peace just and stable as well as to redress the injustice which prompted the conflict which restricted conceptions will avow, we might also require just ex-combatants

(b) to take full responsibility for their fair share of the material burdens of the conflict's aftermath in constructing a just and stable peace which, among other things, acknowledges the moral culpability of just combatants for the damage they have caused to help their former enemies rebuild their societies. Because all war is evil, there must be a commitment to try to avoid resort to war in future which thus could ground a requirement (perhaps the most strikingly novel when compared with more traditional formulations of JWT)

(c) to pursue, where possible and reasonable, national and international political initiatives for conflict prevention (and/or, sub-optimally, conflict containment) and post-conflict reconstruction.

And, finally, where atonement of some kind may be most manifest on both sides, the just must be prepared

(d) to take full and proactive part in *two-way* ethical and socio-cultural processes of forgiveness and reconciliation that are central to the construction of a just and stable peace.[25]

These principles, or what might be done to substantiate them in practice, may seem pale requirements in response to the horrors of war but what atonement requires very often seems inadequate to the enormity of what is being atoned for. Conversely, the bitterness that wars cause may make these requirements impossibly demanding for the survivors. But, insofar as JWT is, in the first instance, a theory for political leaders, those with war-making powers, it is incumbent upon them to transcend such feelings. The tragic conflicts of political leadership are well known, and never more extreme than in circumstances of war. Sometimes, leaders may have to embark on just wars but they must afterwards always try, as best they can, to build a just and stable peace in which the evil of war is never revisited. And it must never be forgotten that this heavy responsibility arises in crucial part from the fact that, by going to war, they denied many from sharing this hoped-for, longed-for better world.

Notes

1 Hannah Arendt, *Responsibility and Judgment,* ed. Jerome Kohn (New York: Schocken Books, 2003), pp. 35–6.
2 Immanuel Kant, 'Perpetual Peace: A Philosophical Sketch', in H. Reiss (ed.) *Kant: Political Writings* (Cambridge: Cambridge University Press, 1991), pp. 93–130, at p. 105.
3 See Steven Lukes, *Power: A Radical View* (London: Macmillan, 1974).
4 Hannah Arendt, 'Nightmare and Flight', in Hannah Arendt, *Essays in Understanding,* ed. J. Kohn (New York: Harcourt Brace, 1994), p. 134.
5 Thus I think that 'evil' should be added to the list of things John Gray finds astonishing in their absence from Robert Goodin and Philip Pettit's *Companion to Contemporary Political Philosophy,* in his *Enlightenment's Wake* (London: Routledge, 1995) chapter 2.
6 Hannah Arendt, *The Origins of Totalitarianism* (Cleveland and New York: World Publishing: Meridian Books, 1958), p. 459.
7 Hannah Arendt, *Eichmann in Jerusalem: A Report on the Banality of Evil* (Harmondsworth: Penguin, 1994), pp. 287–8.
8 Arendt, *Origins of Totalitarianism,* p. 459.
9 Arendt, *Origins of Totalitarianism,* pp. 447f.
10 James Turner Johnson, *Just War and the New Face of Conflict* (Lanham, MD: Rowman and Littlefield, 2005), p. 36.
11 I should here add that I am persuaded of the view that the degree of direct culpability vis-à-vis the unjust cause does make a difference to the moral evaluation of the killing of an unjust combatant. Perhaps killing members of genocidal death squads is not as horribly regrettable as the killing of teenage conscripts. But you should still regret that they have to be killed, and that *you* have to be the one to kill them. Your hands are still dirty even when it is the blood of mass murderers on them.
12 In some conflicts, at least, leaders might claim that it is not they but their enemies who are responsible for the evils inflicted upon their soldiers and civilians – and there is obviously some truth to this. But I contend that an adequate ethic of political responsibility would not let such leaders absolve themselves of all responsibility for the consequences of using violence.
13 Sometimes, perhaps it is not problematic to say that it is a good thing that someone is killed: had Hitler died in a bombing raid in 1944, say, I think we would readily call this a good outcome. But I am talking in general terms here.
14 One could formulate all manner of counterfactual hypothetical situations

in which an intervention inadvertently triggers an even worse catastrophe. This is a tactic that could be indiscriminately used to undermine any justi-fication, of course. But there are times when such counterfactuals are suf-ficiently implausible for us not to be perturbed by them, and I submit that this is one of those times.

15 It is not insignificant that such views are often bedded in theistic doctrines that regard moral purity as significant with respect to prospects in the 'afterlife', or the next life – which changes substantially the moral land-scape here.

16 There are, of course, other moral considerations to be weighed before a war can be justified.

17 Jeff McMahan, 'The Ethics of Killing in War', *Ethics*, 114, 2004, pp. 693–733, at pp. 730–1.

18 Christopher Gowans, *Innocence Lost* (Oxford: Oxford University Press, 1994), p. 226.

19 Michael Stocker, *Plural and Conflicting Values* (Oxford: Oxford University Press, 1990), p. 28.

20 I am not saying that there can never be acts of individual heroism, or what-ever, in war but even a large sum of such acts would not amount to the claim that war itself is a heroic enterprise.

21 JWT is, in the first instance, a theory of moral deliberation for leaders although I think it is for citizens and combatants as well. But I leave aside discussion of the implications of my analysis for the latter to revisit on another occasion.

22 Stephen de Wijze, 'Tragic Remorse: The Anguish of Dirty Hands', *Ethical Theory and Moral Practice*, 7, 2004, pp. 453–71. I say 'among the attitudes' as it cannot be the sole one. Leaders of a just war must also manifest stead-fastness, for example, and I do not deny that these attitudes may conflict: to let remorse dominate one's feelings may undermine steadfastness, for example. Such a possibility, however, should not cause us to abandon insistence upon tragic remorse altogether.

23 See my 'Balancing Peace, Justice and Sovereignty in *Jus Post Bellum*: The Case of Just Occupation, *Millennium*, 36: 3, 2008, pp. 533–54; and 'Moral Responsibilities and the Conflicting Demands of *Jus Post Bellum*', *Ethics and International Affairs*, 23: 2, 2009, pp. 147–64.

24 Richard Swinburne, *Responsibility and Atonement* (Oxford: Clarendon Press, 1989), p. 81.

25 These criteria are discussed at greater length in Evans, 'Balancing Peace' and 'Moral Responsibilities'.

Chapter 8

EVIL AND THE LEFT

Eve Garrard

Some people on the political Left are very reluctant to deploy the concept of evil, and distrust the use to which others put it. This reluctance and distrust are, I shall argue, unnecessary. What I hope to do here is to outline a case for evil and the Left – that is, a case for saying that the Left can legitimately appeal to the concept of evil, and that it can be of some use to them.

I don't intend to offer a complete theory of evil here: it's a highly disputed area, and the case for saying that the Left can legitimately deploy the idea of evil shouldn't depend too much on the details of any specific theory. But a broad characterisation of it, based on our common understanding of the term, can be provided, and should be enough to underpin the argument for the viability of the term in the lexicon of the Left. Similarly, I won't attempt to offer a watertight definition of what it is to be on the Left – it's most unlikely that any such definition exists. I'll treat the Left as being that large group of people who are especially concerned, in the political arena, with equality, diversity, democracy, the reduction of suffering, concerns about class, and concerns about human rights. A member of the Left will be a person who is particularly committed to these things, or at least to some largish subset of these things.

We need to start by noting that we use the term 'evil' in at least three different ways, only one of which is germane to this discussion.[1] We sometimes use 'evil' to mean anything at all that's bad or harmful, and in that sense we can talk quite comprehensibly about earthquakes, say, as being a natural evil. In contrast, we sometimes reserve the term 'evil' for cases of human agency, and use it to denote any actions that are morally wrong. 'The evil that men do lives after them', we say. But there are occasions when we use 'evil' to refer to a much more restricted range of actions and, in this kind of usage, we want to contrast evil actions with (merely) wrong ones. We hear of some dreadful torture, and say in horror: 'That's not just wrong, it's truly *evil!*' It's this last usage that I want to focus on, to see if it's congruent with a broadly Left picture of the world.

So the concept of evil which we're examining here is a fairly narrow one, according to which certain actions are especially terrible in ways which aren't adequately captured by saying that they're wrong or prohibited. (There's widespread agreement that all evil actions are wrongful but not all wrongful actions are evil – evil acts form a subset of wrongful ones.) And one reason for thinking that we do have a legitimate conception of evil is that we all use the term fairly easily. If someone says to you that torture is evil, you know at once what they mean, even if you don't agree with them about every specific case. In this usage, we reserve the term 'evil' for prohibited actions which are especially dreadful in some way – a way in which it is the job of a theory of evil to elucidate. There is a difference between evil and merely wrongful acts, and many, though not all, philosophers think this is a qualitative difference.[2] We use the term 'evil' to mark out some special class of wrongful actions; what characterises that class is the subject matter of theories of evil.

These theories set out to say what evil actually is – what it is for an action (or a person) to count as an evil one. They can be grouped into three broad classes: first, theories that identify evil acts in terms of the badness of their outcomes – typically, in terms of the harm they produce for the victim; second, theories that identify evil acts in terms of the state of mind of the agent – his malice, his sadism, his indifference or worse to the victim's suffering; third, hybrid theories that seek to combine aspects of both of the previous types of account.[3] But there is general agreement that there is something special about evil actions: they produce in those who contemplate them a special reaction of outrage and horror, and often a sense of hideous excess which is difficult to articulate clearly; and in virtue of the features, whatever they are, which produce this reaction, they warrant our most serious moral condemnation and rejection.

The two questions which I want to address are these: firstly, can this conception of evil find a place within a picture of the political world which is informed by the concerns I listed earlier as being those of the Left? Is thinking of some group of actions as being peculiarly horrific and reprehensible, as especially to be shunned and condemned, in any way incompatible with left-wing commitments? And secondly, can this conception of evil actually be of use in left-wing thought? Can it do any intellectual work for the Left?

My strategy in trying to handle these questions is an extremely simple one: we should go along with the phenomenology unless there are insuperable objections to what it delivers. We do seem to use the term 'evil' in mutually comprehensible ways – we can disagree about which actions fall under this heading, and we couldn't have such disagreements if we didn't have some common understanding of the terms they're couched in. And, furthermore, most adults have had the experience gestured at earlier: we see some horror, some atrocity, and reach for a way of describing it that's adequate to its dreadfulness, in a way in which the term 'wrong', or even 'very wrong' is not. That is, evil appears already to be part of our moral phenomenology. There are, as we shall see, various objections to the deployment of this concept coming from the general terrain of the Left. But since the moral phenomenology seems to endorse the use of the concept, then, if (though only if) the objections can be satisfactorily dealt with, we should accept what the phenomenology delivers.

The first objection is one arising from secularism: surely the use of the term 'evil' reveals a commitment to the existence of a supernatural being – the Devil? But the Left is largely (though not exclusively) secularist, and rejects these metaphysical implications. Indeed, even religious members of the Left don't always want to buy into a commitment to a personal source of evil – not all believers believe in the Devil, and many liberal Christians find talk of satanic forces something of an embarrassment. On this view, the concept of evil contains a metaphysical commitment which isn't compatible with the picture of the world endorsed by a large section of the Left.

But this objection misses its target. No doubt the concept of evil had its original home in a theistic view of the world. But so do many of our moral concepts – guilt and atonement, for example – and yet secular thinkers today have a use for them and, indeed, can't do without them if they're to address pressing moral and political issues. Entirely secular thinkers use the term 'evil', and their secular readers know what they mean, whether they do or don't agree with a particular attribution. And the concept is certainly in common usage among non-religious people, for whatever weight one wants to put on that. Furthermore, there are several entirely secular theories of evil currently available in the intellectual marketplace, and though they're no doubt open to a variety of objections, incomprehensibility isn't really one of them. Although we need a good secular theory of evil to help us analyse and reflect on our understanding of the term, nonetheless there's no doubt that we do use and, to some large extent, understand it unreflectively, and this usage is as available to the secular Left as it is to anyone else.

The second objection is encapsulated in the claim that the concept of evil is part of the nature/nurture debate, and not a part which a left-winger would want to endorse. In this debate, the Left usually comes down fairly strongly on the side of nurture, and of explanations of human traits and action in terms of environmental pressures and forces. This stems in large part from standard Left ideas about oppression, and the way in which its effects not only restrict people's freedom and cause them suffering but also go deep into their moral character. There is also the Left aspiration to extend human solidarity and sympathy as widely as possible, encouraging us to see wrongdoers, especially those in unjust situations, as being victims as well as perpetrators and, indeed, in some cases extending this view to oppressors themselves. In contrast to this ensemble of attitudes, the concept of evil (so it is said) makes an appeal to the idea of people being immutably evil, independently of what happens to them – 'evil will out', we say, in a way which implies that whatever the environmental forces acting on the evildoer, nonetheless his ingrained and unalterable evil nature will show its face sooner or later.

This is a rather old-fashioned line of attack on the concept of evil and, again, it misses its target: we may or may not know what the causes of evil are but the concept itself is silent about this aspect of the phenomenon which it picks out. Nothing in the concept of evil requires that its causes be genetic ones, or in some way inherent in the individual agent rather than being a product of his or her circumstances. Indeed, many of the paradigmatic cases of evil action are clearly very context-sensitive – no one supposes that the circumstances created by the totalitarian reach and power of the Nazi government had no causal bearing on the many, many evil acts that were carried out by non-Nazis under its rule. It's a commonplace of moral thought that some of us who are currently blameless might have done evil had we been in those circumstances but this thought in no way lessens the applicability of the concept of evil to the actions in question.

The 'nature' side of this argument generally takes a genetic form these days but this doesn't, in fact, strengthen anti-nurturist explanations of behaviour as much as it might appear to do at first sight. Genes are always expressed in an environment, so a different environment may preclude their expression entirely (as in the case of the genetically determined disease phenylketonuria whose dreadful effects can be avoided by altering the nutritional environment of the bearer of the relevant genes). Perhaps evil is like that, too – if the potential for evil is carried deep inside some or all of us, then the realisation of that potential may be highly dependent on the physical and social environment in which we find ourselves. At any rate, nothing in the concept of evil settles the question of its origins, and the flat polarity – nature versus nurture – needed for this objection to get going isn't really available to us. The Left can accommodate genetic influences on behaviour without erosion of its concern for the effects of an oppressive environment; similarly nothing need prevent it deploying the concept of evil even if the possibility of some inherent evil propensities in the human blueprint remains an open one.[4]

The third objection is really a group of objections which, though they are structurally very dissimilar, nonetheless share something in common, namely a concern (often a laudable concern) that we shouldn't be too harsh on others. The first of these is a worry about responsibility: the concept of evil suggests that ultimate responsibility for evil acts lies with the evil agent but, surely, when people act dreadfully, there are often extenuating circumstances, so that it's wrong to hold them fully responsible for what they do? Furthermore, the very idea of 'ultimate responsibility' may not be tenable in the light of the kind of causal stories we can increasingly tell about the origins of wrongdoing. There are various responses which can be made to this kind of objection. Firstly, there's nothing in the concept of evil that requires that the agent be fully responsible and blameworthy – this may or may not be the case (and it may very well vary from one evil act to the next); indeed, we acknowledge this when we talk with (justified) horror of the children in some parts of the world who are kidnapped for the purposes of making them into child soldiers. Such children can go on, both in their childhood and into their adulthood, to do truly terrible things, acts which we rightly call evil; but it's hard to hold them fully responsible or blameworthy for what they do.[5] In other cases, however (perhaps, indeed, in the case of those adults who decide to kidnap children with a view to turning them into killers) blame seems entirely appropriate. Many evil actions are no doubt fully blameworthy but it doesn't follow, and is not entailed by the concept, that all of them are. And if we go any further down this road, and worry about the external forces acting on competent adult agents, draining away the responsibility and hence the blame from them, we'll come to a problem that is in no way unique to the phenomenon of evil. It's the issue of free will, which is a problem for all the moral concepts, so whatever answer we give for the rest of them can be adopted for the concept of evil. That the concept of evil raises problems of rightly attributing responsibility and blame can't be a reason for refusing to use it since these problems arise for all the moral concepts, and we certainly can't do without all of them.

Next up is another worry about judging others too harshly. It often takes the form of a question: who are we to say that another's conduct is evil, since very probably it won't seem so to the evildoer herself? There are (at least) two different ways of construing this question: firstly, it can be seen as making reference to our epistemic frailty, and the likelihood of our getting judgements wrong about the misdeeds of others. We can all agree with such concerns about the nature and extent of our epistemic frailty but this is a problem for all moral attributions. Something which is a worry about all our moral concepts can't be a special reason for abandoning just one of them. If the concept of evil is threatened by our epistemic frailty, so too will be the concept of injustice, for example. And we can't seriously imagine the Left not wanting to make constant appeal to the concept of injustice.

It might be said that getting our attributions wrong will matter more with respect to judgements about evil, precisely because of the severity of condemnation which they imply. Perhaps that's right – but it should be handled by being exceptionally careful about the deployment of the concept, rather than by abandoning it altogether. If there's a particular problem with judgements about evil because of their moral weightiness, then that tells on both sides of the argument: if evil is especially terrible, then it's especially important not to be blind to its existence or presence.

A different way of construing the question 'Who are we to judge others evil?' is to see it as making a claim about moral metaphysics rather than about moral epistemology. The thought here is that moral judgements, insofar as they are true or legitimate or appropriate (I'm trying to remain as neutral as possible about the truth value of moral judgements) are true or legitimate or appropriate only for certain speakers in certain conditions. It may be true or appropriate for me to say that certain acts are evil but it doesn't follow that it must be true or appropriate for you to do so, much less for those other people over there in a completely different culture from ours. This is effectively the claim made by the moral relativist but it is misplaced as a criticism of the concept of evil. This is because, once again, if it's a problem at all then it's a problem about all the moral concepts, not just one of them. And in any case, although relativism seems to me to be a bad idea for the Left (and, indeed, for anyone else) a relativist can nonetheless deploy the concept of evil just as she deploys other moral concepts – whatever is the basis of morality relativistically construed, it will underpin the concept of evil just as it underpins the concepts of right and wrong. Of course, extreme relativism occasionally leads people into something much closer to moral nihilism, a position which isn't vulnerable to the remarks I've been making here. But whatever strengths moral nihilism has are irrelevant to this debate, since a Left which was morally nihilistic wouldn't look much like the kind of Left which has any claim at all on our political attention.

Two further versions of the objection of over-harshness include the claim that calling another person, or his actions, evil is tantamount to writing him off, to giving up hope on him altogether. There is, in fact, a very quick reply to this charge, which is to point out that it's manifestly untrue. We know that people can and do repent of doing evil – see, for example, the unforgettable account of such a case in Eric Lomax's *The Railway Man*, his memoir of the time he spent in a Japanese prisoner-of-war camp during World War II, and the terrible effects which the torture he suffered there had on him.[6] A central figure in the book is that of one of his Japanese tormentors, who came eventually to repent of his evil deeds, and to devote the rest of his life in trying to memori-alise some of those who had suffered so terribly at his hands and those of his compatriots. However one judges his later repentance, it doesn't seem to be morally negligible, so seeing his earlier actions as evil needn't involve ruling out the moral significance of any later repentance, or of the person who has the potential so to repent. (Of course, just as people can turn away from evil, so they can turn towards it – but that's a problem about mutability which is well beyond my remit here.) Another way in which it's clear that the charge of evil isn't tantamount to writing the agent off, or giving up all hope for him, arises from the fact that some evildoers who don't, in fact, ever repent of their actions may nonetheless be admirable, maybe even heroic, in other respects. Our acknowledgement of this very disturbing fact is sufficient to show that there's no necessary connection between the attribution of evil and the complete moral rejection of the evildoer.

Closely connected to this worry about giving up on people is the view that to call a person's actions evil is to declare that the actions and/ or the agent are unforgivable. But this seems too harsh, so the objection goes – we shouldn't rule out anyone from the possibility of forgiveness. There is, indeed, a question about the forgivability of evil acts, an issue on which people have quite widely differing views. But once again, there's nothing in the concept of evil itself which implies unforgivability: doctrines of universal or unconditional forgiveness can be found among people, such as the early Christians, for whom evil is a central moral term. Ultimately the answer to the question of whether evil acts can ever be forgiven is more likely to arise out of our theory of forgiveness rather than out of our account of evil. So here again, the characteristic Left concern to maintain and widen the scope of human solidarity and compassion needn't be threatened by the concept of evil – we can regard actions as evil without totally rejecting the agents who commit them (though, of course, whether this refusal to reject the evildoer is, indeed, what we ought to do in response to evil is itself a very troubled and troubling question).[7]

The final objection from harshness which I'll consider is the claim that to call another evil is to treat her as a moral monster, someone quite unlike the rest of us; and to treat an evildoer as the Other in this way is hypocritically to bolster our own self-image by contrast with a wicked alien allegedly entirely different from our own good selves. No doubt such things do sometimes happen – hypocrisy appears to be a human constant. But the Othering implications of the use of the term 'evil' follow only if we're sure that we ourselves could never commit evil acts or behave monstrously. But are we sure of that? Have we good reason to be sure of that? We can call another a monster, without implying that he's radically different from us, if we believe that we, too, in a not too distant possible world, could also have acted in that way. The claim that we could never in any circumstances have acted evilly is, so it seems to me, a claim that few of us want to make about ourselves, and even fewer could make it truthfully. And after a century or so of art and theory inspired by the insights of Nietzsche and Freud, and by the work of historians of the twentieth-century genocides, few of us are likely to be too surprised by the idea that monstrosity and normality aren't so very far apart.

None of this is to deny the responsibility of the evildoer, or to say that we're all in some vague way to blame for the evil act – an assertion which all too often turns out to mean that actually nobody is to blame. We can be sure that we're not to blame for horrors which we had no hand in producing but, at the same time, we can acknowledge that in other circumstances we, too, could have been or could have become a person ready to commit evil; and, had we done so, we, too, would have been fully to blame.[8] Attributing evil to the acts of another person isn't tantamount to saying that he or she is utterly and completely unlike ourselves – there is far too much evidence that such a claim would have no basis in fact. But neither does the acknowledgement of our own dark possibilities in any way lift the burden of responsibility from the one who actually does do evil – not unless we want to say that any act which we ourselves could have done can't be fully blameworthy. Few people, particularly on the Left, would want to make that remarkably complacent claim.

There is one further objection to the idea of evil which needs to be addressed but I'll leave it till the end because it has a rather different structure from the other ones that I've canvassed.[9] So far, I've argued that the principal objections to the concept of evil arising out of broadly left-wing sympathies are either false or they apply to all the moral concepts in which case they can't be a reason for abandoning the concept of evil alone. Now let me turn to considering the positive case for the concept of evil, the case that it can actually be of some use to the Left.

The idea of evil captures a very widely held intuition that some moral wrongdoings are in a class (a very terrible class) of their own. If this is something delivered to us by the phenomenology, and if there are no conclusive objections against it, then we have reason to accept it as part of our moral ontology. But is it really delivered to us by the phenomenology? To try to establish this, we might consider, for example, the treatment of women in some of the world's most terrible conflicts. The systematic use of rape as a weapon of war, and the further infliction of the most hideous tortures on these women, such as shooting them through the vagina, or forcing them to collect up the body parts of their slaughtered and dismembered husbands so that they may be raped on top of the dismembered limbs, strikes many people as involving something well beyond ordinary wrongdoing. The element of hideous excess, the terrifying moral blindness involved in such actions, incline us to reach for some special category of condemnation which will reflect the special horror that they evoke in us. It would not, unfortunately, be difficult to provide many further and even worse examples of man's inhumanity to woman, and to man as well. The great genocides of the twentieth century yield a rich seam of pickings, and there are also cases on the personal rather than on the military or political level that produce a similar reaction of horror and fear, and a sense of moral diminution and disgust.[10] Many people feel that actions displaying this kind and level of inhumanity are in a special category of wrongdoing; if this is right, then evil is the appropriate term for this category. The Left has had a special concern for the rights of oppressed racial and gender groups, who have historically been on the receiving end of some of the most terrible actions which humans can commit. The concept of evil allows them to adequately categorise the nightmare of suffering which has been endured by some members of these groups (and by others too), and it helps to express more precisely the kind of condemnation which ought to be provided for the infliction of that suffering.[11]

A point of general importance arises from the philosophical claim that the legitimacy of a concept depends on its explanatory power. The concept of evil does have explanatory power, like the other moral concepts, such as courage, or generosity, or arrogance. These are concepts which play a central part in our understanding of others. We often appeal to them to account for the way people act, and evil is no different in this respect. Of course, there will be occasions where the appeal to evil doesn't do much explaining – for example, if our question is 'Why did A do so evil a thing?' then the answer 'Because he's an evil person' will have very little explanatory power. But, similarly, if we ask 'Why did A act so courageously?' then the answer 'Because he's a courageous person' also has little explanatory power – how explanatory a concept is depends in part on what it's being asked to explain. If, however, we ask, 'Why did A do this act whereas B didn't?' then appeal to evil may be part of the explanation. Of course, just what explanations are provided by appealing to evil will depend on what we think evil actually is – that is, it will depend on our theory of evil. For example, theories of evil which locate it in the psychological state of the agent will be able to explain the fact that one agent acts evilly where another one doesn't by appeal to the motives or intentions or grasp (or failure to grasp) of moral considerations of the agent in question. Clearly, different theories will have different explanatory and predictive powers. It's certainly true to say that appeal to the idea of evil will rarely if ever provide a full explanation of the phenomenon in question. But that hardly marks out the concept of evil in any distinctive way – very few, if any, concepts have this kind of explanatory power, partly because very few, if any, events are explicable with reference to only one cause or kind of cause. But a secular theory of evil will have some explanatory power, and this will be as available and as useful to thinkers on the Left as to any others who hope to understand better the atrocities which darken human history.[12]

Finally I want to consider one further objection to the idea of evil. This is the claim that, if we allow ourselves to deploy the concept of evil, it's likely that we will abuse it in order to gain some personal or political kind of advantage; and, given how weighty the judgement of evil is in terms of rejection and blame, such abuses will be serious enough for us to have reason to abjure the use of the concept altogether. What's distinctive about this objection is that it acknowledges, or certainly is compatible with, the existence of genuine cases of evil, cases which do genuinely fall under the concept. This claim about the likelihood of abuse is an entirely plausible one – we can see exactly this kind of abuse in the case of the term 'genocide' whose horror has to some extent been dissipated by the readiness of some people to appropriate it for activities which, though they may involve genuine and serious wrongdoing, fall very far short of genocide. At the other end of the moral spectrum, 'democracy' is another term which has been stretched in this abusive and ultimately vacuous way.

The reasons for such abuse, and the advantages which accrue to the successful abuser, are fairly transparent, so there's no need to develop them further here. But if there is such a thing as evil, then the appropriate response to abuse of the concept is to refrain from abusing it, and to criticise others when they do so. Rather than abandoning the concept, we should insist that it is used appropriately (a satisfactory theory of evil would be extremely helpful here). We need a richer rather than a poorer moral vocabulary, more moral distinctions rather than fewer ones. But does the Left, it may be asked, need this one, the concept of evil, in particular? To answer this question, we need only look at the history of the terrible twentieth century, and the way in which the twenty-first century is shaping up to be appallingly like its predecessor. Can we, and in particular the Left, do even descriptive justice to the horrors – profound, diverse, and hideously inventive – which some people have had to undergo at the hands of others, *without* appeal to the idea of evil?

Notes

1 See Eve Garrard, 'The Nature of Evil', *Philosophical Explorations*, 1: 1, 1998, pp. 43–60.

2 Theorists who regard the difference as a qualitative one include Stephen De Wijze, 'Defining Evil: Insights from the Problem of "Dirty Hands"', *The Monist*, 85: 2, 2002, pp. 210–38; Eve Garrard, 'Evil as an Explanatory Concept', *The Monist*, 85: 2, 2002, pp. 320–36; Daniel Haybron, 'Moral Monsters and Saints', *The Monist*, 85: 2, 2002, pp. 260–84; Hillel Steiner, 'Calibrating Evil', *The Monist*, 85: 2, 2002, pp. 183–93; in contrast, Luke Russell argues that it is a quantitative difference, in 'Is Evil Action Qualitatively Distinct from Ordinary Wrongdoing?', *Australasian Journal of Philosophy*, 85: 4, 2007, pp. 659–77.

3 For a fuller discussion of these categories see Paul Formosa, 'A Conception of Evil', *The Journal of Value Inquiry*, 42, 2008, pp. 217–39.

4 For argument from the Marxist Left which affirms the possibility of evil being inherent in human nature see Norman Geras, *The Contract of Mutual Indifference* (London: Verso, 1998).

5 For discussion of the moral liability of child soldiers, and the terrible circumstances in which they are recruited, see Jeff McMahan, *Killing in War* (Oxford: Oxford University Press, 2009) esp. chapter 4, pp. 198–202.

6 Eric Lomax, *The Railway Man* (London: W. W. Norton and Co., 1995).

7 On this issue see, for example, Simon Wiesenthal, *The Sunflower*, revised edn (New York: Schocken Books, 1997); Jean Amery, *At the Mind's Limits: Contemplations by a Survivor on Auschwitz and its Realities* (New York: Schocken Books, 1986, 1990); Thomas Brudholm, *Resentment's Virtue: Jean Amery and the Refusal to Forgive* (Philadelphia: Temple University Press, 2008); Charles Griswold, *Forgiveness: A Philosophical Exploration* (New York: Cambridge University Press, 2007) esp. chapter 2; Eve Garrard and David McNaughton, 'In Defence of Unconditional Forgiveness', *Proceedings of the Aristotelian Society*, 103: 1, 2003, pp. 39–60; Eve Garrard and David McNaughton, 'Conditional Unconditional Forgiveness', in Christel Fricke (ed.), *The Ethics of Forgiveness* (Routledge, forthcoming).

8 The truth of this counter-factual seems to me to have rich and substantive moral implications, but they can't be adequately dealt with here.

9 For further discussion of general objections to the idea of evil, see Paul Formosa, 'The Problems with Evil', *Contemporary Political Theory*, 7, 2008,

pp. 395–415; Luke Russell, 'Evil-Revivalism Versus Evil-Skepticism', *Journal of Value Inquiry*, 40: 1, 2006, pp. 89–105.

10 For some individual cases see the examples cited in Marcus Singer, 'The Concept of Evil', *Philosophy*, 79, 2004, pp. 185–214.

11 I don't intend to imply that all theories of evil locate it in the production of great suffering, since this certainly isn't the case. But it's doubtful that any theorists would deny that the kind of action described above would count as evil, partly in virtue of the suffering produced. The role played by suffering, or more broadly harm, in the nature of evil is a central topic of discussion among theorists which I can't do full justice to here but see, among many others, Claudia Card, *The Atrocity Paradigm: A Theory of Evil* (New York: Oxford University Press, 2002); Russell, 'Evil-Revivalism versus Evil-Skepticism'; De Wijze, 'Defining Evil'; Adam Morton, *On Evil* (New York: Routledge, 2004); M. H. Kramer, *The Death Penalty Redux: A Philosophical Investigation* (Oxford: Oxford University Press, forthcoming), chapter 6.

12 For further discussion of the explanatory power of evil, see Garrard, 'Evil as an Explanatory Concept'.

Chapter 9

THE GLAMOUR OF EVIL: DOSTOYEVSKY AND THE POLITICS OF TRANSGRESSION

John Horton

A

Probably the most famous contribution to the discussion of the nature of evil in the modern world over the last half-century, at least in the field of political theory, is that of Hannah Arendt. Her thesis regarding 'the banality of evil' set out in the course of her reflections on the Eichmann trial in *Eichmann in Jerusalem*, first published in 1963,[1] is widely celebrated and much invoked, if not always unambiguously favourably. Exactly what she meant by this captivating but misleadingly simple phrase is less easily understood than is sometimes thought and has been the cause of heated debate.[2] One thing that Arendt's perceptive and sometimes brilliant argument unquestionably brought to the fore, however, is an insufficiently appreciated feature of the guise of evil as manifested in the modern world: this is its routinisation and bureaucratisation. What is striking about such evil is, paradoxically, the apparent ordinariness of its mien. She found in Eichmann not the kind of moral monster or political fanatic typically associated with evil in the popular imagination but, instead, a rather dull and anonymous functionary 'conscientiously', as he (not entirely convincingly) maintained, fulfilling his duties within the bureaucratic system of the Nazi state. She argued that what those, like Eichmann, who willingly served in the Nazi system lacked was primarily the imagination and reflectiveness to question it: Arendt presents him as literally 'thoughtless'. He was not, at least in any straightforward sense, 'mad', depraved, a vicious sadist, or a fanatic, nor it seems was he even motivated by any particular animus towards the Jews, either individually or collectively, holding throughout that he had 'nothing personal' against them. It was this very 'routinisation' of the organisation and administration of the Nazi death camps, and the impersonal thoughtlessness of those like Eichmann, which Arendt saw as a distinctive feature of the modern form of evil that they embodied.

It is clear that Arendt was not seeking in any way to minimise or diminish the moral repulsiveness of the Nazi regime; and nor, I believe, did she want to deny the guilt of those who knowingly served it. She was not claiming that people like Eichmann were not really engaged in evil, nor arguing that those who were deeply implicated in the murderous system should be excused because they were 'obeying orders' or only 'doing their job', although she has sometimes been (mis)understood as erring in that direction. Rather, she was (among other things) pointing to the inadequacy of a common way of thinking about evil, and trying to show how evil, even on such an appalling scale, could reveal an apparently mundane face; how otherwise 'normal' people could become complicit in evil on such a scale without seemingly being in the least morally troubled by what they were actually doing. While some Nazis and their supporters were no doubt close to the caricatured fanatics of popular misconception, most were not; rather they were 'ordinary' people who, had they found themselves living in different circumstances, would likely have led lives of blameless bourgeois rectitude (or no more blameworthy than the lives of most of the rest of us). From his defence at his trial, something like that seems to be pretty much how Eichmann thought of himself. But that does not mean that he and others were blameless because, in fact, they did not live such a life but instead, knowingly and voluntarily, chose to act in ways that helped to sustain and advance a system that quite deliberately perpetrated the most terrible human suffering. That they were in some sense 'blind' to what they were really doing is not an excuse but itself a particularly serious kind of moral failing.

Arendt's analysis is relevant beyond the immediate Nazi experience of totalitarianism more generally in helping us to understand how ordinary people, motivated neither by overwhelming fear nor fanatical devotion to an ideology or cause or even by a ruthless desire for personal advancement, are able with an apparently clear conscience to serve as effective functionaries in malign and evil enterprises. It is, furthermore, an analysis that is disturbing, for it is far easier for us if evil does, so to speak, show itself on the face of the culprit; if we are dealing with people who can be readily identified as moral monsters and clearly different from 'normal' people (the rest of us, as we like to think). One of

Arendt's greatest achievements, though, is precisely her undermining of this comforting illusion, and her exploration of this altogether more deeply unsettling, yet also blander, face of evil. In so far as the perpetrators of such evil are much like us, we are denied the easy consolation of a Manichaean division that separates 'evil' people from the rest of us. Moreover, in so far as we focus on the kind of bureaucratic system in which people like Eichmann were functionaries, then we can also see how these systems work to facilitate such actions while also effectively shielding people from having to acknowledge responsibility for what they are doing. Her insights can also be extended by, for example, focusing on the way in which a sanitised bureaucratic language can help to disguise from people, or make more palatable to them, what they are really doing. Thus, collateral damage seems a lot less morally troubling than the killing of innocent civilians, and water boarding can sound more akin to surfboarding than to the torture that it undoubtedly is. They can also lead us to ask questions about how simple-minded categorisations of regimes (the evil empire, the axis of evil and so on) and people (between evil suicide bombers and decent presidents who, nonetheless, use nuclear weapons or resort to pre-emptive strikes) are made. These were not issues that Arendt herself pursued and they are not ones that will be explored further here.

There had certainly been intimations of Arendt's line of thought earlier, perhaps most profoundly in the strange logic of the fictional worlds of Franz Kafka. But Kafka was more interested in a metaphysical condition than a political one and, although his work easily came to bear a pregnant political reading, that does not seem to have been his principal intent. And, as an extremely well-educated central European Jew, Arendt was clearly aware of many of these ideas, but there is no denying her originality. For not only did she come up with the remarkably evocative phrase, 'the banality of evil', she also pursued its logic in non-fictional context in a way that represented a genuinely original insight into how evil can insinuate itself into modern social and political systems. This is not to suggest that what she says in this regard is not open to criticism but, again, I shall not pursue such criticisms here, for this homage to Arendt is essentially an apology for largely neglecting her in the remainder of this chapter. For, as should be clear, without wishing in any way to deny the importance of her insights, I want to focus on a very different and, perhaps in some respects, more traditional, aspect of evil – its allure.

First, though, we will need to backtrack a little, for I have so far written about evil as though the whole idea of it is unproblematical; and, of course, that is not the case. There is a real question, at least for those who are non-religious – though perhaps not only for the non-religious – of what evil can mean under the disenchanted and secular conditions of modernity. Indeed, in such a context, it is quite hard to see how the concept of evil can be seriously thought to have either an explanatory or analytical role. Many will hold that, in any strong or distinctive sense, the concept is long past its use by date, out of place and reeking only of the musty superstitions of an earlier age. The problem here is not so much about trying to define evil – something that Arendt, for example, sensibly does not attempt – but about making it real for us as something genuinely distinctive or 'special'. If the idea of evil as something like an active force in the world or even as marking a phenomenologically distinct form of activity is no longer credible, what exactly is it? Even as a label or term of disapproval, it may appear to have lost any of the real power it once had. One, admittedly rather trivial, instance of this is that, at least among young people in the West, 'evil' seems to be going, or perhaps to have already gone, much the same way as 'wicked', with its almost comic penumbra of associations and a reversal of meaning. Thus, to give one example, in an interview, the violinist Nigel Kennedy describes the guitar playing of Jeff Beck as 'like, really evil, man', and he is unproblematically understood to be praising the power of Beck's mastery of the guitar. Nor, among a large number of people, does such a usage cause the least surprise or offence. And such examples could be multiplied many times over.

It is also true, however, that the term 'evil' still figures often enough, even in secular discourse, in something like its more traditional guise, if without any theological underpinning. For example, it is a staple of lurid tabloid headlines and commonly to be found in the pronouncements of judges when sentencing those who have committed particularly horrific crimes. It is also to be found flourishing in the moral fables of popular culture where a Manichaean divide between 'good' and 'evil' often continues to rein unchecked. Yet, it is often hard to take such uses altogether seriously, to avoid the sense that such uses have about them the air of pantomime villainy or are more than a crude straining for emotional effect; equally, though, it cannot be denied that they are also meant to be taken seriously by at least some of those who resort to the language of evil. This suspicion towards the concept does not arise because we think that the actions or events to which they are attached are anything other than morally appalling – we will usually share that feeling – but because the use of the term 'evil' seems to add little, if anything, to our ability to understand or explain them. Where evil is used with serious intent to characterise people or their actions, it functions mostly as no more than a term of especially strong disapproval within the rhetoric of condemnation.

In short, it seems to be difficult to see exactly what the uses of the language of evil can amount to, at least for those who see themselves as part of a modern secular age which, it must be acknowledged, is by no means everyone even in the most secular of current societies. As has been remarked, 'evil' is not understood by those of us who have this trouble in getting to grips with it as an active force in the world; and nor is it informed by a religious, or (I suggest) even moral, metaphysics. While it is worth noting that a number of political theorists, such as William Connolly, Nel Noddings and John Kekes among others, have written about evil with perhaps surprisingly little embarrassment, they do not ultimately appear to mean anything very distinctive by it.[3] For, without wishing to claim that the term cannot still be used seriously or carry with it at least some of the horror that was once its natural accompaniment, it is hard to see what it denotes beyond an especially extreme form of wrongdoing, or a set of especially vicious intentions, or natural misfortune on a grand scale. Indeed, it would seem that, generally, we tend to be least uncomfortable or self-conscious in using the term to describe states of affairs, which may or may not be caused by human beings, rather than people or actions per se. Typically, in this sense, phenomena such as civil war, genocide, famines, epidemics and earthquakes are described as great evils. I am not suggesting that there is anything unintelligible or morally or intellectually objectionable with so using the term, and it may even be useful sometimes to have a special word to mark the extreme of dreadfulness. But, in the absence of a theodicy that gives rise to 'the problem of evil', or a discourse in which it functions as a genuinely malign force, there also seems to be little, if anything, that is very special or distinctive about such a use. And, where it is applied to people rather than to events, it seems not to fit very easily with a modern psychological understanding of human agency. Evil thus appears to be, at best, potentially redundant and, at worst, simply inappropriate in helping to *explain* or *understand* any acts or events in the world.

These doubts whether there is a plausible, viable or useful secular concept of evil that is in some way truly distinctive or different from either merely a label for the very bad or a way of expressing our horror or disapproval naturally give rise to the question of whether we should dispense with the concept altogether? Is it best to consign it to an antiquated metaphysics as more likely to mystify or mislead than illuminate anything? There is probably little that can be said to someone so inclined to show that they are making some kind of mistake if that is how they respond. On the other hand, it is also possible to understand, if much less easy to articulate convincingly, how such a response might leave one feeling slightly dissatisfied, as though the abandonment of the concept of evil would be a genuine loss and not merely the jettisoning of the superstitious language of a bygone age. Although it need not do so, the notion of evil can still have resonance and seemingly be experienced as a phenomenological reality even for people who are unsure whether it really has any defensible place in our moral or conceptual universe.

In what follows, therefore, I shall, so far as possible, be agnostic about what precisely is entailed in deploying the language of evil in the hope that what I go on to discuss makes sense whatever one's exact attitude towards the concept. Even those resolutely opposed to any continued employment of it should have no problem translating my use of the concept into something like: an exceptionally serious form of harm perpetrated by some human beings upon others. On the other hand, those who have some sort of metaphysically inflected commitment to a more robust conception of evil will hopefully at least find nothing in what I say that is seriously inconsistent with their understanding.

B

The title of this chapter comes from the Roman Catholic Easter vigil service when baptismal vows are renewed, and one of the questions asked by the priest conducting the service is: 'Do you reject the glamour of evil?' There are undoubtedly different ways in which this question can be interpreted, and I claim no particular authority for the use I make of it. As I understand it, however, the premise of the question strikes me as a bold and intriguing one, even for those who do not subscribe to its specific religious meaning: evil is taken to be alluring and enticing, something to which we could understandably be drawn, and not necessarily something that we are naturally inclined to shy away from. We are invited to reject that which we might also find attractive. It may remind us that the traditional Christian agent of evil – the Devil – was a fallen angel, God's favourite no less, of the temptations felt by Augustine, and of the long history in imaginative literature from at least Milton to Stephen Adly Guirgis, for instance, in which the Devil is a compellingly attractive presence and often charismatic figure – Lucifer, a beacon of (deceptive) light, whose dazzle blinds. On a secular plane, too, the fascination with evil is ubiquitous in popular culture: whether it is fictional serial killers, such as Hannibal Lecter, or real ones, such as Jack the Ripper or Peter Sutcliffe; or in supernatural horror stories in which evil may or may not take a human form. Indeed, though it is not a point I shall pursue, it may perhaps be worth noting briefly how evil is represented within the popular imaginary. For, overwhelmingly, it does not appear there in the register of Arendt's banality of evil, not least for the obvious commercial reason that it is unlikely in such a form to engage a mass audience. (Of course, this is partly what Arendt was concerned to challenge.) While evil is presented in such contexts as a spectre that shocks and perhaps frightens us, it is typically not *just* shocking or frightening. There is something that also attracts us (and that helps to keep us reading, listening or watching). There are, it should be conceded, many exceptions to such a gross generalisation but, in the popular imagination, evil often possesses this Janus-faced or dual aspect, as having a fascination that is simultaneously both repellent and attractive.

This leads, naturally enough – given that whatever we mean by evil it is supposed to be bad, indeed, the very worst kind of bad – to what it is that makes it attractive. Why is it that, even for 'decent', ordinary people, it can have this insidious attraction? There is, no doubt, no single answer to this question but the one I want to examine is that the glamour of evil lies, at least in part, in its relationship to the transgressive. The transgressive is also typically connected with power. This is partly because power is what makes the transgressive a viable possibility but also, more interestingly, partly because it is the possession of power that can motivate the desire to transgress. That is, power acts not merely a means to be used in effectively perpetrating evil but also, in a sense, as an inspiration for it. The transgressive becomes an explicit manifestation, even validation, of power – the greater the evil, the greater the power. It is, I shall suggest, its transgressive character that helps to explain the allure (as well as the horror) that evil has for us. In this respect, evil can be the very antithesis of the banal: it is a source of excitement and vitality. In this respect, it stands against the diurnal and mundane, which are also the stuff of a certain kind of pragmatic 'bourgeois' politics, commonly associated, for example, with parliamentarianism, constitutionalism or liberalism, and to which I shall return at the very end of the chapter.

The 'transgressive' involves the intentional crossing of acknowledged boundaries, acting outside of rules or accepted norms. But, more than that, at least as I want to use the notion, it involves these actions on a grand scale although this is a far from precise idea. In so far as it specifically relates to evil (and not all transgressions, of course, need be bad) it is close to what is sometimes called 'radical evil'.[4] Any crime, even the most minor, is in some sense transgressive: indeed, crimes are called legal transgressions. Indeed, any intentional violation of a rule or norm is by definition a transgression against it. In the sense in which I want to employ the term, however, breaches of norms that are merely trivial or entirely commonplace are not relevantly transgressive. (They can still be seriously damaging: it was Flaubert, I think, who described adultery as the most conventional form of unconventionality, and there is statistically at least nothing very exceptional about it in many modern societies, but it can still destroy lives and relationships.) Similarly, breaches of norms undertaken for motives that are routine and easily understood, such as personal gain (for instance, injuring or killing someone with the sole purpose of stealing their property) and which do not involve a denial of the validity of the norm are also not really what I have in mind, although they can be so extreme as to shade into the kind of cases that are of concern. Rather, an important feature of the form of the transgressive in play here is that it is typically associated with something like an avowed contempt for the very norm or boundary that is being crossed. The transgressive is above all bold: it makes a statement. And therein lies an important part of its glamour or allure. It is a refusal to be bound by the conventions, by the ordinary, by the normal, by the same standards as everyone else; and is instead a stepping beyond or outside of the safe, the routine or the familiar: the transgressive is the exceptional, the extraordinary.

If one focuses on some of the most obvious political evils of the last century – Nazism, Stalinism (and I mean Stalinism, not Communism), the Pol Pot regime in Cambodia or many dictatorial regimes in Africa, for instance – one can see that, although the motives were various, they all involved a contempt for fundamental elements of what (for want of a better term) might be called a minimal level of moral concern and human decency. In all these cases the initiators of these evils saw either themselves or what they thought they stood for as exceptional, above or beyond the small-mindedness of mere 'conventional morality' and the mundane pettiness of 'normal' politics. While their followers were no doubt variously motivated, there seems to be little doubt that, in some cases, especially, but not only, among the senior apparatchiks and enthusiasts, they shared this sense of being part of something different and exceptional. While many of the participants may have been similar to Eichmann, it appears highly improbable that Eichmann or his like could have initiated or inspired such regimes.

While, as I mentioned earlier, even some contemporary political the-orists have not been shy about writing about evil, it is psychologists and psychoanalysts, on the one hand, and novelists, poets and dramatists, on the other, who have been most engaged with the aspect of evil that interests me here. Thus, although I also believe that there is something quite profound in what she says, I cannot entirely agree with Simone Weil when she writes that:

> Imaginary evil is romantic and varied; real evil is gloomy, monoto-nous, barren, boring. Imaginary good is boring; real good is always new, marvellous, intoxicating. Therefore, imaginative literature is either boring or immoral (or a mixture of both).[5]

One problem is that this leaves us without any explanation for the attractions of real evil. Another is that, although Weil perceptively alerts us to the dangers of aestheticising evil, she unfairly tarnishes all imagi-native literature with the same brush. Some works of art succeed in ways that Weil fails to acknowledge, and thus she denies us the chance to learn from it. Thus, *Don Giovanni* is perhaps one *locus classicus* or archetype of a work that belies her claim, revealing as it does the con-fluence of freedom and power, evil and allure that the transgressive can elicit in us (and if one does not feel the visceral attraction of the Don then one has either seen a duff production or missed the point). Moreover, the opera, written only a couple of years before the start of the French Revolution, is suffused with political significance, and not just in the more obvious areas of class and gender but in the enigmatic and, in some respects, perplexing *viva la liberta* at the close of the first act,[6] and in the wonderfully complex finale, notwithstanding the strand of conventional sentiment whereby it is proclaimed that the evil get their just deserts. And there are numerous literary (and cinematic) figures that also come to mind – Conrad's Kurtz, for instance, and also his brilliant re-imagination by Coppola and realisation by Brando in his (widely underappreciated and misunderstood) performance in *Apocalypse Now*. These are not immoral works because the seductive-ness of evil is presented within a controlling moral intelligence which also captures its repulsiveness. Rather than range widely over a variety of artistic forms or even different writers, however, in order better to focus the discussion, I have chosen to explore the issues through a single novel: *The Devils*.

C

One of the greatest imaginative writers, and one who had a profound sense of the reality of evil and its relationship to the transgressive, is Dostoyevsky. He wrote very much in a Christian context even if, for him, affirming his (Russian Orthodox) faith was at best a continuing and difficult struggle. Yet that struggle also surely helped him to attain the moral and psychological insight into how human beings relate to good and evil that is an omnipresent feature of his novels. Moreover, it does not seem to me that, for the most part, one needs to *subscribe* to any Christian doctrines or precepts to appreciate Dostoyevsky's imagi-native engagement with it although, no doubt, at least a modest sym-pathy with a religious sensibility is in this regard desirable (and some knowledge of the Bible and the iconography of Christianity is essential to understanding his work). But one of Dostoyevsky's achievements as a novelist – as distinct from his frankly rather tedious and distasteful writings as a political pamphleteer and commentator – is that, even if he did not give the Devil *all* the best tunes, he certainly gave him his fair share. Because of this, and as one of the most acute moral psycholo-gists who has ever written, he succeeded in portraying with remarkable effectiveness the allure and seductiveness of evil, its multitudinous forms and disguises and its social and psychological destructiveness.

His insights into such matters can be found in pretty much all of his novels and stories, including most famously through his remark-able portrait of the Grand Inquisitor in *The Brothers Karamazov* and the character of Raskolnikov in *Crime and Punishment*. The latter novel can plausibly be seen as Dostoyevsky's most focused engagement with the attraction of transgressive behaviour, and Raskolnikov as probably offering his most acute dissection of its psychic mechanisms. I want to focus on a slightly less well-known novel, however, Dostoyevsky's most explicitly political fictional work, *The Devils* (sometimes more evocatively but less accurately translated as *The Possessed*). The novel, first published in serial form in 1871 and 1872, was loosely inspired by the extraordinary activities of the remarkably charismatic, revolutionary nihilist, Sergey Nechaev, many details of which are fairly accurately woven into the plot of the novel, including his cold-blooded murder of one of the members of his revolutionary cell for failing to obey his orders. Nechaev himself is also supposedly a model for one of the central characters, Peter Verkhovensky but, in this case, the resemblance is very approximate for, as we shall shortly see, his literary equivalent had little of the almost universally acknowledged impressiveness of the man himself. Furthermore, Dostoyevsky had direct personal experience of a radical, utopian political group in his youth through his association with the Petrashevsky Circle. Although the precise extent of his involvement with the group is unclear and to some degree contested, it was his relations with them that resulted in his decade-long exile to Siberia, an experience that for a much briefer time Nechaev – the maiden name of Dostoyevsky's mother, as coincidence would have it – also underwent, and which had the effect of transforming Dostoyevsky from young radical to increasingly reactionary *Slavophil*.

The novel is set in an unnamed provincial Russian town in Dostoyevsky's own time. It traces the activities of a radical political group and the resulting breakdown of social order within the town which clearly functions for Dostoyevsky as a microcosm of Russia more generally. His own lack of sympathy with the political radicals in the novel is very evident throughout and, for some readers, this seriously mars the novel, but it must be said that the representatives of the established order fare little better; and it can hardly be described as a tract for political conservatism or even obviously supportive of his own strong Slavophil sympathies. The tone, as with most of Dostoyevsky's fiction, combines black humour, including biting irony and caricature, with an unquestionable seriousness of purpose and an at times unremitting bleakness, and it has legitimate claims to be regarded as the most pessimistic of all his novels. Dostoyevsky is often labelled a realist writer and, to some extent, this is apt enough but such a categorisation can also be deeply misleading: *The Devils* operates on many levels and is suffused with Christian imagery and symbolism. As with any great novel, it is open to a diversity of readings although I shall treat it as a moral and political fable as much as anything else.

The central metaphor of the novel is given in a passage from Luke that Dostoyevsky uses both in the story and as an epigraph to the novel as a whole:

> And there was there a herd of many swine feeding on the mountain: and he besought them that he would suffer them to enter into them. And he suffered them. Then went the devils out of the man, and entered into the swine: and the herd ran violently down a steep place into the lake and were choked. When they that fed them saw what was done, they fled, and went and told it in the city and in the country. Then they went out to see what was done; and came to Jesus, and found the man out of whom the devils were departed, sitting at the feet of Jesus, clothed, and in his right mind: and they were afraid. They also which saw it told them by what means he that was possessed of the devils was healed. (Luke 8: 32–6)[7]

In a sentence, it is a novel about the social and political disintegration consequent on the moral corruption of the Russia of the time, as Dostoyevsky saw it, and by implication the need for spiritual cleansing and renewal. But it advocates no clear political solution, and whatever precisely 'sitting at the feet of Jesus' amounts to, it is far from evident in the novel, beyond perhaps a certain Christ-like humility, generosity towards one's fellow human beings, and a consciousness that we are all flawed and sinners and in need of forgiveness. Arguably, and interestingly, what Dostoyevsky seems to set most strongly against all the mayhem and destruction is not an alternative ideology or theory but the miracle of human life itself, represented by the birth of the child of Shatov (the character, incidentally, whose political views in some respects appear to be closest to those of Dostoyevsky), the most troubled of the 'revolutionaries', though Shatov himself, like Nechaev's erring follower, is ultimately murdered at the initiative of Peter Verkhovensky, the malign instigator of much of the action.

The power of the novel, however, does not lie in any positive message that might be discerned, even if one can be detected. Instead, in my view, it is better appreciated as a 'diagnostic' novel in which Dostoyevsky seeks to analyse and challenge both the 'liberal' sentiments – we are dealing with liberalism of mid-nineteenth century Russia, not John Rawls! – of the Westernised intelligentsia and especially the radicalism of the emerging 'new class' in Russia. It engages with the central political debates of the age, such as between idealism and materialism, faith and rationalism, the aesthetic and the utilitarian, Westernisers and Slavophils, and the iconic image of 'the superfluous man', as well as much else, as the liberal and romantic but politically ineffective generation of the 1840s is seen to be not merely succeeded by but to have a causal role in the emergence of the more ruthlessly militant, rationalistic, materialist and utilitarian generation of the 1860s: the latter also issued in one of the earliest and most impressive of modern terrorist movements, one that not too fancifully can be claimed to have some interesting similarities to al-Qaeda. John Gray has even gone so far as to say that 'if Osama Bin Laden has a precursor, it is the nineteenth century Russian terrorist Sergei Nechaev',[8] who, as we have already noted, was one of the principal inspirations for *The Devils*.

This generational conflict had also been the subject of Turgenev's earlier novel, *Fathers and Sons*, where the emerging generation is embodied in its most famous literary representative, Bazarov.[9] But Bazarov is ultimately ineffective, although possibly a harbinger of the future, and the novel concludes with rather more comforting and sentimental images of domestic contentment and metaphysical musings expressing the insignificance of human life and the consolations of religion:

> However passionate, sinful and rebellious the heart hidden in the tomb, the flowers growing over it peep at us serenely with their innocent eyes; they speak to us not only of eternal peace, of the vast repose of 'indifferent' nature: they tell us, too, of everlasting reconciliation and of life which has no end'.[10]

Dostoyevsky not only offers us no such reassurance, he goes well beyond Turgenev's more domestically oriented exploration of the political dimensions of the ideological conflicts that they both dissect with remarkable perceptiveness. Inevitably, I shall not be able to do justice even to all the relevant and important features of what is an immensely rich (and very long) novel and, in any case, such selectivity also reflects the fact there are some aspects of Dostoyevsky's fictional analysis that I find less persuasive and will return to only towards the end.

The theme that is of particular concern here is the ethical vacuum at the heart of a provincial community that loses its moral bearings, ultimately consumed by an apocalyptic (literally a foreshadowing of the Apocalypse) orgy of destruction, and the at least temporary triumph of evil, as the community is seduced by the transgressive impulse. Although all levels of society are eventually complicit in this process, two characters in the novel are effectively the proximate causes of the evil that transpires. One intentionally, the other not, though no less culpable; and it is the unintentional agent whose presence is, in a sense, the spiritual source of the crisis that besets the town, and in whom even the more explicitly destructive character reposes his illusions. The lesser but also more direct and active of these forces, as we might say, is Peter Verkhovensky. He is the neglected and estranged son of Stepan Verkhovensky, one of the ineffectual liberals of the generation of the 1840s, and also loosely based on a real character, T. N. Granovsky, an influential historian and Westerniser. Stepan is one of Dostoyevsky's most masterful comic creations – a 'liberal' whose liberalism is really no more than skin deep, an affectation along with his continual propensity to break into French, expressing his disconnection with the very people he claims to champion; and whose claims to be a serious scholar are undermined by his laziness and love of the comforts of an easy life. Furthermore, his self-image as a dangerous political dissident under permanent police surveillance is little more than a self-flattering illusion and undercut by his ready resort to the police when genuinely fearful. He is, in short, the very embodiment, in caricatured form, of a familiar kind of intellectual and political poseur, intrinsically harmless perhaps (and even presented with some affection as well as ridicule by Dostoyevsky) but whose irresponsibility is seen (literally) as the breeding ground for something altogether more dangerous.

Thus, his son, Peter, is a very different kettle of fish. Whereas his father is full of ideas but at best no more than a quixotic dreamer, Peter is a man of action, although interestingly one motivated by no clear political ideology. In this regard, Dostoyevsky perhaps shows how it is the opportunists rather than the ideologues that are ultimately politically effective. While he, too, can be seen as a cynical and superficial character, that cynicism, manifested in his refusal to take (almost) anything seriously, makes Peter a powerful and effective force for destruction. He is a transgressor initially in the rather petty way that he consistently and contemptuously ignores all the conventions of manners and everyday morals that provide the standards of good behaviour. What begins, though, as often trivial transgressions, rudeness, crassness and such like, take an increasingly extreme form, including but not limited to the murder of Shatov mentioned earlier. Peter's motivations as a character are often opaque and are subject to dispute but he seems almost to embody unconstrained wilfulness, and symbolically functions as a destructive demiurge once norms and conventions are perceived as there only to be broken. For Peter, transgression is its own reward. But even the apparently nihilistic and iconoclastic Peter, who otherwise shows no respect to anyone, acknowledges one inspiration.

This inspiration is Nicholas Stavrogin. His mother is a minor aristocrat but a 'progressive one'; she is the last word in radical chic in her desire to be au fait with the new and most 'advanced' ideas and to mix with the fashionable and trendy younger generation while also retaining her own privileges and sense of social superiority:

> She was in favour of big agricultural estates, the aristocratic element and the increase of the Governor's prerogatives and, at the same time, of the democratic element, the new institutions, law and order, free-thinking, and social reforms; the strict etiquette of an aristocratic salon and the free-and-easy, almost public house manners of the young people who surrounded her.[11]

She is also the patron of the aforementioned Stepan Verkhovensky, who acted as her son's tutor and surrogate father. Nicholas has returned to the town from a period away in the West (always a bad sign in Dostoyevsky) as have several other prominent figures in the novel, including Peter (and Kirilov, an extraordinarily complex character, a quasi-existentialist *avant la lettre*, who fascinated Albert Camus). While other characters in the novel typically ramble on interminably – it is a very 'talky' novel – Stavrogin remains largely silent and inscrutable. We learn nothing about his inner life or what motivates him – at least until we hear the enigmatic contents of his letter to Dasha, his putative fiancée, and what is effectively his suicide note about three pages from the end of a seven hundred-page novel (and by a wonderful coincidence that would surely have amused Dostoyevsky himself it is on page

666 of the Penguin edition). Throughout he is a shadowy character, surrounded by rumours and stories of extraordinary, sometimes shocking but mostly morally ambiguous acts, the truth of which is never vouchsafed to the reader. The one chapter that did appear to shed a little more light on his past history was cut by the censor and (in my view, rightly) never restored by Dostoyevsky. Yet, Stavrogin is also an intensely charismatic figure of enormous personal magnetism whom virtually everyone in the novel, though in different ways, has great expectations. He is in part a Byronic figure, part a proto-Nietzschean *Übermensch* and a pretender (with its particular significance for a Russian readership), a false messiah for those around him. Stavrogin embodies a combination of personal magnetism, overweening pride and heartless apathy, and his challengingly transgressive actions appear to be almost a form of experimentation to test his own reactions and feelings or, rather, whether he has any at all. It is a portrait of the glamour of evil, manifested not in evil intentions but in his indifference and lack of concern: he is the hollow man.

Stavrogin is able to have the effect that he does, however, not because he has aspirations to be a leader but in large part because of the context in which he finds himself. There is a firmament of ideas, a craving for the new, and an existing social order in which nobody has any real conviction. Motivated by their own, alternately petty and absurdly grandiose designs, Stavrogin is a Rorschach blot for others: people discover in him what they want to find. Moreover, and here there is rather surprisingly a potential connection with Arendt, Stavrogin's emptiness is also a manifestation of a form of rationalism. It is his lack of passion or commitment to ideas, people or a cause, being 'neither 'hot nor cold', which distinguishes him from all the other characters who populate the novel. Through the character of Stavrogin, Dostoyevsky presents what he perceives to be a deep-rooted affinity between what he sees as a desiccated rationalism and nihilism. If we can understand Stavrogin as an embodiment of evil, it is evil as indifference. Stavrogin is not cut out to be a leader, and has no desire to be, but his alluring and charismatic nihilism represented, not as a doctrine or philosophy so much as a way of life, is the ultimate source of the evil that reaches its crescendo as the novel proceeds. It is only when he hangs himself – portrayed implicitly in his last letter as the final meaningless gesture in a meaningless life: 'a delusion in an infinite sequence of delusions'[12] – that there is any prospect that things could start to return to normal in the town although,

interestingly, one of the few central characters to survive the confla-
gration of death and destruction is Peter Verkhovensky, and hence the
death of Stavrogin, though necessary, is not much cause for optimism.
Indeed, the judgement of the doctors on Stavrogin's suicide that 'it was
most definitely not a case of insanity'[13] is the enigmatic but hardly reassuring words with which the novel ends.

Around the principal figures is a diverse cast of characters, including the various revolutionaries. There is, for example, the theoretician
Shigalyov, a man whose love of humanity fails to embrace a concern
for any actual human beings other than himself, and who becomes so
confused he has to admit that 'my conclusion is in direct contradiction
to the original idea with which I start. Starting from unlimited freedom,
I arrived at unlimited despotism,' but still insists 'that there can be
no other solution of the social formula than mine'.[14] This may seem
ridiculous which, of course it is but also as an unfair caricature of the
serious revolutionary; although anyone who has spent much time in
small radical political sects theorising the revolution may feel a pang of
recognition. But Dostoyevsky is using caricature, as Dickens whom he
much admired does, to make a serious point: this is, that life is resistant
to theory, and theorising is no substitute for lived experience. A striking
feature of the novel is how many of the characters are absorbed by their
own ideas and theories. It is a veritable maelstrom of abstract ideas
that float free of any real roots, as if it is for every individual to create
ex nihilo a theory to explain the point of their own existence or how
social life should ideally be organised. The attempts to do so, though,
are not merely an absurd hubris, they are also dangerous. It is another
manifestation of the impulse to transgress, often manifesting itself as
supposedly rational argument, with moral and intellectual confusion
the inevitable result. Existing norms are dismissed as old hat and ridi-
culed accordingly but there are only vain and incoherent speculations
and pseudo-theories conjured up in minds unconstrained by any sense
of reality to replace them. In a novel obsessed by theories and ideas, the
last thing we need is yet another theory.

The Devils is far richer, more complex and subtle than my decidedly selective discussion of it may suggest, and I am conscious that
I have conveyed only very poorly what seem to me to be some of its
seminal insights: they are no substitute for reading the novel. What I
want to draw from the novel here, however, is how Dostoyevsky helps
us to understand at least one form of what I have called 'the glamour

of evil', and some of the circumstances in which it flourishes. It is not difficult to understand how the logic of transgression that is to be found to varying degrees in so many contexts in the story leads to a kind of disintegration of the normative order that issues in fire, murder and destruction (although more problematically, in my view, he also presents these events as potentially purgative, which risks succumbing to the very logic that he is challenging). Moreover, Dostoyevsky enables us, as readers, to feel the pull, without, we hope, succumbing to it, of the impetus to transgression. In doing so, he is neither explicitly nor implicitly offering a defence of the status quo, nor seeking a return to some supposed golden age. He is, rather, reminding us – and here I think another connection can be made with Arendt – of the precariousness and fragility of the normative structures that are crucial in restraining, both psychically and socially, a barbarism to which the glamour of evil draws us. Dostoyevsky unquestionably had in mind Nechaev, as we have seen, but also the theories of Bakunin as well as many lesser figures of his own time. But his concerns are not limited by his time. The idea that the transgressive impulse is a positive one has a vigorous life in a variety of contexts, and not least in the post-Nietzschean tradition of political theorising which has considerable currency in the contemporary academic world, but also more broadly in a culture that can make a fetish of the ideals of freedom and individuality. Dostoyevsky, I believe, challenges us to think seriously and realistically about what the implications of such ways of thinking and theorising might be.

D

Evil can be 'banal', and sometimes in just the way that Arendt so acutely captures, but it can also be attractive and seductive, not least when dressed in the alluring garb of the transgressive. It can seem to offer us excitement, to break the shackles of the routine of our everyday lives and to afford us the opportunity to be different, to stand out from the crowd and make a distinctive mark in the world. Evil on a grand enough scale has a fair chance of being remembered, for, as Mark Antony sagely remarks, 'the evil that men do lives after them; the good is oft interred with their bones'. A life of merely average goodness or unremarkable rectitude, by contrast, may appear, especially to those with imagination and ambition, second rate and more than a tad dull and unadventurous. The norms and rules that govern our lives can be experienced as constraints on our desire to assert ourselves or to secure a place in posterity. But such a way of thinking, which is fertile soil for the transgressive, is potentially dangerous both to those who think this way and those who do not. None of us is an *Übermensch* and we should not be tempted to think that we can be if only we were freed from inhibition and restraint, or to feel that we are necessarily failures because we are not. Seductive thoughts that promise radically to transform the mundane and quotidian lives that we lead are no more than siren calls.

At a political level, moreover, the potential for evil associated with radical transgression becomes considerably more serious for the obvious reason that politics is generally played out on a much bigger stage and its reach correspondingly much greater. When inspired by 'ideals' or motives that anyway seem to most of us self-evidently repulsive and inhuman, transgression will no doubt look similarly unappealing. Even where the initial motivation may appear (to some at least) altogether more benign, however, and perhaps simply 'rational', or even inspiring, attempts to remake humanity in ways that take no account of human imperfection and fallibility, or of diversity and difference of culture and values, and which show only contempt for the norms and restraints that govern an admittedly often deeply flawed politics of negotiation, compromise and mutual accommodation, is, as history has often enough shown, to be led along a path that risks great evils. In practice, when pursued with any rigour or single-mindedness, for instance, communism seems more likely to result in some form of authoritarianism than to realise any worthy ideals of freedom and equality.

This is not, it must be insisted, to counsel fatalism and acquiescence in every ill, whether misfortune or injustice, with which we are confronted. It is rather, and here I part company with Dostoyevsky to some extent, to seek the feasible: that is, to limit and to reduce the causes of the most serious suffering and to undertake remedial actions that are viable; it is to accept that, although politics can help to create conditions more rather than less favourable to decent and worthwhile lives, it cannot bring it about that we actually succeed in living such lives. Still less can it provide us – at least in any way that is truly desirable – with the kind of transcendence that will sublimate the often petty and disappointing features of our day-to-day lives that the politics of transgression may seem to promise.[15] Yet, there is a twist: this is that it also has to be acknowledged that even a politics of ameliorative pragmatism has its limits when confronted by evil. For such a politics is largely bereft of effective resources for responding to evil once it has attained some significant measure of political power. Just as it is possible benignly to tolerate the intolerant only so long as they are not in a position to exercise their intolerance; so, while a resolutely non-utopian politics of pragmatic bargaining and compromise is perhaps the best way of keeping at bay the destructiveness of a politics of transgression, it seems much less able to resist when it is already in full flow. That, perhaps, is one lesson that can be learnt from the experience of Weimar Germany. In situations where evil is already to a significant extent in control of the levers of political power, it seems that a very different kind of response is necessary if it is to be effective. But it is not clear that Dostoyevsky is of much help here either.

Dostoyevsky, while brilliantly bringing out the dangers of a romantic or eschatological politics, especially when deceptively dressed in the form of secular rationalism, also found it hard to appreciate the merits of a pragmatic politics of negotiation and compromise. It is partly because he clearly felt the pull of a more ambitious conception of political life that he is able to portray both its allure and its dangers so vividly. It also accounts for a deep paradox in *The Devils*. This is that, though remorselessly critical of utopianism and theorising generally, the novel is clearly fascinated by ideas and apocalyptic in spirit. True, Dostoyevsky does not appear to think in terms of any kind of secular political transformation but rather of a spiritual change in people's hearts and attitudes to others. But, while it is never clear that this is exactly what Dostoyevsky has in mind, it would be no less of a utopian illusion to believe that such a spiritual change could potentially displace the need for a mundane politics of negotiation and compromise. Although, as I have tried to show, we can learn much from reading *The Devils*, and indeed the rest of his fictional work, we should be careful not to divest ourselves of our critical faculties and succumb entirely to his vision, for Dostoyevsky, too, can be a source of temptation to transgress: we need to read both with and against him.[16]

Notes

1 H. Arendt, *Eichmann in Jerusalem: A Report on the Banality of Evil*, revised and enlarged edition (Harmondsworth: Penguin, 1976).
2 B. Lang, 'Hannah Arendt and the Politics of Evil', in L. P. and S. K.

Hinchman (eds) *Hannah Arendt: Critical Essays* (Albany: State University of New York Press, 1994).

3 W. E. Connolly, *Identity/Difference: Democratic Negotiations of Political Paradox* (Ithaca: Cornell University Press, 1991); J. Kekes, *Facing Evil* (Princeton: Princeton University Press, 1990); J. Kekes, *The Roots of Evil* (Ithaca: Cornell University Press, 2007); N. Noddings, *Women and Evil* (Berkley and Los Angeles: University of California Press, 1989).

4 A. Ferrara, 'The Evil That Men Do: A Meditation on Radical Evil from a Postmetaphysical Point of View', in M. Lara (ed.), *Rethinking Evil: Contemporary Perspectives* (Berkeley and Los Angeles: University of California Press, 2001).

5 S. Weil, *Gravity and Grace,* trans. E. Craufurd (London: Routledge, 1952), pp. 62–3.

6 A. Arblaster, *Viva La Liberta! Politics in Opera* (London: Verso, 1992), p. 30.

7 F. Dostoyevsky, *The Devils,* trans. D. Magarshack (Harmondsworth: Penguin, 1953), p. 20.

8 J. Gray, *Al Qaeda and What It Means to Be Modern* (London: Faber and Faber, 2003), p. 21.

9 I. Turgenev, *Fathers and Sons,* trans. R. Edmonds (Harmondsworth: Penguin, 1965).

10 Turgenev, *Fathers and Sons,* p. 295.

11 Dostoyevsky, *The Devils,* p. 348.

12 Dostoyevsky, *The Devils,* p. 667.

13 Dostoyevsky, *The Devils,* p. 669.

14 Dostoyevsky, *The Devils,* p. 404.

15 J. Horton, 'A Qualified Defence of Oakeshott's Politics of Scepticism', *European Journal of Political Theory,* 4: 1, 2005, pp. 23–36.

16 An earlier version of this chapter was presented to the panel organised by the editors of this volume at the Manchester Workshops on Political Theory in 2009. I am grateful to them and to the other contributors to the discussion for a number of useful comments, and especially to Bruce Haddock for some exceptionally helpful suggestions about how to improve the penultimate draft.

Chapter 10

THE RHETORIC OF MORAL EQUIVALENCE

Richard Shorten

Evil in contemporary politics has an important rhetorical dimension. Whenever instances of wrongdoing are contested in the public realm, the relevant actors are liable to call upon a familiar store of resources for persuading audiences to respond in particular ways. These resources can be expected to consist in recognisable rhetorical tropes and figures, a predictable range of 'commonplaces', and the manipulation of definitions according to recurring patterns of argument. They can be envisaged to entail, too, the arousal of a characteristic series of emotions. The actors themselves, in the relevant sense, might also be variously composed. They may be perpetrators of the wrongdoing, they may be subjects of the harm either intended or inflicted, or they may be third parties, of varying shades of disinterestedness. In each case, however, the terms in which evil and wrongdoing are excused or exonerated, condemned or vilified, and understood or tolerated will likely share routine inflections.[1]

The aim of this chapter is therefore to begin to establish what it is that is distinctive about the scope and content of the rhetorical repertoire that belongs to wrongdoing. It proposes to do so by focusing consideration upon a specific case: the rhetoric of moral equivalence. An account of a single case, of course, no matter how representative, can only ever hope to provide a partial perspective upon the wider picture. On condition, though, that the account is found to resonate sufficiently, then it might at least give pause for thought as to the possibilities for exploring a rhetoric of wrongdoing in its broader directions. This, accordingly, is the tenor in which the chapter proceeds. Moral equivalence is suggested to be no more than a single strategy for impressing upon public opinion the case for conceiving particular instances of wrongdoing according to specific moral complexions. But, as I will also seek to show, it is a strategy which throws light upon the general possibilities, constraints and demands which attach to the contestation of wrongdoing, especially those of the kind brought into view by a rhetorical conception of the study of political thought.[2]

INTRODUCING MORAL EQUIVALENCE

Moral equivalence is an important – though often neglected – feature of political argument. The term itself has an interesting history. It was first introduced to a general political lexicon by the American philosopher William James who is widely credited with having coined the expression in his 1906 address at Stanford University, 'The Moral Equivalent of War'.[3] James meant to denote a pair of objects in which one object was a function of the other. Hence, in the parameters of his particular speech, the 'martial virtues' (chiefly, discipline and obedience) were presented as dependent upon war itself for their very existence. Effectively, these virtues were the socially beneficial counterpart of war. Ever since, the term has tended to imply a comparative relation between two objects rather than a functional connection. It is conventionally used to picture an equivalence between two or more actions, practices, or states of affairs, and almost invariably when it is wrongdoing which is in dispute, as opposed to the apportionment of commendable qualities.

 This type of juxtaposition allows predictable acts of persuasion to be performed according to the subject positions typical of the relevant actors. First of all, perpetrators of particular wrongs will try to deflect or diminish anticipated criticism though in such a way that gives tacit recognition to the status of those wrongs. Specifically, they will appeal to the discomfort experienced by the communities meanwhile condemning those wrongs, by calling to attention the comparable actions committed in their own pasts or presents. This move tends to echo the biblical sentiment 'let he who is without sin cast the first stone'.[4] By way of an example, Hermann Göring made use of it in extreme form during incarceration at the Nuremberg Trials, in his recorded remark in defence of the record of the Third Reich, that 'even the British Empire w[as] not built up with due regard to the principles of humanity . . . America ha[s] hacked its way to a rich *Lebensraum* by revolution, massacre and war.'[5] Göring's use is common to perpetrator discourse in redirecting condemnation on replicated grounds but in less obviously replicated proportions.

Third parties, by contrast, will conventionally seek to intensify the criticism of wrongs, rather than to exonerate or excuse them. They will, in particular, employ evocative points of reference understood to contain broader moral lessons. The evil of the Holocaust is a case in point. We can in recent memory, for example, think of Ken Livingstone's statement publicised in British media at the time of Israel's 2008–9 offensive against Hamas, that 'Gaza is a ghetto in exactly the same way that the Warsaw ghetto was, and people are trapped in it'.[6] Not being directly implicated in the wrongdoing themselves, third parties have the advantage of being exempt from the same standards of proof and substantiation demanded of perpetrators. They are typically at liberty, therefore, to frame comparisons in self-consciously more provocative ways.

Finally, the subjects of harm will more often than not tend to employ the expression to denote disapproval of the practice it names. They will look to attenuate the apologetics that figure in particular cases, by recalling the distinctions and degrees which ordinarily apply to wrong-doing. Anticipating attempts, for instance, to explain the September 11th attacks by connecting Islamic terrorism to broader political realities, the then New York mayor Rudolf Giuliani signalled disquiet at post hoc rationalisations, when he proclaimed confidently '[t]here is no moral equivalence to this attack. There is no justification for it. The people who did it lost any right to ask for justification for it when they slaughtered four or five thousand [*sic*] innocent people.'[7] The term in this conjunction is given credence in passing, only in order to caricature it in a particular application.

The standing of moral equivalence in political argument exhibits, then, several facets. It is morally controversial. The uses to which it is put are varied, open to adaptation to suit particular agendas. And in the formal sense, nearly all of its uses are vulnerable to the charge of being fallacious; they are usually based upon the logical fallacy of the *tu quoque* (literally, 'you too'), the mistake of rendering an objection to an action or practice redundant by means only of showing that the objection applies equally to the other party to a dispute. Ethical validity, logical coherence, and adaptation in localised contexts of disagreement, however, are all aspects of moral equivalence arguments to be investigated on their own terms. The rhetorical dimension raises rather different questions. The issues it begs, and which are to be pursued in this chapter, are roughly as follows. What are the characteristic rhetorical applications which render moral equivalence arguments compelling in the public realm? How does the enumeration of those applications leave the analyst better placed to understand and interpret these kinds of arguments? And, in a further step, in what ways does that enumeration better equip the theorist to evaluate or criticise them?

To construct the rhetoric of moral equivalence, and to parcel it out into its distinctive elements, I will draw in the rest of the chapter, more systematically than in the instances above, on the evidence from three specific discourses across historical and contemporary political experience: first, from the discourse of memory in contemporary Germany, especially insofar as it is organised around the themes of guilt and victimhood in World War II; second, from the discourse of the Cold War, in particular regard to disputes over the moral standing of 'East' and 'West'; and third, from recent interventions in the Israeli–Palestinian conflict. I begin, however, with a brief discussion of the standing of rhetoric in debates regarding evil in general, before turning, in greater detail, to the considerations that arise when evil and wrongdoing are posed, specifically, in a comparative frame of rhetorical action. At this point, I move to extrapolate the distinctive elements which, taken together, comprise the rhetorical repertoire of moral equivalence. In this I attend lastly, and in sequence, to the recurring tropes and figures; the characteristic use made of commonplaces; the typical manipulations of definitions; and the most prominent emotions which form the target of discrete appeals.

EVIL AND POLITICAL RHETORIC

Evil itself is a word rich in its emotive and, indeed, theological resonances. In a cultural context, where religious languages of politics are largely excluded from the public realm, we might expect evil, too, to bear the mark of anachronism. Yet the word demonstrates a remarkable capacity for resistance. The decline of religion has to be set against the event of Auschwitz.[8] As Tony Judt rightly observed, while 'modern secular society has long been uncomfortable with the idea of "evil"', in the wake of World War II it 'crept slowly back into moral and even political discourse'.[9]

It is not so clear, though, whether the concept of evil admits gradations. When evil is pictured as pure, demonic – 'radical' – the language of evil is presumed to be appealing precisely because it is taken to be geared towards uncompromising absolutes.[10] It is often deemed unattractive for that same reason. What Susan Neiman describes as the 'paralysed moral reaction' to September 11th is an apt illustration. The act of ceding the rhetoric of evil to conservatives had, on her view, the consequence of cutting off 'progressives' from a meaningful vocabulary in which to engage it.[11] Conversely, when evil is pictured not as demonic but as demarcated in varying shades of grey – ordinary, thoughtless, routine and 'banal' – its rhetorical force is ostensibly blunted. Yet this conception of evil opens up rhetorical possibilities of its own.[12] It makes possible, for instance, the denunciation of evils as insidious, deep rooted, and systemic. In a rather different, yet nonetheless closely related way, the idea of 'the lesser of two evils' likewise supposes there to be distinctions in degrees and in kind, and it plays off these distinctions to perform particular political actions; lesser-evil arguments redefine the terms in which moral choices are to be expressed and validated by hierarchically ordering wrongful acts so that certain evils in politics can be exonerated insofar as their commission avoids greater ones.[13]

Evil discourse, in short, points to linguistic acts that are more plural and less constrained than is sometimes understood to be the case. It offers up resources, to be sure, for demonising actions, practices and states of affairs. But it also, in different directions, holds out resources for 'naturalising' them, for 'relativising' them, or for otherwise re-conceiving them. One of the most interesting linguistic possibilities in this connection is recasting wrongful actions through comparison, a move which is open to being analysed as the performance of a particular type of speech act.[14] In consequence, as I next seek to show, comparative claims regarding wrongdoing require decoding in a particular key.

POLITICAL RHETORIC AND COMPARATIVE WRONGDOING

In the context of evil and wrongdoing, the exercise of moral comparison poses two polarised dangers: sacralisation and trivialisation.[15] In practice, these extremes map on to the rhetorical strategies for rendering evil in demonic and banal terms respectively. Sacralisation is often thought to be undesirable because, by implication, it takes wrongs out of rational discussion and places them beyond human understanding (as is often purported to be the case with the Holocaust).[16] It also threatens to desensitise moral reactions to evils in their non-sacralised forms.[17] Trivialisation, on the other hand, is logically the end point of the kind of association that assimilates one action to another in mechanical, uncritical fashion. Claims for the specificity or 'uniqueness' of events need not, however, lapse into sacralisation. Nor need the spectre of trivialisation rule out of hand assertions of similarity. Rather, judgements in particular cases answer to the demands of plausible moral description where plausibility is governed by the weight of the evidence, the abstraction of morally salient features, and the existing moral attachments of the audiences to whom the judgements are directed.

'Equivalence' supposes a specific type of similarity. It occupies the space somewhere between identity and resemblance. It is also far from hostile to claims of uniqueness per se because exemplary status can, in the public realm, often be employed to serve comparative purposes. When the 'unique' evil of Hitler and Nazism is yoked, for example, to Iraq, Iran, and North Korea, as in the 'axis of evil', we have an illustration of a less successful case.[18] In the general drift of modern Western cultural sensibilities we have a more instructive demonstration. As Samantha Power has shown, in contemporary experience and in the wake of events in the former Yugoslavia, Rwanda and Darfur, we tend to recognise an understanding of the present as 'the age of genocide'[19] and, paradoxically, the sense that genocide – a comparative category – expresses a universal evil distinctive in its moral gravity usually affirms the uniqueness of the Holocaust at the same time by making the Holocaust genocide's paradigmatic case.[20] In this particular respect, uniqueness and comparison prove quite capable of hanging together.

The conventional appeal of moral-equivalence arguments is, however, to a specific type of similarity – similarity by analogy. The threat of trivialisation rather than sacralisation becomes the main obstacle to their capacity to move audiences to particular feelings and opinions in ways envisaged.[21] In the discourse of memory in contemporary Germany, for example, moral-equivalence claims function with the aim of calling attention to German wartime suffering, through its association with the suffering imposed by Nazism, on proscribed categories of non-Germans, as well as others. Banalisation is an intrinsic danger here because, for obvious reasons, the reception of Nazism is likely to carry immense symbolic resonance, especially in a context where the audience principally intended is assumed to owe its legacy special recognition.[22] Other pertinent cases likewise affirm the need for plausible accounts of moral equivalence to negotiate the same predicament. Within the discourse of the Cold War, for instance, 'East' and 'West' were the principal terms of reference for the kind of equivalence projected, particularly in sections of opinion sympathetic to communism in some sense; getting arguments of that order to stick for wider audiences was, in one respect, a matter of doing so without giving the impression of depreciating those more pernicious aspects of Soviet society which had no ready parallel in Western countries.[23] The task facing assertions of moral equivalence in connection with the current-configuration Israeli–Palestinian conflict is, once more, of the same dimension. It is, among other things, to manage to censure certain Israeli reprisals against Palestinian actions as being 'terrorist' in design and content, albeit without belittling terrorism in more conventional guises in the process.[24]

The propensity towards trivialisation might be expected, therefore, to diminish the persuasive force of moral-equivalence claims in advance. The terms of their public assessment are, however, within the bounds of being carefully delineated from the point of articulation, which offers an opportunity to balance out the potential invalidation by trivialisation. In this sense, analogy rather than either resemblance or identity is the representative type of similarity engaged. The relevant actors tend to ask, implicitly, that the comparative claim being made be judged according to the standards demanded of analogy rather than according to any other set of criteria and, as such, they arrange the features of two selected cases on that basis. Importantly, they do not attempt to show that the properties of these two actions, practices or states of affairs are alike –'identical'– in each and every respect.[25] Neither do they expect to be held accountable to that ambition. Oppositely, nor are they content to demonstrate, rather more weakly, that a vague and imprecise pattern of correlations and coincidences applies. Instead, consistent with the style of analogical reasoning, the weight of the evidence is expected to point towards a particular kind of inference. Namely, the evidence is anticipated to support the inference that, because two instances can be agreed to share several largely *un*controversial features in common, they will more than likely share a further – more controversial – feature in common.[26] The representative claim proceeds on this basis. Hence, the protagonists of German victimhood assert that the Allied bombing of German cities in World War II led to a loss of human life on a large scale – as did the various strategies of the Axis powers; and they assert, too, that it likely led to the loss of life on a scale in considerable excess of any justification by military necessity (again, as did the broad record of the Third Reich, in particular). But the inference itself is used to betoken the possession of a third property shared by the two cases which is less ostensibly apparent: in this case, the same animating intention and purpose behind Allied war aims and the agenda of National Socialism. Typically, the move to assimilate further features will be controversial because of the differences either in proportion or in kind which are more usually conspicuous, or because of the contradiction by additional properties, which are deliberately left obscure.

The weight of the evidence alone, though, does not shoulder the burden of the entirety of the work being done in support of the representative claim. A rough rule of relevance requires that the features abstracted express a certain degree of moral significance, and that they express that significance for particular audiences. More accurately, it requires that they at least be made *to appear* to express that sort of import as is appropriate to specific settings. Thus, that the use of modern technology was a feature of the Holocaust is a matter of historical fact; whether that fact carries moral salience in and of itself is a rather different matter which rests upon particular interpretation according to specific contexts of reference.[27] The distinction is important for the construction of meaningful analogies because, say, whether 'East' and 'West' are two equivalent, superpower blocs which imitate one another in their internal dynamics and mutual interaction becomes a rather more consequential issue if the implications of that imitation are cashed out in ethical terms.[28] The detail of that cashing out must cohere with the constraints imposed by the relevant bodies of public opinion: in any given case, it is likely to entail an important appeal to the background commitments of the audience intended. Existing moral attachments typically serve as the repository in which the connections being brought into focus are expected to find resonance. Audiences are first of all reminded why it is that they regard a familiar action, practice or state of affairs according to a particular moral complexion. They are then subject to suasion that the reasons for holding the object in that instance in a condemnatory light apply equally to the object in contestation. Hence, in the Gaza/Warsaw ghetto analogy, public opinion is reminded that the moral objections at issue are to confinement, the restriction of movement, and the deprivation of the basic means of subsistence, each of which is relayed as being equally present in the Israeli treatment of Palestinian civilians.[29] Accordingly, as Hiliard Aaronovitch remarks, the strategy of justification which analogical argument generates in politics has a specific linguistic form: 'don't you see, this is really like that which you already accept and do not want to go back on'.[30] In a curious way, moral-equivalence arguments appeal to a certain kind of continuity and consistency even while ordinarily being put to provocative use in encouraging the rethinking of received ideas and assumptions. The typical type of situation is one in which audiences are invited to challenge a prevailing consensus on how wrongful actions should be ordered and classified, a consensus which, from the point of view of the rhetorical actor, has the capacity to be unsettled and restructured.

There is one final aspect to note before turning to the rhetorical repertoire itself. As I have sought to demonstrate so far, the terms of moral comparison which are engaged in moral-equivalence arguments threaten, by their very nature, to lapse into trivialising the more familiar actions to which contested actions are being attached. In practice, this danger is usually offset. Analogy is implicitly employed as the measure of success – a move which tends to lower the threshold against which comparisons become permissible and, in the further sense envisaged, authoritative. Further, as I have tried to indicate, analogies will conventionally be constructed out of whichever materials happen to be immediately available. Some properties of evil and wrongdoing, however, can be generalised irrespective of context and, in any given case, the allocation and 'ranking' of these properties are likely to be decisive.[31] It is worth briefly recapitulating those properties, once again with a view to how they figure in the possibilities for rhetorical action.

Both the ordinary understanding of evil and evil's place within the philosophical canon are useful reference points for elaborating the generic properties of wrongdoing. Most conventionally, there are two properties of wrongful political actions which are pitted against each other in assessments of their moral gravity: intention and scale. Thus, for example, in the broad sketch of the political history of the twentieth century, Hitler's Nazism is routinely compared against Stalin's Communism whereby Stalin is (negatively) distinguished according to a basic arithmetic of mass murder while Hitler is ascribed the baser moral intention. In this comparison, Nazism is generally found to have (im)moral elements lacking in the case of Stalin's Communism: the explicit division of humanity into fixed racial groups and the deliberate policy of extermination as enacted in the death camps.[32] In the more rigorous philosophical sense, the three significant traditions of moral philosophy isolate three distinct properties to be allocated moral priority in each case: virtue ethicists emphasise agents; Kantians emphasise motivations; and consequentialists emphasise outcomes (within which the scale of wrongdoing is to be understood as one type of outcome).[33] With this series of properties in view, the matter of legitimating comparisons between discrete actions becomes, finally, an exercise in arranging the moral significance of these properties in a suitable hierarchy so that their application to the empirical features of two cases brings the pair of actions within the same range of condemnation.

On the one hand, this opens up the scope for discarding the properties which may show two instances in rather different moral complexions. When it is the character of 'evildoers', for instance, which is selectively interpreted to be at stake, differences in the maxims standing behind their deeds, or the consequences arising from those deeds themselves, both fall off in their moral register. The corresponding rhetorical application is likely, quite crudely, to be to appeal to a psychological account of two particularly maladjusted individuals, assumed for whatever reason to be central to the wrongful actions in dispute. On the other hand, there is nothing intrinsic to a rhetorical frame of action which demands that particular traditions in moral philosophy be appealed to in a pure form.[34] Intended consequences, in practice, are often made to 'count' more than *un*intended consequences. More generally, properties are likely to be weighted and ranked in more complex configurations, according to the demands made with reference to the specific analogies proposed. The generic properties of wrongdoing can be pictured as being elevated or downgraded as suited to particular ends in mind, as well as subdivided and again reordered where secondary considerations prove useful: the moral significance of a harm inflicted can, for example, be traded off against its quantitative dimension, the number of persons affected.[35]

In sum, the rhetorical resources for substantiating comparative claims in regard to political evil and wrongdoing begin, in the first place, with the options for framing similarities and contrasts in ways which are sensitive to the terms of their projected reception in the public realm. Moral equivalence is a particular type of comparative claim which, prior to anything else, makes use of the rhetorical possibilities contained within analogies. To this point, however, the account that I have constructed might reasonably be viewed as undeveloped, in its failure thus far to give due consideration to the broad range of techniques for rendering arguments compelling which are elucidated within the classical tradition of rhetoric. The remaining part of this chapter therefore picks apart the distinct elements of the relevant rhetorical repertoire borrowed from this tradition, illustrated once more in connection with the three discourses being drawn upon.

THE RHETORIC OF MORAL EQUIVALENCE

Rhetoric, in Aristotle's famous conception, consists in the ability 'to observe the persuasiveness of which any particular matter admits'.[36] It provides the resources via which, in addition to the basic stating of a case, one might hope to bring others to one's own point of view, where views may be held in greater or lesser amounts of sincerity but which, regardless, confront the general disinclination to revise and rethink existing and sometimes inherited habits of thought.[37] In the Aristotelian account, there are three generic categories potentially at work in rhetoric, and across which the available means of persuasion for any viable discourse may be found. *Ethos* refers to persuasion through personality and stance; *logos* refers to persuasion through reasoning; and *pathos* connotes persuasion through the arousal of emotions.[38] For Aristotle, there are also several branches of oratory which will be more or less well suited to the performance of specific rhetorical tasks.

In the strict sense, moral-equivalence discourses belong to the 'forensic' branch of oratory.[39] Moral-equivalence arguments are concerned with the task of establishing the 'justice' of their subject matter by finding ways to diminish the blame and censure attached to relevant actors in virtue of their having followed particular courses of action. With this task in view, *ethos* is an important category because much turns upon the disposition of speakers towards their audiences. As a rule of thumb, speakers will seek to give the impression of impartiality (even more so if they are third parties to the dispute); they will seek to speak with moderation; and in light of the need to avoid being perceived to trivialise the gravity of the object to which the action in dispute is being analogised, they will refrain from unnecessarily maligning opponents and, in particular, the victims of the wrong in question.[40] The techniques for establishing *ethos* are, then, fairly predictable. In a certain sense the elements of *logos* are also transparent. Moral-equivalence claims are always underpinned by a pattern of reasoned argument which appeals to the inconsistency of condemning one action while exonerating, or otherwise moderating, another. Yet some of its rhetorical devices are more complex. These require parsing out with careful reference to the tropes and figures available, the employment of 'commonplaces', and the manipulation of definitions. The appeal to particular emotions is also worth dissecting although a general rule stands that moral-equivalence claims will principally attempt to elicit sympathy and indignation towards the relevant parties and, more specifically, seek to reapportion the quantities of each from their existing and familiar distributions.

1. The tropes and figures

The classical tradition of rhetoric distinguishes tropes from figures. Tropes are semantic in function and exercise linguistic effects through the use of particular words in non-literal ways. Figures are syntactic and operate through the ordering of words.[41] Both, however, pertain to the ornamental and decorative aspects of rhetoric. In general, the rhetoric of moral equivalence makes recourse to two distinct sets of devices: first, the techniques of amplification (mainly, though not exclusively, performed via particular tropes of degree); and second, the schematic language of repetition. The use of moral-equivalence arguments in specific contexts also comprises the appropriation of more particular devices, as are suited to the varying materials available.

Techniques of amplification, as Quentin Skinner notes of the rhetorical canon, encompass the various means for arousing the emotions 'by way of stretching the truth'.[42] In application to wrongdoing they therefore have several potentially forceful uses. They might, for example, be adapted in order to render permissible actions into impermissible actions. Or they might, with a slightly more modest ambition in mind, be used for the purpose of prompting an audience to begin to consider an action which is generally understood to be morally neutral within a more forthrightly condemnatory light. In this connection, moral-equivalence arguments have a more distinct feature. They employ amplification in the sense that they seek either to ratchet up or to ratchet down the measure of disapprobation attached to two cases respectively, thereby narrowing down the range within which they stand in proximity to one another, by casting their basic, evident features according to particular interpretive moves. Hype or exaggeration (hyperbole) – the use of extravagant terms for emphasis – is one apposite trope for eliciting this effect.[43] We find hyperbole at work in moral-equivalence discourses whenever the assumed moral reaction to the more moderately felt event is presented as a reaction of shock and horror as opposed to unease and disquiet. (We also find it in use whenever, for rather different effect, the extent of resistance facing any particular claim for equivalence is 'reported' in exaggerated fashion; when, for example, the contents of a projected comparison, typically as invoking the Holocaust, are described as being taboo and off limits, instead of simply unavailable both for credible and rather more assailable reasons.) Conversely, understatement (litotes) can lead an audience to infer what amounts to the same, that the speaker might reasonably have expressed the point in stronger terms, and is to be commended for having refrained from so doing.[44] Paradiastole, however, is the trope that Skinner himself picks out for portraying actions in more and less censurable complexions – though properly speaking it belongs to the manipulation of definitions.[45] In archetypical use, it refers to the kind of euphemism which is deployed for disparaging virtue and excusing vice but which also lends itself to excusing contested actions through comparison, by attenuating the qualities which show those actions to be wrong.

Amplification, in sum, enables the framing of a comparative claim in ways that magnify the wrongful aspects of one action while minimising those of another. The schematic language of repetition is further apt for stimulating those effects by patterning statements in rhythmically attractive sequence and, especially, by building towards discursive crescendos. It is, as a result, of special persuasive force when the interest is in 'ranking' wrongful actions in ways that challenge conventionally accepted hierarchies.[46] *Incrementum* – sometimes climax or *gradatio* – is, for instance, an expedient figure for structuring any argument through a 'mounting series of increments'. Moral-equivalence claims will make effective use of it in the form of 'from "bad" to "worse" to "worst"',[47] as when, for example, familiar orderings are reversed by altering the ethical nuances attached to the agreed criteria. (Good intentions with malevolent consequences can, for example, easily be represented to count as 'worse' than bad intentions with malevolent consequences which is often the case of those indictments of communism that veer close to apologetics for Nazism.)[48] Epistrophe, which refers to a repeated word at the end of several sentences, can likewise be put to good use in this remit.[49] Jean Baudrillard used it after September 11th in the following arrangement: 'Terrorism is immoral and it is a response to a globalisation which is itself immoral'.[50] A final schematic device – antithesis – also necessarily underwrites moral-equivalence arguments because the interest is always in posing a contrary relationship.[51] Antithesis, moreover, is indispensable in the appeal to the emotions because getting an audience to feel '*we* are like this, but *they* are like that' is not only the recurrent form of these arguments but is also a convenient way of smuggling a more controversial insinuation into the same terms of acceptance.[52]

More miscellaneously, moral-equivalence arguments in connection with the Israeli–Palestinian conflict give special space to the application of irony – and for particular reason. Whenever Palestinian acts of violence are coupled with the Israeli response to those acts, an ambiguous victim/perpetrator relationship tends to be pictured. In this relationship, the state of Israel both assumes the mantle of historical victimhood of the Jewish people and on that basis is deemed, especially by its critics, to be accountable in its actions according to the elevated moral status which that mantle entails. Accordingly, the resonances of past suffering are deliberately tapped in order to prompt certain emotive responses to the impositions of the Israeli occupation in the present: the 'irony' of victims morphing into perpetrators is made to fix the attention of third-party audiences with rather more immediacy than is the presence of saliently shared features of wrongdoing in similar degree.[53] More generally, irony is successfully employed to push assessments of wrongdoing in desired directions when there is something to be gainsaid for affecting a tone of derision, a practice which often yields the further result of implying a message with greater force precisely in virtue of leaving it unstated.[54] Again, metaphor is often put to work in substantiating equivalence claims, and it is a trope which belongs neither to the traditional techniques of amplification nor to the strict language of repetition. Rather it can be effected as particular occasions demand. In a certain sense, the metaphorical manipulation of meanings underwrites assertions of moral equivalence in structural form, since it is 'through metaphor [that] analogical extensions are made'.[55] Metaphors, though, can also shape the more specific qualities within actions that are being abstracted for comparison, discreetly seeking to control how they are conceptualised. Hence, in one example widely judged as especially insidious, Jörg Friedrich attempts explicitly to appropriate the idiom of the death camps in order to draw connections between 'Dresden', 'Hamburg' and the Holocaust. In Friedrich's narrative in *The Fire*, burning buildings, cellars and air-raid shelters all become 'crematoria', RAF bomber command is substituted with

'*Einsatzgruppe*', and densely populated areas are displaced by 'extermination spaces' (*Vernictungsraum*).[56]

2. The commonplaces

The structural form of metaphor is usefully expanded further with reference to the next element of the rhetorical repertoire of moral equivalence, the status of 'commonplaces'. Commonplaces are, literally, the common 'places' (loci) of rhetorical argument.[57] For Aristotle, they had an important place in the general process of 'invention' (*inventio*) that leads to the discovery of any argument in its basic form, prior to its development via more decorative arrangements by means including tropes and figures.[58] As Quentin Skinner notes, in the Roman rhetorical tradition, commonplaces had two principal senses: either they were general forms of reasoning to be applied in individual cases or they were everyday stock themes to be adverted to more indirectly.[59] Both types of commonplace can be seen to be operative in moral equivalence arguments.

Metaphors are structured around a 'source' and 'target'.[60] Moral-equivalence claims belong, as we have seen, to the broad categories of moral analogies and, as Markus Kornprobst has shown on the basis of Cicero's account of analogical reasoning, the composition of all moral analogies begins with the careful choice of what amounts to the 'source' in any given case.[61] Expanding on this account, the choice of this source will be determined by two things. First, it will be conditioned by its appropriateness to the object – or 'target' – intended for illumination. Second, it will be steered by the background commitments of the designated audience where, strictly speaking, it is here that the general store of commonplaces comes, importantly, to delineate the relevant range of options. The prudent rhetorical actor who wishes to intervene in the public assessment of wrongdoing will therefore wish to consult, consider and select from across this store. The rhetorical actor may, for example, in the first sense of commonplace identified by Skinner, and if the case to hand concerns the justification of specific, militant courses of action, choose from among the ready-made arguments for defending political violence: that recourse is a last resort for communities having exhausted all other viable means; that it is the only strategy open, granted a set of external considerations; or that violence is indistinct from other forms of political struggle.[62] Or again, for example, should the point at issue involve the identities to be ascribed to 'superpowers', then the relevant actors may select from among the available terms and vocabularies for contesting modes of political domination: 'hegemony', 'imperialism', 'dictatorship', 'authoritarian', and so on.[63] In both these cases, corresponding to the rhetorical situations confronting actors in the Israeli–Palestinian conflict and the Cold War discourse respectively, it is the general forms of reasoning which are available that vie for status as the commonplace most suited to challenging accepted norms. Alternatively, in Skinner's second sense, when it is stock themes being invoked rather than abstract principles, the choice instead will typically consist in weighing up the utility of established reference points drawn out of practical experience. While the protagonists of German victimhood, for instance, have often preferred to frame comparisons in connection with the Allied 'area bombing' of German cities, there are viable commonplaces equally suggested by prevalent public discourses on other contemporaneous episodes, notably the behaviour of the invading Red Army and the post-war expulsions of ethnic Germans in the East.[64]

   The selection of a suitable commonplace does not mark the end point, however, of the rhetorical possibilities for constructing moral analogies (excepting their composition via the relevant tropes and figures). Once the commonplace is fixed within the generic structure of any moral-equivalence argument, the three further stages that order their articulation and reception follow logically: the commonplace is given selective interpretation according to the political ends in view; the 'target' in dispute is inserted; and the target is juxtaposed with source – or commonplace – in the act of drawing the analogical inference itself.[65] Across these stages there is ample space for intervening upon how the projected audience might conceive the target itself, above all by means of manipulating the relevant definitions that might be made to carry force.

3. Techniques for manipulating definitions

Definitions can be manipulated in two main directions. Either the existing set of empirical criteria for admission to any given definitional term may be revised – in which case the typical rhetorical action concerned will be to enlarge the range of instances which the term covers. Or else it may be the moral complexion of whatever term is at stake that is subject to attempted alteration.[66] In connection with wrongdoing, it is the application of 'evil' itself that will often be in contest, both in its salient properties (intention, consequence, agency) and its moral register (radical or banal). Moral-equivalence claims are more specific. The task in mind will be to bring the disputed target closer to the chosen source by getting the same definitions to apply.

There are several strategies open here for effecting the change in empirical criteria as required. One is to eliminate any particular criterion according to which two actions markedly differ, so that otherwise significant differences are made insignificant. Conversely, the opposite holds true: the definitional content of a term can be extended in order to cover two cases more meaningfully. Hence, Soviet apologists in the Cold War discourse sometimes sought to expand the scope of human rights, so that the West also became guilty of 'abuses', in its case by denying citizens the full range of 'economic' as well as 'constitutional freedoms'.[67] Another strategy is more disingenuous. It involves papering over differences with the deliberate employment of 'vagueness' about the criteria being appealed to.[68] Genocide, for instance, is a concept for which the admissible threshold is notoriously imprecise, it being unclear whether a genocidal 'intention' is sufficient (in the event that this intent is left only partially realised in practice) and whether genocides can properly be said to occur only when their victims are racially defined.[69] In a related method, rather than to admit openly that the equivalence being asserted will not stick by the accepted standards, one of the most effective means for getting new criteria accepted is simply to talk in ways that imply that those being proposed are *already* the operative standards.[70]

The strategies available for changing the moral complexion of concepts, and that of the objects to which they are being made to refer, correspond to devices which have more formal recognition in the rhetorical tradition. One of these has already been specified in connection with techniques of amplification, paradiastole. Paradiastolic redescription is apt for bringing two actions into association through a particular kind of word substitution – substitution by adjacent terms. Moral-equivalence claims will seek to subsume two actions under the same evaluative term, whenever the concept more usually applied to the action in dispute is a rival – yet neighbouring – term. For instance, this is the move employed when the record of Allied aerial bombardment is lifted out of the category of 'war crime' and assigned to the yet

more ignominious category, 'crimes against humanity'.[71] Catachresis
denotes a more radical possibility. When the target of moral analogies
is something for which no generally agreed term exists at all (rather
than an agreed term which the rhetorical actor wishes to challenge)
the 'catachrestical speech act' is representative of the type of statement which – in the absence of hegemonic meaning – refers a new
and unknown problem in political life to contexts which *are* known.[72]
As Ernesto Laclau summarises the act in question, 'the name becomes
the ground of the thing'.[73] In a moral-equivalence claim catachresis
can function effectively, therefore, to displace the emphasis from the
mode of response anticipated. We might find this at work, for instance,
when Israeli reprisals against Palestinian actions are named 'terrorist',
in advance of their contrary designation as 'counter-terrorist'; or when
the broad thrust of American policy in response to September 11th is
named 'imperialist'.[74]

4. The appeal to emotions

Tropes, figures, commonplaces, and definitions are all rhetorical devices
for constructing reasoned arguments through which to contest acts of
wrongdoing – albeit devices which also seek to arouse strong emotive
reactions. Finally, it is worth unpacking the principal emotions being
appealed to. Sympathy and indignation will invariably play a central
part in due measure but the broader picture is one in which a range of
responses is projected around these two representative emotions, and
where particular relations between and across victims, perpetrators, and
third parties will present specific kinds of demands. A great deal hinges
upon the collective acts of subjective 'identification' being performed
in specific cases. An important dimension of the political rhetoric of
wrongdoing is the fashioning of the standpoints of wronged parties in
an emotively wrought key. Identification, accordingly, engages empathy
in various capacities: third parties are asked to imagine themselves as
experiencing first hand the harm either intended or inflicted, in an
enlargement of perspective which may be achieved through a range of
rhetorical possibilities.

The 'logic of equivalence' as it is thematised, in particular, in post-
Marxist discourse analysis is a useful point of reference for drawing
out these possibilities, and in special connection with the dynamics
engaged in moral equivalence arguments. Laclau and Mouffe's inves-

tigations grant an important space to the affective aspect of their principal theme, the antagonistic construction of group identities.[75] In their idealised scenario, diverse demands and interests in politics prove susceptible to being linked together in 'chains of equivalences' via careful discursive moves. Primarily, these equivalential chains are pictured as bringing together collective social actors who share – experientially – in specific exclusions or deprivations, though the same logic can be thought to apply when one of those sets of actors stands at further remove from events. It is not actions as such that are rendered equivalent in this connection; rather the association projected is between victim groups and more disinterested spectators. Thus conceived, third parties to wrongdoing are the intended audience, and the identification with other subjects as required demands that emotions be aroused in specific directions and proportions.

Emotions, in general, are complex because they can be understood to be both dependent upon social interaction and linked to cognition and judgement.[76] Aristotle defines emotions as 'those things *by the alteration of which* men differ with regard to those judgments which pain and pleasure accompany'.[77] There is an important relation to cognition here because these judgements will at the same time rest upon more reason-oriented appraisals of the objects in question.[78] But audiences can also be persuaded to revise these judgements as is consistent with the emotional pitch of the messages received about the same. Furthermore, Aristotle enumerates an inventory of emotions that relate to rhetoric, many of the more negative of which routinely animate moral-equivalence claims and, moreover, according to the understandings that Aristotle had in mind: notably, the *anger* of aggrieved parties towards perpetrators of past and present actions; the *fear* prompted by the 'expectation' of future suffering; and the *shame* of perpetrator communities, whose 'reputation' is debased.[79] *Pity*, however, and its opposite, *indignation*, are central to the mechanisms at work, being the emotions exclusive to forensic oratory. Pity, which in Aristotle's inventory comes closest to sympathy, is the type of 'pain occasioned by [. . .] pain's occurring to one who does not deserve it, which the pitier might be expected to suffer himself';[80] its arousal is especially keyed to third parties because it is not those who have 'already suffered' who pity, rather, it is their 'acquaintances', 'equals' and 'contemporaries' who are constituted variously 'by character, by habit, by esteem, and by birth'.[81] Relatedly, the scope for constituting these relationships presents an important opportunity for appealing to *pathos*. Conversely, the same holds for repudiating relationships with the authors of wrongful actions, when the pitier is moved to feel indignation and 'grief over undeserved good fortune'.[82]

Emotions, in this distinctive sense, can be pictured as being called into play in their capacity as 'the "glue" of solidarity'.[83] Sympathy and indignation are, in a more accurate designation, the 'reactive' emotions thereby in contest: both are made to stimulate immediate responses to new events in the ways envisaged (or else to new disclosures regarding past events). There is a prior, more consequential level, however, in which, on the basis of the sympathy and indignation touched off, the relevant (and ongoing) 'affective' emotions are summoned to effect:[84] principally, loyalty and allegiance. The cases having been considered here bear out this pattern of response. For instance, in the Cold War discourse, the intent behind moral analogies framed in the vocabulary of imperialism is to 'detach the identifications and affections' of citizens in the West from liberal democratic institutions, by casting their practices as fraudulent and in contradiction with professed values: the fidelity of states and governments to particular moral principles is thereby put to test.[85] In the memory discourses in contemporary Germany, the attempt is to shift the identification of the audience intended from one set of victims to another. 'Germans' are wrested out of the category of 'perpetrators', by reinscribing identification with 'Germans-as-victims' in place of 'Jews-as-victims', thereby forging a new collective identity at the same time.[86] In short and in sum, the rhetorical structure of moral-equivalence arguments makes space for the intervention of emotional appeals at various points. An audience can be persuaded that anger and fear are not exclusive to victims but should be shared; indignation can be directed at what is identified as the perpetrator community; sympathy for victims can be aroused, solidarity affirmed, and allegiance to wrongdoers undermined through shame.

CONCLUSION

At the beginning of this chapter it was suggested that extrapolating the distinctive elements of the rhetoric of moral equivalence might serve as a spur to investigating the rhetorical dimension of wrongdoing in political life within a broader perspective. It is to be hoped that enough has been said to stake out some levels of analysis for doing so. Arguments concerning moral equivalence engage the same representative actors as will all claims regarding wrongdoing which are contested in the public realm and, within this category, they draw upon the distinctive rhetorical resources for disputing prevailing norms and ideas through carefully managed comparisons, sharing this feature in common with lesser-evil type arguments in particular. Trivialisation, accordingly, poses something of an occupational hazard and, in several connections, it is this problem which the recurring rhetorical devices are intended to get around. Couching moral-equivalence claims as suggestive 'moral analogies' is the basic strategy employed to this effect. Around it is organised a range of techniques borrowed from the classical tradition. Its tropes and figures relate to amplification and repetition; the typical use of commonplaces draws from vocabularies and stock themes established in the public imagination; relevant definitions are manipulated either in their empirical or their normative senses; and the prominent emotions appealed to are sympathy and indignation, and loyalty or allegiance. The uses to which an appreciation of these techniques might be put are principally intended as interpretative and explanatory but there are implications for a more explicitly prescriptive agenda as well. In the former aspect, there are important pointers contained here for how 'mapping' arguments about evil and wrongdoing ought to proceed. In the latter aspect, making use of the prescriptive dimension requires greater recognition of the rhetorical character of political argument in general than currently carries sway. Exposing the dependence of moral-equivalence arguments upon a particular rhetorical repertoire, which is otherwise in danger of being dismissed as mere 'surface', might help to lessen the force of their appeal and, at the same time, modify the wider discourses of wrongdoing in ways that open them up to more critical modes of evaluation.

Notes

1 For the purposes of this chapter, 'wrongdoing' is employed as a broader category than 'evil' as such. Evil, however, is taken to denote an end point within that category.

2 The rhetorical analysis of political ideas represents an increasingly influential agenda within the discipline of political studies broadly conceived. See esp. Alan Finlayson, 'From Beliefs to Arguments: Interpretive Methodology and Rhetorical Political Analysis', *British Journal of Politics and International Relations*, 9: 4, 2007, pp. 545–63.

3 William James, 'The Moral Equivalent of War', in *Memories and Studies* (London: Longman Green and Co., 1911), pp. 267–96.

 4 G. A. Cohen, 'Casting the First Stone: Who Can, and Who Can't, Condemn the Terrorists?', in Anthony O'Hear (ed.), *Political Philosophy* (Cambridge: Cambridge University Press, 2006), pp. 113–36.

 5 G. M. Gilbert, *Nuremberg Diary* (New York: Farrar, Straus and Co., 1947), p. 202. See also Laughland, *A History of Political Trials: From Charles I to Saddam Hussein* (Peter Lang: Oxford, 2008), pp. 103–18.

 6 Cited in David Aaronovitch, 'Hamas or Hannas, they're not Black and White', *Times*, 6 January 2009.

 7 See Judith Butler, 'Explanation and Exoneration, or What We Can Hear', *Social Text*, 20: 3, 2002, p. 184.

 8 Richard Bernstein, *The Abuse of Evil: The Corruption of Politics and Religion since 9/11* (Cambridge: Cambridge University Press, 2005), p. 4.

 9 Tony Judt, *Reappraisals: Reflections on the Forgotten Twentieth Century* (New York: Penguin, 2008), p. 16.

10 Jean Copjec (ed.), *Radical Evil* (London: Verso, 1996); Bernstein, *Radical Evil: A Philosophical Interrogation* (Cambridge: Polity, 2002).

11 Susan Neiman, *Evil in Modern Thought* (Princeton: Princeton University Press, 2004), p. 285.

12 Hannah Arendt, *Eichmann in Jerusalem* (London: Penguin, 1994); Zygmunt Bauman, *Modernity and the Holocaust* (Cambridge: Polity, 1991); Christopher Browning, *Ordinary Men: Reserve Battalion 101 and the Final Solution in Poland* (New York: HarperCollins, 1992). The allusion to 'shades of grey' here is a reference to Primo Levi's account of evil. See Levi, 'The Grey Zone', in *The Drowned and the Saved*, trans. Raymond Rosenthal (London: Abacus, 2008), pp. 22–51.

13 E.g. Michael Ignatieff, *The Lesser Evil: Political Ethics in an Age of Terror* (Edinburgh: Edinburgh University Press, 2005); Alex J. Bellamy, 'Dirty Hands and Lesser Evils in the War on Terror', *British Journal of Politics and International Relations*, 9 (3) (2007), pp. 509–26. The idea of 'the lesser of two evils' generally gains far greater attention within political studies than does the idea of moral equivalence. The lack of attention is not entirely paralleled in other fields, however. There is a prominent use of the term in applied ethics, where there is a particular debate concerning whether 'killing' and 'letting die' are morally equivalent. See Jonathan Glover, *Causing Death and Saving Lives* (Harmondsworth: Penguin, 1977); Peter Singer, *Practical Ethics* (Cambridge: Cambridge University Press, 1993), pp. 175–218; and F. M. Kamm, *Morality, Mortality*, Vol. II, *Rights, Duties and States* (Oxford: Oxford University Press, 1996), esp. pp. 17–121.

14 See J. L. Austin, *How to Do Things with Words* (Oxford: Oxford University Press, 1975 [1962]). Specifically, moral-equivalence claims can be under-

stood to be speech acts of 'admonition' which reprove and censure rather than, for instance, commend.

15 Tzvetan Todorov, 'The Uses and Abuses of Comparison', in Helmut Dubiel and Gabriel Motzkin (eds), *The Lesser Evil: Moral Approaches to Genocide Practices* (London: Routledge, 2004).

16 See, for instance, Peter Novick's polemic against 'the sacralisation of the Holocaust' in *The Holocaust in American Life* (New York: Houghton and Mifflin, 1999).

17 Jeffrey C. Alexander, 'On the Social Construction of Moral Universals: The "Holocaust" from War Crime to Trauma Drama', *European Journal of Social Theory*, 5: 1, 2002, pp. 5–85.

18 Judt, *Reappraisals*, p. 17.

19 Samantha Power, *'A Problem from Hell': America and the Age of Genocide* (London: HarperCollins, 2003). For the debate on the 'uniqueness' of the Holocaust, see esp. Dan Stone, 'The Historiography of the Holocaust: Beyond "Uniqueness" and Ethnic Competition', *Rethinking History*, 8: 1, 2004, pp. 127–42.

20 Berel Lang, 'The Evil in Genocide', in John K. Roth (ed.), *Genocide and Human Rights* (Basingstoke: Palgrave Macmillan, 2005), p. 8.

21 Generally, it should be noted that the threat of trivialisation implicit in moral-equivalence claims is to some degree tempered by the convention that they fall into the category of 'excuses' rather than 'justifications'. As Michael Walzer observes, excuses have the distinction of giving implicit recognition to the 'evil' of the actions at hand. See Walzer, *Arguing About War* (New Haven and London: Yale University Press, 2004), p. 52.

22 A discourse of German victimhood has become increasingly prevalent in the period since German reunification, in which context the 'air wars' of World War II have been a recurrent point of focus for developing moral-equivalence arguments. For the primary sources, see Jörg Friedrich, *The Fire: The Bombing of Germany, 1940–1945,* trans. Allison Brown (New York: Columbia University Press, 2008); and W. G. Sebald, *On the Natural History of Destruction*, trans. Anthea Bell (London: Hamish Hamilton, 2003). For other significant interventions see Dagmar Barnouw, *The War in the Empty Air: Victims, Perpetrators and Postwar Germans* (Bloomington: Indiana University Press, 2005), A. C. Grayling, *Among the Dead Cities: Was the Allied Bombing of Civilians in WWII a Necessity or a Crime?* (London: Bloomsbury, 2006), and Maja Zehfuss, *Wounds of Memory: The Politics of War in Germany* (Cambridge: Cambridge University Press, 2007). For more general, critical commentary see Daniel Johnson, 'Breaking the Silence', *Times Literary Supplement*, 25 April 2003, pp. 7–8; Christian Schütze, 'On that Terrible Night', *London Review of Books*, 21 August 2003, pp. 28–9; Ian Buruma, 'The Destruction of Germany', *New York Review of Books*, 21 October 2004,

pp. 8–12; and Mary Nolan, 'Germans as Victims during the Second World War: Air Wars, Memory Wars', *Central European History*, 38: 1, 2005, pp. 7–40.

23 The ideological debates of the Cold War typically posed left-wing intellectuals against neoconservative authors. For a neoconservative commentary see esp. Jeanne Kirkpatrick, 'Dictatorships and Double Standards', *Commentary*, 68, 1979, pp. 34–45, and Kirkpatrick, 'The Myth of Moral Equivalence', in *Legitimacy and Force: Political and Moral Dimensions*, Vol. 1 (New Brunswick, NJ: Transaction, 1988), pp. 74–84. In particular see also Dominic Tierney, '"Pearl Harbor in Reverse": Moral Analogies in the Cuban Missile Crisis', *Journal of Cold War Studies*, 9: 3, 2007, pp. 49–77.

24 For a partisan rejoinder to all moral-equivalence arguments in the post-September 11th context in general, see William J. Bennett, *Why We Fight: Moral Clarity and the War of Terrorism* (New York: Doubleday, 2002).

25 E. J. Lowe, 'What is a Criterion of Identity?', *Philosophical Quarterly*, 39, 1989, pp. 1–21.

26 See Wesley C. Salmon, *Logic* (Englewood Cliffs, NJ, Prentice-Hall, Inc., 1963), p. 70.

27 Lawrence Blum, '*The Holocaust in American Life* as a Moral Text' in Eve Garrard and Geoffrey Scarre (eds), *The Holocaust and Moral Philosophy* (Aldershot: Ashgate, 2003), pp. 261–2.

28 E.g. see Kirkpatrick, 'The Myth of Moral Equivalence', pp. 74–84.

29 See Sigrid Rausing, 'The Code for Conspiracy', *New Statesman*, 23 April 2009, p. 19.

30 Hiliard Aronovitch, 'The Political Importance of Analogical Argument', *Political Studies*, XLV, 1997, p. 88.

31 On ranking, see Michael Freeden, 'What Should the "Political" in Political Theory Explore?', *Journal of Political Philosophy*, 13, 2005, pp. 130–1.

32 See esp. Jonathan Glover, *Humanity: A Moral History of the Twentieth Century* (London: Pimlico, 2001); Avishai Margalit, *On Compromise and Rotten Compromises* (Princeton: Princeton University Press, 2010), pp. 175–98.

33 See William D. Casebeer, 'Knowing Evil When You See It: Uses for the Rhetoric of Evil in International Relations', *International Relations*, 18: 4, 2004, pp. 441–51.

34 Berel Lang, 'Comparative Evil: Degrees, Numbers and the Problem of Measure' in Dubiel and Motzkin (eds), *The Lesser Evil*, p. 102.

35 Not only does harm break down into its quantitative and qualitative dimensions but wrongful intentions also bifurcate into the presence (or absence) of intention itself and the type of intention (or 'motive') at work. See Card, *The Atrocity Paradigm: A Theory of Evil* (Oxford: Oxford University Press, 2002), p. 3.

36 Aristotle, *The Art of Rhetoric*, trans. H. C. Lawson-Tancred (London: Penguin, 2004), p. 74.

37 Victoria McGeer and Philip Pettit, 'Sticky Judgement and the Role of Rhetoric', in Richard Bourke and Raymond Geuss (eds), *Political Judgement* (Cambridge: Cambridge University Press, 2009), pp. 65–70.

38 Robert Cockcroft and Susan Cockcroft, *Persuading People: An Introduction to Rhetoric* (Basingstoke: Palgrave Macmillan, 2006), p. 4. See also Herbert Gottweis, 'Rhetoric in Policy Making: Between Logos, Ethos and Pathos', in F. Fischer, G. J. Miller and M. S. Sidney (eds), *Handbook of Public Policy* (London: Taylor and Francis, 2006).

39 Aristotle, *The Art of Rhetoric*, pp. 79–82.

40 See esp. Quentin Skinner, *Reason and Rhetoric in the Philosophy of Hobbes* (Cambridge: Cambridge University Press, 1996), pp. 127–33.

41 Richard Lanham, *A Handlist of Rhetorical Terms* (Berkeley and Los Angeles: University of California Press, 1991), pp. 78, 154–7.

42 Skinner, *Reason and Rhetoric*, p. 136.

43 Lanham, *Handlist*, p. 86; Cockcroft and Cockcroft, *Persuading People*, pp. 183–4.

44 Lanham, *Handlist*, pp. 95–6; Cockcroft and Cockcroft, *Persuading People*, p. 184.

45 Skinner, *Reason and Rhetoric*, p. 136.

46 See esp. Jeanne Fahnestock, 'Series Reasoning in Scientific Argument: "*Incrementum* and *Gradatio*" and the Case of Darwin', *Rhetoric Studies Quarterly*, 26: 4, 1996, pp. 13–40.

47 Cockcroft and Cockcroft, *Persuading People*, pp. 182, 184.

48 See, for instance, François Furet and Ernst Nolte, *Fascism and Communism*, trans. Katherine Golsan (Lincoln and London: University of Nebraska Press, 2001), p. 69.

49 Lanham, *Handlist*, p. 16.

50 Jean Baudrillard, *The Spirit of Terrorism*, trans. Chris Turner (London: Verso, 2003), p. 12.

51 Cockcroft and Cockcroft, *Persuading People*, p. 176.

52 Kenneth Burke, *A Rhetoric of Motives* (Berkeley, CA: University of California Press, 1969), p. 165.

53 See, for instance, David Aaronovitch, 'Hamas or Hannas', and Howard Jacobson, 'Let's see the "criticism" of Israel for what it really is', *The Independent*, 18 February 2009. For a general survey of moral equivalence as depicted in Steven Spielberg's 2005 film *Munich*, see Henry Siegman, 'The Killing Equation', *New York Review of Books*, 53: 2, 9 February 2006, pp. 18–19.

54 Lanham, *Handlist*, p. 92.

55 Kenneth Burke, *Permanence and Change: An Anatomy of Purpose* (Berkeley, CA: University of California Press, 1984), p. 194.

56 See Friedrich, *The Fire*, and in particular the commentary on Friedrich in Johnson, 'Breaking the Silence', p. 7 and Buruma, 'The Destruction of Germany', p. 12.

57 Lanham, *Handlist*, pp. 169–70.

58 Jennifer Richards, *Rhetoric* (London: Routledge, 2008), pp. 32–41.

59 Skinner, *Reason and Rhetoric*, pp. 111–19.

60 Jonathan Charteris-Black, *Politicians and Rhetoric: The Persuasive Power of Metaphor* (Basingstoke: Palgrave Macmillan, 2005), pp. 8–20.

61 Markus Kornprobst, 'Comparing Apples and Oranges? Leading and Misleading Uses of Historical Analogies', *Millennium*, 36: 1, 2007, pp. 29–49.

62 See Walzer, *Arguing About War*, pp. 53–60.

63 For a good discussion of the conceptual vocabularies for contesting modes of political domination in general, see Melvin Richter, 'A Family of Political Concepts: Tyranny, Despotism, Bonapartism, Caesarism, Dictatorship, 1750–1917', *European Journal of Political Theory*, 4: 3, 2005, pp. 221–47.

64 E.g. John Bendix, 'Facing Hitler: German Responses to *Downfall*', *German Politics and Society*, 25(1) (2007), pp. 70–89; Günter Grass, *Crabwalk* (London: Faber and Faber, 2003).

65 Kornprobst, 'Comparing Apples and Oranges?', pp. 36–40. See also some of the standard criteria for evaluating analogical arguments discussed in Aronovitch, 'The Political Importance of Analogical Argument', p. 81. For instance, analogies are likely to be effective if the properties shown to be common are expressed in similar proportion, greater rather than fewer in recurrence and frequency, and contradicted by as few uncommon properties as possible.

66 Skinner, 'Some Problems in the Analysis of Political Thought and Action', *Political Theory*, 1: 3, 1974, pp. 296–8.

67 Kirkpatrick in William Barrett et al., 'Human Rights and American Foreign Policy: A Symposium', *Commentary*, 72, 1981, p. 43.

68 See esp. R. Keefe and P. Smith (eds), *Vagueness: A Reader* (Cambridge, MA: MIT Press).

69 See Steven Lee, 'The Moral Distinctiveness of Genocide', *Journal of Political Philosophy* (forthcoming), and the various contributions in Roth (ed.), *Genocide and Human Rights*.

70 J. O. Urmson, 'On Grading', *Mind*, 59(234), 1950, p. 166.

71 A. C. Grayling, *Dead Cities*, p. 231; Donald Bloxham, 'Dresden as a War Crime', in Paul Addison and Jeremy A. Crang (eds), *Firestorm: The Bombing of Dresden, 1945* (London: Pimlico, 2006).

72 Ernesto Laclau, *On Populist Reason* (London: Verso, 2007), pp. 71–2, 100; Alan Finlayson, 'Rhetoric and Radical Democratic Theory', in Adrian Little

and Moya Lloyd (eds), *The Politics of Radical Democracy* (Edinburgh: Edinburgh University Press, 2009), p. 28.

73 Laclau, *On Populist Reason*, p. 100.

74 E.g. Noam Chomsky, *Hegemony or Survival: America's Quest for Global Dominance* (London: Hamish Hamilton, 2003).

75 Ernesto Laclau and Chantal Mouffe, *Hegemony and Socialist Strategy* (London: Verso, 2001).

76 Simon Clarke, Paul Hoggett and Simon Thompson, 'The Study of Emotion: An Introduction', in Clarke, Hoggett and Thompson (eds), *Emotions, Politics and Society* (Basingstoke: Palgrave, 2006), pp. 6–7.

77 Aristotle, *The Art of Rhetoric*, p. 141; italics added.

78 James Jasper, 'The Emotions of Protest: Affective and Reactive Emotions in and around Social Movements', *Sociological Forum*, 13: 3, 1998, pp. 397–424.

79 Aristotle, *The Art of Rhetoric*, pp. 142–6, 153–61.

80 Aristotle, *The Art of Rhetoric*, p. 163.

81 Aristotle, *The Art of Rhetoric*, p. 164.

82 Aristotle, *The Art of Rhetoric*, p. 165. See also Peter Lyman, 'The Domestication of Anger: The Use and Abuse of Anger in Politics', *European Journal of Social Theory*, 7: 2, 2004, p. 137.

83 Randall Collins, 'Stratification, Emotional Energy, and the Transient Emotions', in T. D. Kemper (ed.), *Research Agendas in the Sociology of Emotions* (Albany: State University of New York Press, 1990), p. 28.

84 Jasper, 'The Emotions of Protest', p. 398.

85 Kirkpatrick, 'The Myth of Moral Equivalence', p. 84.

86 See esp. Zehfuss, *Wounds of Memory*, p. 109.

Chapter 11

BANAL BUT NOT BENIGN: ARENDT ON EVIL

David Boucher

Hannah Arendt is one of the most revered and reviled philosophers of the twentieth century. Almost sixty years after the publication of *Eichmann in Jerusalem*, her conclusions still have the power to provoke extreme reactions. For example, David Cesarani accuses Arendt of being deeply contemptuous of the Jews of Poland and Russia because of her bourgeois German Jewish background. Barry Gewen, reviewing the book in the *New York Times*, dismisses Cesarani as 'a writer in control of neither his material nor himself'. Arendt could certainly be dismissive, contemptuous and excessively judgemental of those outside her circle, and yet her flashes of brilliant insight elevated her above the ordinary. Her characterisation of the banality of evil is probably one of the most memorable, and most controversial, of her observations on the human condition.[1] Eichmann's refusal to judge the moral veracity of his superiors, or what we may call his suspension of judgement, is what precipitated Arendt's remark about the banality of evil. A weak, vain, mediocre man in appearance and intellect, with a propensity to speak in clichés, was an accomplice in one of the most monstrous crimes in history. Eichmann's suspension of judgement is in contrast with Arendt's tendency to be severe in her own judgements. Not only Eichmann, she thought, but many of the German people were equally complicit, and just as deserving of condemnation were the *Judenräte*, the Jewish councils, efficient and systematic accomplices in the murder of their own people.[2]

The aim of this chapter is to examine one of the most infamous attempts to make evil intelligible, namely that of Hannah Arendt. First I will construct Arendt's 'theory' of the banality of evil. This will entail revisiting the site of the crime and re-examining the reasons why Arendt's attempt to make Eichmann's evil acts intelligible precipitated hostile reactions. Second, I will explore the nature of the hostile reactions to Arendt's book. Third, I will look at the particularist implications in the context of the civilised nations. I contend that what Arendt actually did was to make Eichmann and his kind, and not the evil he committed, intelligible. In this respect, she fulfilled one of the objectives that she believed the court in Jerusalem failed to achieve, namely an understanding of the new type of criminal capable of committing such crimes.[3] Finally, I want to ask if her understanding of evil, or to be precise the monstrous crimes Eichmann committed, may be universally condemned, or more controversially, is the perpetration of the evil in which Eichmann indulged contingent on certain conditions? If the process in which evil is manifest is the enjoyment and depravation of citizenship rights, as I will argue Arendt contends, then we cannot condemn with the same moral force or conviction the slaughter of groups of people who have not yet reached a level whereby citizenship rights and civil society have been attained. I will argue that the implication of Arendt's position is that it is not enough to be human to meet the qualifying threshold for the enjoyment of genuine rights, namely citizenship or social rights. Without such an attainment, Arendt gives us grounds for believing that genocide in such circumstances is less heinous an evil, for example, against black Africans, than against those who have had citizenship rights revoked and are systematically slaughtered, as were the Jews.

A

Whether from the theological or secular point of view, the manifestation of evil raises questions about the intelligibility of the world. In modern thought there are two broad answers that morality dictates. On the one hand, it is claimed that morality demands that we make sense of evil and render it intelligible. On the other, it is contended that morality demands that evil is inexplicable, senseless, capricious.[4] Evil may be rendered intelligible by suggesting that the perpetrators conformed to a different moral code of conduct as, for example, has been suggested of Nazi Germany. No one at the Nuremberg trials, however, wished to defend that code, and deflected the blame on to everyone else, declaring that they had always been against it. Alternatively, evil is rendered unintelligible by pronouncing the evil doers as mad or insane.[5]

Susan Neiman identifies the Lisbon earthquake of 1755 and

Auschwitz as the beginning and end of the modern conception of evil. Lisbon is emblematic of the moment of recognition that traditional theodicy offered little hope in the face of evil; we could no longer attribute it to God's intention to punish our sins. In other words, the earthquake destroyed the idea of divine punishment for human crimes. The apparently arbitrary and destructive earthquake decimated contemporary moral frameworks that attributed natural evil (suffering) to moral evil (sin). It simultaneously gave birth to the nascent distinction between catastrophic natural and unaccountable disaster on the one hand and human accountability for moral evil on the other. Auschwitz taught us that having taken responsibility for evil, attributing it to human intention, that such substitute explanations were even more hopeless. Neiman contends: 'If Auschwitz leaves us more helpless than Lisbon, it is because our conceptual resources seem exhausted.'[6]

What is shocking about Arendt's account of Eichmann's evil is that he appeared unaware of his wrongdoing. Conscientiously doing his duty, in conformity with the laws of the land, he was an accomplice in the most heinous crime ever committed. Arendt almost completely undermines the idea that evil is irrevocably attached to the human will and human responsibility, hence its banality.

Karl Adolf Eichmann escaped justice at Nuremberg by fleeing Germany and remaining in hiding in Europe until 1950, after which he escaped and lived under an assumed identity in Argentina.[7] He was illegally detained in Buenos Aires by Israeli Mossad operatives and flown to Israel nine days later on 20 May 1960 to face trial in the District Court in Jerusalem. Stripped of his authority, the Mossad operatives were surprised at how ordinary he looked, not at all imposing or sinister, as one would expect the incarnation of evil to be. The trial began on 11 April 1961 culminating in his execution on 31 May 1962. While not the architect of the 'final solution', nor among the highest-ranking Nazis, Eichmann efficiently organised the transportation of its victims to the death camps, apparently without any qualms of conscience. He claimed he had not personally killed, nor ordered the killing of, any person.

In 1964 the Canadian poet Leonard Cohen published a book of poems entitled *Flowers for Hitler*. In the poem 'All There Is to Know about Adolph Eichmann', he describes as medium: the colour of his hair and eyes; weight and height; and intelligence. Eichmann had the normal number of fingers and toes, and had no distinguishing features.

Cohen ends: 'What did you expect? Talons? Oversize incisors? Green saliva? Madness?' In these few words he conveyed the extraordinary ordinariness that so unnerved the Mossad operatives, and so struck Hannah Arendt in reporting the case for the *New York Times*.[8] She published a book based on the articles in 1963, and revised and expanded it in 1964.

Arendt herself disavowed any suggestion that her book was a 'theoretical treatise on the nature of evil'.[9] Yet the subject matter of her book, the Holocaust and the Nazi desire to 'cleanse' the world of the mentally ill, gypsies and, above all, Jews, has become the epitome of evil, not only for the twentieth century, but for all time. The book itself has become a touchstone for almost every attempt theoretically to understand the nature of evil because it is so chilling in its conclusions. While it does not present itself as a theoretical treatise, one may nevertheless extrapolate a theory from it by relating it to pertinent evidence from her other works.

Eichmann and the human predicament

Arendt rejects Natural Law as the foundation of the notion of crimes against humanity on the grounds that it is obsolete. It posits a fixed human nature and thus falls foul of the metaphysics of substance. Instead of the language of human nature, Arendt favours that of the 'human condition'. She contends that, 'the human condition is not the same as human nature'.[10] Heidegger's insight is that *Dasien* is the only being for which the question of its existence is meaningful, that is, our factuality, or our abandonment by the drama of the past into a world as it is. In other words, we are situated in a plot not of our own making. We are thrust into the midst of an ongoing performance. The human condition refers to the context in which life is bestowed upon human beings. Arendt argues that: 'Whatever touches or enters into a sustained relationship with human life immediately assumes the character of a condition of human existence. This is why men, no matter what they do, are always conditioned beings.'[11] The circumstances constrain but do not determine our choices.[12] We are the makers of the world. The universals are not human rights or human nature, nor even human reason, but plurality, in which we are all the same, yet uniquely different. Plurality is part of the structure of life; we have no choice in the matter but how this plurality is manifest is not easily predictable.[13] As

Andrew Vincent argues, for Arendt, 'there is no universal moral foundation for human rights. There was nothing inevitable about any such order. There was neither any universal order of nature nor any objective good to be discovered. There was rather the historical contingency of certain nation states . . .'[14]

Eichmann, then, was thrust into a drama, not of his own making, and the constraints that bounded his parameters, his situatedness, are the context in which his actions are explicable. Arendt's analysis of Adolf Eichmann as a study in evil needs to be located in this background and understood through an exploration of the relation between thinking and acting, and the importance of thinking for the political.[15] Eichmann stood trial for his part in the final solution of the Jewish problem. While there is no doubt of Eichmann's guilt, the fact of a nation intent on revenge, resorting to illegal kidnapping, allowing no defence witnesses, and focusing on the suffering of the Jews rather than upon bringing Eichmann to justice for what he did, tainted the whole proceedings.[16] The trial, in Arendt's view, was of limited success because it failed to address adequately three fundamental issues, all of which had been to the fore of discussion since Nuremburg. First, there was the issue of tainted justice, victor's justice. Second, there was an inadequate definition or understanding of the idea of a crime against humanity. And third, there was no clear recognition of the new type of criminal capable of such crimes.[17] The trial was an exercise in indoctrination, and contributed little to the stimulation of thinking. Eichmann was found guilty of 'crimes against the Jewish people' and of intending to eradicate them from the face of the earth. He was hanged for his crimes.

What the court needed to declare, in Arendt's view, was that Eichmann was guilty of deciding who could and who could not inhabit the earth, and that led him to behave in a manner suppressive of the sphere of appearance, the political, and to disregard elements of humanity as unnecessary – this was his crime, a crime against humanity. Indeed, the court at Jerusalem was faced with the problem of on what formal grounds should he be charged and of determining a moral or psychological motive or explanation for why he became an instrument of the Nazi's final solution. Is Arendt attributing any responsibility to Eichmann or was he just a pawn in the totalitarian game?

What does Arendt mean by the term 'banality of evil', which serves as the subtitle of her book *Eichmann in Jerusalem*? Although Arendt purports not to have a theory of evil, and claims that her account of

Eichmann's trial is 'factual', observations on what was self-evident from the proceedings, she does certainly have a view about the nature of evil. In her letter to Mary McCarthy she says that 'evil never has depth', and to the distinguished scholar of Judaism, Gershom Scholem, she wrote that 'evil is never "radical"... it is only extreme and ... possesses neither depth nor demonic dimensions'.[18] Furthermore, she suggests that, for Eichmann, crime was innately repugnant and that any of his compatriots could have been like him. There was nothing specific about him, his character, or activities that singles him out. Eichmann was, she suggests, the revealer of truth for generations to come in that he was the exemplification of the banality of evil.[19] In the posthumously published *The Life of the Mind*, she returns fleetingly to the banality of evil in the introduction. By the phrase, once again applying it specifically to Eichmann, she claimed she did not put forward a thesis or doctrine but was, nevertheless, vaguely aware that it deviated from the conception encountered in our literary, theological and philosophic traditions of thought. It was the manifest shallowness of the perpetrator of the undeniably evil deeds which made it impossible to detect the roots of or motives for the crimes. The deeds were without doubt monstrous but their perpetrator 'was quite ordinary, commonplace and neither demonic nor monstrous'.[20]

She was not suggesting that the acts of humiliation and extermination, or the principles that lay behind them, were 'banal'. It was Eichmann's ordinariness, his thoughtlessness and his remoteness from reality that wrought a havoc far more frightening than all the evil intentions put together. In her view, that was, in fact, the lesson one could learn in Jerusalem. But it was a lesson, neither an explanation of the phenomenon nor a theory about it.[21] It was this particular evil that was banal, not evil per se.[22] For Arendt, Eichmann's inarticulateness was evidence of his inability to think, especially from the perspective of someone else.[23] His evil was not intentional. It was unthinking which contributed to rendering other humans superfluous.

Some years earlier Arendt had identified one of the most remarkable features of our time, namely thoughtlessness. She characterised it in terms of hopeless confusion, heedlessness and recklessness, or complacently repeating received truths which were vacuous and trivial.[24] Eichmann, then, was the exemplification of the tendency of the times. The remedy, was obvious: to think what we are doing.[25]

Eichmann was pronounced normal by the psychiatrists who

examined him, and considered by the prison minister to have some positive qualities. Eichmann exemplifies the disturbing conclusion that an ordinary person can be incapable of discerning right from wrong. Eichmann had acted within the context of the Third Reich and saw no reason to judge his actions as criminal. Arendt shows that, throughout his career, Eichmann exhibited a habit of behaving without thinking, that is, an inability to think from the standpoint of someone else.[26] To be normal requires behaviour and not thought. He tended to speak in clichés and officialese, using euphemisms such as 'final solution' and 'special treatment' instead of 'killing'.[27] He was given 'language rules' by which he disguised the truth, and which sheltered him from believing he was engaged in wrongdoing.

Arendt implied that Eichmann was more or less a pawn in the totalitarian game. His thoughtlessness, his unthinking, made him, too, a victim. Indeed, the banality and thoughtlessness of those complicit in the Holocaust stripped evil of the character we usually attribute to it – temptation. Eichmann was not even conscious of his own wrong-doing.[28] She portrays Eichmann as a 'clown', a vain man incapable of detecting contradictions in his speech, and almost incapable of articulating his thoughts because he had very few. He would make grand gestures, and then immediately contradict them, as, for example, when he stated boldly that he would never take another oath because eventually, however sincere, there would be consequences for him. No one, he said, would ever make him take an oath again. He was then asked if he would like to give his evidence under oath, or if he preferred not to, and he declared that he would give evidence under oath. There is no doubt that Arendt found him a pathetic, ridiculous man.[29]

Arendt explicitly maintains that 'this trial had to take place in the interests of justice and nothing else'.[30] Despite the fact that the crime was previously unknown and the criminal of the likes that no court, except Nuremberg, had seen before, Arendt contends that her report 'deals with nothing but the extent to which the court in Jerusalem suc-ceeded in fulfilling the demands of justice'.[31] And again she says: 'on trial are his deeds, not the sufferings of the Jews, not the German people or mankind, not even anti-Semitism and racism'.[32] The chief prosecu-tor, however, Gideon Hausner had a wider agenda. His case was to play on what the Jews had suffered and not upon what Eichmann had done. Nuremberg had not focused on the 'final solution' but instead on crimes committed by the defendants against various nations. The simple reason for this was that Eichmann was not there.

On the trial Arendt contends that it was a show trial, emphasising drama, creating an atmosphere of suffering, the details of which were often irrelevant to the charges against Eichmann. While her criticisms of the prosecutor Hausner are fair, she nevertheless does more than merely apply the question of justice. After all, this was a new type of crime, and Eichmann was like most soldiers obeying orders, but the law that he obeyed was of a different kind. Eichmann's defence pleaded 'acts of state' rather than superior orders.

On the question of the Israeli motive for conducting the case in the manner of a show trial, it is clear that Eichmann was a symbol, not merely of Nazism, but of centuries of anti-Semitism, in order to lie heavily upon the conscience of nations in protecting the Israeli state. Arendt accused the Israeli government of pursuing political advantage rather than justice. It was a mistake in her view to charge Eichmann with crimes against the Jewish people. It downgraded his crime and brought into question the complicity of the Jewish people. Indeed, the Israeli authorities tried to establish at the trial the futility of Jewish resistance against the Nazis because they could not rely on the backing of a Jewish state, because no Jewish state existed. It was a veiled justification for the state of Israel itself.

In the conduct of the trial the more general picture of anti-Semitism formed the backdrop but this merely served to obscure the fact that only Eichmann was on trial for his life, and to confuse his trial with that of the Nazi system clouded the issue of individual responsibility.

Arendt believed that the Israelis failed to recognise the enormity of the novelty of the Nazi threat. In portraying Eichmann as committing crimes against the Jews, they placed the actions of the Nazis within a long tradition of anti-Semitism. The Jerusalem court failed to see the clear distinctions between discrimination, expulsion and genocide. It saw such actions as part of the same age-old process of anti-Semitism. There is a big difference between expulsion and genocide. Expulsion is 'an offence against fellow-nations, whereas the latter is an attack upon human diversity as such, that is, upon a characteristic of the "human status" without which the very words "mankind" or "humanity" would be devoid of meaning'.[33] She goes on to argue that: 'the physical extermination of the Jewish people, was a crime against humanity, perpetrated upon the body of the Jewish people, and that only the choice of victims, not the nature of the crime, could be derived from the long history of Jew-hatred and anti-Semitism'.[34]

For Arendt, however, the reasoned and rationalised murder by the Nazis of whole populations portended a new set of frightening and horrific possibilities, superseding anti-Semitism. In other words, the Nazi atrocities were not the last chapter in anti-Semitism but the first chapter in modern totalitarianism.[35] Bruno Bettelheim argues that, despite the questions of the legality of the trial, because of the kidnap of Eichmann: 'It brought the world face to face with those dangers of totalitarianism that it seems all too willing to avoid examining.'[36]

Even the introduction of the concept of 'genocide' to cover Nazi crimes inadequately characterised what was done and the overall implications. Massacres of whole peoples were not unknown in antiquity, and colonisation and imperialism provided plenty of examples.[37] .

In Arendt's view, the category of 'crimes against humanity' was invented to describe a new act, the act of genocide against a people because of the mere fact that it existed on this earth as a particular type of people.[38] The possibility of future genocide must make every nation alert to its own vulnerability and realise that its continued existence is better assured with the protection of international law.[39]

Arendt does not attempt to make the victims into saints. The murdered Jews are not portrayed as martyrs but straightforwardly as men, women and children. They were not offered the option of renouncing their religion and choosing to save their lives by adopting the state religion. In applying her uncompromising standard of justice how fair is she being to the Israelis, the judgement of the court, and to the memory of the victims? And second how adequate is such a standard as a response to the events?

Daniel Bell contends that a subtle but powerful transformation of the link between words and what they signified, between language and the world, was perpetrated by the Nazis. Words with unfavourable pejorative connotations were replaced by a more innocuous vocabulary, designed to make the same abhorrent actions palatable. Similarly, the perpetrators of individual acts of atrocity were made to feel that their actions were part of a higher cause or purpose. Eichmann himself knew what was happening when in his final statement to the court he talked of the 'revaluation of values prescribed by the [Nazi] government'.[40] Eichmann believed he was acting from conscience because he did his duty, namely obeyed the law, even if it was against his inclinations.

Morals became transformed in Nazi Germany, conscience dictated thou shalt kill, and evil 'lost the quality by which most people recognise it – the quality of temptation'.[41] What in other societies was regarded as good became temptation in the Third Reich – not to betray one's neighbour was a temptation. Such transformations in the meaning of words and the undermining of ordinary morality were not, of course, unprecedented. Thucydides, in his *History of the Peloponnesian War*, described a similar process, following the Corcyrean civil war when nearly all of the Hellenic world became embroiled in intrigues and disputes. In Thucydides' view, it was 'Love of power, operating through greed and through personal ambition' which brought about the evils he detected.[42] Once the struggles broke out, a violent fanaticism came into play. While consolidating aristocracy, leaders of parties duped the people into thinking they were promoting political equality for all. Neither justice nor considerations of the interests of the state deterred the excesses to which men went. Their criterion and motive for action was pleasure. There was no room for conscience in a city where those who were valued were those who could put forward clever arguments to justify disgraceful acts. Citizens who held moderate views were held in suspicion and eliminated for not taking sides. The less intelligent triumphed over the more intelligent by launching themselves straight into action and thus gaining the advantage over those who deliberated before acting.

Nazi Germany differed from ancient Corcyra in its ability to mobilise the masses. Totalitarianism had a much greater capacity to direct populations to the achievement of ideas or ideals, perhaps not for long periods of time but for long enough to bring about horrific consequences. What the rediscovery of evil in Nazi Germany exposed was the prospect that centralised powers could manipulate vast numbers through state coercion and that totalitarianism is always potentially a threat.[43]

B

There were those who thought Arendt gave us a tremendous insight into a new kind of mass murderer. Frederick S. Burin remarked of Arendt's book: 'Not only does it do justice to Miss Arendt's reputation for brilliant insight and critical imagination, it reflects great courage, great independence of mind, and – other reviewers to the contrary notwithstanding – a shining humanity.'[44] On the whole, however, Arendt's critics were legion, as she acknowledges in the postscript to the 1964 revised edition. The title, let alone the content of the book, was hugely controversial: *Eichmann in Jerusalem: A Report on the Banality of Evil*. She was vilified throughout the world by those Jews who found it objectionable that she should so explicitly argue that the Jewish Councils were complicit in the final solution, and without them it would not have been as successful and efficient as it was. To many it appeared that she was denying the concept of personal responsibility in describing Eichmann as unthinking. Nuremberg had fought hard to establish personal responsibility as grounds for conviction of Nazi war criminals.[45]

Jacob Robinson could barely contain his contempt in his attack on the veracity of Arendt's judgements, her grasp of the facts, and understanding of international law.[46] In his view, Arendt's conclusions were inconsistent with the evidence and frankly perverse. He contended that Eichmann was a man of 'extraordinary driving power, master in the arts of cunning and deception, intelligent and competent in his field, single-minded in his mission to make Europe "free of Jews" (*judenrein*) – in short, a man uniquely suited to be the overseer of most of the Nazi program to exterminate the Jews'.[47] In reviewing Robinson's book, Walter Laqueur declared that many thought 'the entire tenor of her work was deplorable, that the murder of six million people was not a fitting occasion to display cleverness, occasionally even flippancy'.[48]

Lionel Abel criticises Arendt for applying an aesthetic rather than a moral standard to Eichmann and, as a consequence, of grossly diluting the enormity of the evil. Abel takes issue with Arendt's background contentions: first that the Jewish Councils set up by the Nazis in Europe were imperative instruments for the destruction of Jewry in Europe; and, second, that Eichmann was a replaceable facilitator of the programme, and not its central perpetrator. Abel accuses Arendt of crimes of omission. In relation to the first 'terrible charge',[49] Abel denied that the Jewish leadership was as complicit in the destruction of Jewry as Arendt contends. In establishing that no Belgian Jew was deported from Belgium because there was no Nazi-inspired Jewish Council, Abel argues that Arendt neglects to point out that there was an Association of Belgian Jews subject to Nazi directives. In other words, there was a Jewish leadership yet no Belgian Jews were deported.

What of the Jewish leadership? Daniel Bell suggests that it is a matter of regret that Arendt takes the historical fact of Jewish complicity and converts it into a moral condemnation. In retrospect, non-cooperation may have been a better strategy but there was no knowing, and divisions had arisen among Jews as a result of becoming more bourgeois and losing a sense of solidarity as a people. Hence, some were prepared to sacrifice non-nationals, or those who had not served Germany in the previous war, for the sake of their own safety.[50]

The more serious omission for Abel was that Arendt neglects to discuss the slaughter of over half a million Jews in the Ukraine between November 1941 and June 1942. This happened despite a complete lack of organisation among the Jews. In other words, the mass destruction of Jews was not dependent upon the complicity of Jewish leaders. Bell points out, however, that the Nazi policy in Russia was different and entailed wholesale shootings, often failing to discriminate between Russians and Jews.[51]

A further charge that Abel makes is that Eichmann comes off so much better than his victims in the book because Arendt is making an aesthetic, rather than a moral, judgement. Abel contends that Arendt's judgement would have been sounder had she taken on board Simone de Beauvoir's point when writing of the war criminal Laval in 1946. The man in the dock is weak and broken, worn down by the press attention and the incessant questioning, and perhaps has doubts about the rightness of what he did. Whereas the real Laval who needs to be on trial is the Laval who wielded such power and who collaborated in the designs of Hitler. Arendt is accused of being insensitive to this distinction and of projecting the broken sorrowful Eichmann back into his past role, without portraying his Nazism as a conspicuous ideological decision, but claiming that his sympathy to Zionism was reasoned.

Furthermore Abel suggests that characterising someone as mediocre and comic, as Eichmann undoubtedly was, is not in contradiction with describing him as morally reprehensible, that is, a monster who boasted that he would go to his grave laughing knowing that he had the deaths of five million Jews on his conscience. The difference is in the norms of judgement being employed. As Bell points out, however, to portray Eichmann as a 'perverted sadist' and monster is too comfortable a judgement. It allows us to think that such behaviour is an aberration and that the wickedness of Nazism and Stalinism, of torture and extermination camps, is the work of madmen who had hijacked the apparatus of the state and terrorised ordinary citizens into silence or acquiescence.[52]

Daniel Bell characterises Arendt's enterprise as one of applying objective and universal standards of justice. She rejects tribal or parochial identification. Although the crimes of Eichmann were against the Jews, she thinks that his sentence of death was deserved not because of what he did to the Jews but because of his crime against humanity. Abel, Bell implies, is confusing law and morality when he accuses Arendt of making an aesthetic judgement. The law, as are aesthetic judgements, is separate from morality. Eichmann was not on trial in Jerusalem for the actions of the state he served. The legal system that tried him did not permit it. Had that been the case, hundreds of thousands of others would have been deemed culpable. Those who set up the Nuremberg trials realised that, in order to avoid putting limitless others to trial, personal responsibility had to be established. Eichmann was tried as a person, albeit an extraordinary evil monster. As part of a monstrous system he certainly was but as a man he clearly was not.[53] Bell maintains, however, that: 'The agony of Miss Arendt's book is precisely that she takes her stand so unyieldingly on the side of disinterested justice, and that she judges both Nazi and Jew. But abstract justice, as the Talmudic wisdom knew, is sometimes too "strong" a yardstick to judge the world.'[54]

C

In this section I want to draw out the implications of Arendt's characterisation of evil for the 'civilised' world, that is, the particularism of the argument, and in the next the extent to which it lacks universality.

The study of Eichmann shows that the gross violations of human rights that totalitarian regimes are capable of perpetrating do not depend upon mad psychotic lunatics but upon people like Eichmann who many psychiatrists pronounced perfectly normal in his affections and attachments to people and who, in his vanity, detachment from reality, and stupidity, was swept along in the tide of the machinery of the final solution, implementing his orders with dutiful enthusiasm. It is a warning that human rights are fragile, and that modern states with far greater potential for centralisation of power and communications constitute an ever-present threat.

Arendt's description of evil as banal, based upon her observations of Eichmann at his trial, is nevertheless a generalisation based upon one instance. We have to be careful that we do not take one facet of the Holocaust and mistake it for the whole. Nazi Germany produced three sorts of people capable of perpetrating the most evil of crimes, the eradication of a whole people and systematic violation of their right to life. First, there were those who formulated the policy with deliberative intent, in the full knowledge of the consequences of their actions, orchestrating the complete subversion of morals, assisted by unrelenting propaganda, such as Hitler and Goebbels. These are the producers of the fundamental and operative ideology which provides the reasons for motivating the actions of subordinates. These would include, secondly, those who implemented the policies faithfully, such as Eichmann, who neither initiated the genocide, nor engaged in any of the killings. They may have shielded themselves from the horrors, as Arendt contends Eichmann did, by a lack of imagination. Other SS officers closer to the implementation of the ideology, generally well educated and intelligent, instead of saying to themselves what terrible things they did to people, declare instead that, in pursuance of their duties, they were forced to witness horrible things which weighed heavily on their shoulders.[55] And thirdly, there were those who engaged in the brutal killing of Jews, gypsies and the insane, such as the guard known as Ivan the Terrible at the Polish extermination camp, Treblinka. He forced into the gas chambers over 29,000 prisoners, occasionally hacking the reluctant with a sword. Or, Dr Josef Mengele, known as the 'Angel of Death' at Auschwitz, who selected victims for extermination, and conducted notorious macabre experiments, especially on twins, often without anaesthetics, almost invariably followed by their murder. Such killers may well be best explained by reverting to categories such as madness, monstrous and psychopathic.

In Arendt's view, the distance one stands from the crime gives little indication of culpability. She contends, in general, that the degree of responsibility increases the further we draw away from the person who pulls the trigger.[56] On this scale of evil, Hitler and Goebbels are more evil than Eichmann, and Eichmann is more evil than Mengele and Ivan the Terrible.

Eichmann is, indeed, emblematic of the Holocaust but he should not be taken to be representative of the kind of people who were its perpetrators. Those who committed the crimes were of many different characters ranging from Eichmann himself to Ivan the Terrible and Dr Mengele. The pathological brutes and sadists, the so called monsters, give us nothing to distinguish the Holocaust from the countless atrocities throughout history but reflection upon the character of Eichmann may add depth to our understanding of essential parts, if not the essence, of the Holocaust. For Arendt, describing Eichmann as banal was not intended to diminish the evil of the Holocaust. Its banality was in some ways even more frightening than her earlier sense of its radicalness.[57] The example of Eichmann demonstrated the consequences of what happens when thinking fails to inform the behaviour of a person and a culture.[58]

In the first and third categories, the formulation of policies and their brutal face-to-face execution, one may attribute intent to the action. As Adolf Hitler contemplated the eradication from the face of the earth of what he believed to be 'vermin', and Josef Mengele devised and performed grotesque experiments on humans, as if animals in a laboratory, it would be perverse to describe either as unthinking and lacking intent. They thought, and they acted, and what they did was evil, knowing the likely consequences of their actions, death and unconscionable suffering. Both escaped punishment, the former by suicide, and the latter by fleeing to Argentina and dying from drowning following a massive stroke in Brazil in 1979. Eichmann is different in that he had no intention of committing acts that were evil (according to Arendt), that he was himself a victim of the Nazi system, but he was nevertheless punished. On what justification?

Arendt acknowledges that pride of place in modern legal systems goes to the establishment of intent, the subjective factor, in the commission of a crime. She suggests: 'Where this intent is absent, where, for whatever reasons, even reasons of moral insanity, the ability to distinguish between right and wrong is impaired, we feel no crime has been committed'.[59] Eichmann, in Arendt's words "*never realized what he was doing*'.[60] Despite lack of intent, it was right that the trial went ahead 'in the interests of justice and nothing else'.[61] The crime was an offence against nature, and only retribution can restore the natural harmony. The wronged collectivity has a duty to punish the criminal on moral grounds.[62] Retribution, however, requires moral or legal guilt, or both for the justifiable infliction of punishment, and guilt assumes intent. One may imagine justifying punishment on utilitarian grounds, that is, making an example of Eichmann in order to send out the message that one may not act unthinkingly on behalf of an evil regime and get away with it.

In her own imaginary verdict, Arendt addresses the prisoner. Because he acted in the name of the regime, which had a policy of mass murder, Eichmann demonstrated his support, whether wittingly or not, for what was effectively the assertion that the regime and its supporters had a right to determine who and who should not share the earth with them. Ultimately, the ground for punishing him is 'no one, that is, no member of the human race, can be expected to want to share the earth with you. This is the reason, and the only reason, you must hang.'[63]

Is this a satisfactory way of differentiating Eichmann from, on the one hand Hitler and Goebbels, and on the other from Dr Mengele and Ivan the Terrible? With increasing secularisation in the West, the concept of wickedness has lost some of its currency but it is exactly the term that allows us to make a conceptual difference between the evil act, and the evil person. An unthinking person, such as Eichmann, who was weak and misguided, may commit evil acts and, indeed, be guilty of a serious character flaw but the lack of intent makes it difficult to attribute the character of a wicked person to him despite the fact that his actions and their consequences were evil. On the other hand, it is perfectly possible to describe someone as wicked despite never having committed an evil deed or act. A person incapable of action, for example a paraplegic, may be bitter and twisted, wishing harm on everyone and rejoicing in their misfortunes. Wickedness assumes a person with a cognitive capacity for imagining an act and its consequences and having an attitude towards it, or what G. E. Moore called an 'emotion'.[64] What Arendt is suggesting is that Eichmann did not have such a capacity. With Richard III, he had no intention of being a villain nor was he an Iago or Macbeth. In fact, he appears to have had no motive for his actions other than personal advancement.[65]

Yet personal advancement to the exclusion of other things, that is, self-interestedness, may be both wicked and evil not because of the end to be attained, such as greater power or aggrandisement, but because it entails a failure or refusal to acknowledge a good which is not self-centred. In Eichmann's case, there was a cognitive disjuncture between the activities he organised and authorised and their consequences. His part of the sequence of events stopped at the point of delivery and what happened to the deportees thereafter was not his responsibility. His rationalisation was that he had personally killed no one nor ordered anyone to be killed. He was doing as good a job as he could in order to ingratiate and advance himself. Self-interestedness, to act as if there is no good other than a self-centred good, is in Kant's view the form that human wickedness most characteristically takes.

Kant contends that the moral law, the law of reason, is not only accessible to any rational person but it is also a motivation or spring of action in however small degree. In this respect, the selfish person, as Eichmann clearly was, is not perversely antagonistic to the moral law. It is not that the moral law cannot motivate such a person but, instead, it becomes subordinate to his or her self-love. As Kant suggests, the person 'makes the spring of self-love and its inclinations the condition of obedience to the moral law; whereas, on the contrary, the latter ought to be adopted as the sole spring, being the *supreme condition* of the satisfaction of the former'.[66] Eichmann was not unaware of right and wrong and, when he witnessed the mistreatment of Jews, as he occasionally did, he was visibly shaken. The moral law existed for him yet it was subordinate to his self-interest and the overall aims of the Third Reich.

Both Barry Clarke and Stanley Benn accuse Eichmann of 'heteronomous evil' and 'heteronomous wickedness', respectively.[67] Both Clarke and Benn argue that Eichmann's defence at Jerusalem was that he obeyed orders and that, therefore, his defence claimed he was absolved of the responsibility of the crimes his superiors directed him to do.[68] In other words, Eichmann allowed others to make the moral judgments on his behalf. The argument, following Kant, distinguishes between acting spontaneously and acting autonomously which is related to three maxims of common understanding. To act spontaneously Kant takes as a given but autonomous action is capable of being developed or retarded. The maxims he presents are those of understanding, that is, to think for oneself; of judgement, to think from the position of everyone else; and of reason, that is, always to think consistently.[69] In Arendt's view, Eichmann failed to act in accordance with any of these maxims.

Was Eichmann incapable of thinking *for* himself, however, and therefore putting the moral law into abeyance? Or did thinking *of* himself precipitate the subordination of the moral law to his self-interest? If so, on Kant's terminology, he was both wicked and evil. Eichmann was certainly capable of thinking for himself. His reasoning often typically displayed instrumental rationality. Logistically, he often overcame significant obstacles in formulating and implementing the means to achieve his ends, that is, manipulating Jewish Councils to round up and deliver Jews to be transported to the death camps. He was not like Aristotle's natural slave, capable of acting on instructions but incapable of formulating them for himself. Indeed, his defence at Jerusalem was not as Clarke and Benn suggest, acting on superior orders, but, as I suggested earlier, immunity for acts of state.

The focus of critics, generally, outraged by Arendt's judgements of Nazis and Jews alike, and her characterisation of Eichmann as extraordinarily ordinary, deflects us from the wider theoretical considerations which are perhaps even more controversial than her observations on Eichmann. Eichmann was complicit in a totalitarian system that stripped people of their citizenship, of their culture and their rights. It took rights-bearing citizens of civil society and placed them outside it. While mass murder and genocide were not uncommon in history, and frequently to be observed at the founding of political societies, genocide in the context of modern totalitarianism was unique precisely because of the systematic undermining of citizenship, culture and rights. The question arises, then, if Eichmann had engaged outside of Europe in the activities he engaged in within, would he have been equally deserving of death. In other words, is Arendt's theory of the banality of evil universal, or geographically contingent?

D

In Arendt's view, to be human is to live the life of a citizen, with all the rights and obligations it entails. The civilised polity is what makes human beings human, and to be stripped of the rights of citizenship and nationality is to tear away the cloak of humanity and render humans on a par with the rest of the natural world. This is the context, for her, in which evil is perpetrated. To strip persons of citizenship rights and nationality is to dehumanise them, rendering their extermination something less in the eyes of the exterminators than murder or genocide. Having witnessed the consequences of denaturalisation of citizens, and the degradation they faced as a consequence, she tenaciously believed that the rights of citizenship provided a much greater safeguard against crimes against humanity than the outmoded notion of natural rights. Arendt is conscious of the extent to which human rights depend upon being first and foremost a citizen enjoying the rights of citizenship. To be deprived of those also effectively stripped you of human rights. If the Rights of Man have a concrete existence, they would belong to everyone unconditionally by the mere fact of being human. [70] To be regarded merely as human is to be regarded as nothing more than a savage, and the fear is that you may quickly come to be regarded as a beast. Arendt wants to insist upon our right to have rights.[71] What this means is a prohibition on states denaturalising individuals by withdrawing protections and citizenship rights.[72] It is for Arendt an unconditional right but quite distinct from universal human rights or the Rights of Man.

The right to have rights, in Arendt's theory, is a double-edged sword: at the same time it reproaches, in different degrees, every particular order of rights; it demands that everyone belong to such an order. The paradox is that we depend upon rights because of our fear that governments will fail to treat us with dignity and respect while, at the same time, depending for those rights on those very same governments or states.[73] Between the two world wars, Arendt argues, denationalisation became a powerful weapon in the hands of totalitarian regimes. The Nazis, for instance, paved the way in its Nuremberg Laws which distinguished between citizens of the Reich and nationals, or second-class citizens who had no political rights, which led eventually by decree to the deprivation of their nationality of all nationals of 'alien blood'.

Arendt's book on Eichmann points to a particular phenomenon which constitutes the occasion on which the evil of crimes against humanity may be perpetrated. The human predicament to which she attributes such evils is the denaturalisation of citizens, followed by systematic degradation and eventually extermination. The threshold from which such crimes begin, then, is that of relatively civilised communities in which citizens have rights that are protected by governments.

The implications of such a theory, however, need not lead us to the conclusions that Arendt drew regarding those who have never enjoyed the benefits of civilisation or associated citizenship rights. For her, it is undeniable that many parts of the world fell far below European standards of civilisation, and their political achievement failed to attain anything recognisable as civil association with consequent citizenship rights. Such a continent was Africa, or the dark continent, populated by black savages, possessing no historical record. In other words, they lacked in almost every respect civil association on the European model. Imperialist adventurers who slaughtered these 'savages' did not think of themselves as committing murder – the very idea appeared ridiculous and inappropriate. How else could one approach such a strangely alien people, Arendt wonders, whose claim to humanity was at best tenuous. Indeed, her sympathies are with the imperialists in this matter, having to face 'a horrifying experience of something alien beyond imagination or comprehension: it was tempting indeed to simply declare that these were not human beings'.[74] In such circumstances murder may seem wrong but the response to a people whose past had not accomplished a human world, and whose future exhibited no purpose, and for whom nature was the overwhelming reality, was not inappropriate. The African past was ahistorical, an exemplification of the worthless activities of natural men who have 'vegetated for thousands of years'.[75] Africans were human beings who lacked a specifically human character. Civilisation had evaded black Africans, evidenced by their general lack of human culture and morality. While the slaughter of Africans by imperialists may be against natural justice, it was not immoral.[76] Natural rights are naturalistic and do not elevate humans above animals. The right to life, and any other right, are not parts of the moral armoury of anyone who has attained no more than the bare minimum condition of human origin. Human status is a function of a moral community that sustains and endows it.[77] The Indians and Chinese had attained human status through the achievement of their civilisations, and therefore their murder by imperialists could not be excused, nor was there any comprehensible reason why they were not treated as human beings.[78]

What makes the Holocaust shocking is the murder of civilised people by civilised people. The right to life and citizenship for the Jews was a juridical fact, eroded and extinguished by a systematic stripping of vestiges of entitlement to enjoy citizenship rights. The Jews were reduced from political citizens to rightless natural animals, jettisoned from civilisation.[79]

Arendt is here setting the threshold very high for the point at which evil may be perpetrated against fellow human beings. Human rights are for her, in fact, citizenship rights. Her argument illustrates a contention I have made elsewhere. Human rights have never been universal. They have always been conditional and, therefore, special rights. The real issues surround the question of who qualifies for them, and why. In other words, who counts as being fully human? Europeans have traditionally been rather parsimonious in conferring the status of full humanity on anyone other than adult white European males. The Native Americans, the Australian Aboriginals, the New Zealand Maori, and black Africans were, in differing ways, deemed to fall short of enjoying full human rights, yet they were all equally as capable of violating them. They had the obligations without the rights. Women and children similarly constituted a problem regarding the attainment of full human status.[80] Arendt was perhaps rather less parsimonious but, nevertheless, complicit in the same process in asking herself, perhaps not explicitly but certainly by implication, who qualifies as human and why in order to endow them with the right to have rights. We should perhaps be rather more shocked at her answer to this question than at her depiction of evil as banal.

Notes

1 Hannah Arendt, *Eichmann in Jerusalem: A Report on the Banality of Evil* (Harmondsworth: Penguin, 1965), revised and expanded. For the examples of vehement vilification see Jacob Robinson, *And the Crooked Shall be Made Straight: A New Look at Eichmann's Trial* (New York: Collier Macmillan, 1965). Walter Laqueur in reviewing Robinson suggests that he is clearly outraged by Arendt, declaring that many thought 'the entire tenor of her work was deplorable, that the murder of six million people was not a fitting occasion to display cleverness, occasionally even flippancy.' Walter Lacquer, 'review of *And the Crooked Shall be Made Straight*', *The New York Review of Books*, 11 November 1965. David Cesarani, *Becoming Eichmann: Rethinking the Life, Crimes, and Trial of a 'Desk Murderer'* (London: Da Capo Press, 2006), p. 345. Barry Gewen, 'The Everyman of Genocide', *New York Times*, 14 May 2006. For a positive review of *Eichmann in Jerusalem* see Frederick S. Burin, review in *Political Science Quarterly*, 79 (1964), pp. 122–5. He contends: 'Not only does it do justice to Miss Arendt's reputation for brilliant insight and critical imagination, it reflects great courage, great independence of mind, and – other reviewers to the contrary notwithstanding – a shining humanity' (p. 122).

2 See Barry Sharpe, *Modesty and Arrogance in Judgement: Hannah Arendt's Eichmann in Jerusalem* (Westport, CT: Praeger, 1999).

3 Arendt, *Eichmann in Jerusalem*, p. 274.

4 Susan Neiman, *Evil in Modern Thought: An Alternative History of Philosophy* (Princeton: Princeton University Press, 2002).

5 Mary Midgley, *Wickedness* (London: Routledge, 1984), pp. 62–3.

6 Neiman, *Evil in Modern Thought*, p. 281.

7 He obtained a passport from the International Red Cross in the name of Ricardo Klement, a native Italian without nationality, but went to no great lengths to suppress his identity while in Argentina, even registering his children, who joined him with his wife in 1952, under the name of Eichmann in a German School.

8 Arendt's article and subsequent book did not directly influence Cohen's poem but he says: 'Hannah Arendt is somehow involved, but I don't recall the circumstances. I didn't read the book, but I may have read a review of the book, or heard of the book. My old friend, Irving Layton and I were certainly discussing these matters, which hung heavy in the air at the time, and I guess the poem rose from those conversations. Irving most probably did read the book. I seem to remember that Hannah Arendt's position was unacceptable in some Jewish circles around Montreal.' E-mail to the author dated 30 January 2011.

9 Arendt, *Eichmann in Jerusalem*, p. 285.

10 Hannah Arendt, *The Human Condition* (Chicago: Chicago University Press, 1958), p. 10.

11 Arendt, *The Human Condition*, 9.

12 Seyla Benhabib, *Another Cosmopolitanism*, with Jeremy Waldron, Bonnie Honig and Will Kymlicka (Oxford: Oxford University Press, 2006), p. 21.

13 Bridget Cotter, 'Arendt and "The Right to Have Rights"', in Anthony F. Lang Jr, and John Williams, eds, *Hannah Arendt and International Relations* (London: Palgrave, 2005), p. 11.

14 Andrew Vincent, *The Politics of Human Rights* (Oxford: Oxford University Press, 2010), p. 166.

15 Patricia Altenberd Johnson, *On Arendt* (Belmont, CA: Wadsworth, 2001), p. 44.

16 Seyla Benhabib, 'Arendt's *Eichmann in Jerusalem*', in Dana Villa, ed., *The Cambridge Companion to Hannah Arendt* (Cambridge, Cambridge University Press, 2000), p. 67.

17 Arendt, *Eichmann in Jerusalem*, p. 274

18 Raimond Gaita, *A Common Humanity: Thinking about Love and Truth and Justice*, 2nd edn (London: Routledge, 2002), pp. 39–40.

19 See Robinson, *And the Crooked Shall be Made Straight*, p. 58, referring to the correspondence between Gershom Scholem and Hannah Arendt.

20 Hannah Arendt, *The Life of the Mind*, two volumes (London: Secker and Warburg, 1978), Vol. 1, p. 4.

21 Arendt, *Eichmann in Jerusalem*, p. 288.

22 Benhabib, 'Arendt's *Eichmann in Jerusalem*', p. 75.

23 Arendt, *Eichmann in Jerusalem*, p. 49.

24 Arendt, *The Human* Condition, p. 5.

25 Hannah Arendt, *The Human Condition*, p. 5. In her later writings, particularly *The Life of the Mind* (Arendt, 1978: 2 volumes), this solution was not so simple because of her separation of willing, thinking and judgement from the realm of action. Like Hume she contends that reason alone cannot move the will. This point is well made by Barry Clarke, 'Beyond the Banality of Evil', *British Journal of Political Science*, 10, 1980, p. 421.

26 Arendt, *Eichmann in Jerusalem*, p. 49.
27 Patricia Altenberd Johnson, *On Arendt* (Belmont, CA: Wadsworth, 2001), pp. 46–7.
28 Arendt, *Eichmann in Jerusalem*, p. 150. Also see Stephen J. Whitfield, 'Hannah Arendt and the Banality of Evil', *The History Teacher*, 14, 1981, p. 471.
29 Arendt, *Eichmann in Jerusalem*, p. 54.
30 Arendt, *Eichmann in Jerusalem*, p. 286.
31 Arendt, *Eichmann in Jerusalem*, p. 298.
32 Arendt, *Eichmann in Jerusalem*, p. 5.
33 Arendt, *Eichmann in Jerusalem*, p. 269.
34 Arendt, *Eichmann in Jerusalem*, p. 269.
35 Bruno Bettelheim, 'Eichmann; the System; the Victims', *The New Republic*, 148, 15 June 1963, p. 27.
36 Bettelheim, 'Eichmann', p. 33.
37 Arendt, *Eichmann in Jerusalem*, pp. 288–9.
38 Benhabib, 'Arendt's *Eichmann in Jerusalem*', p. 79.
39 Arendt, *Eichmann in Jerusalem*, p. 273.
40 Arendt, *Eichmann in Jerusalem*, p. 287.
41 Arendt, *Eichmann in Jerusalem*, p. 150.
42 Thucydides, *History of the Peloponnesian War*, trans. Rex Warner (Harmondsworth: Penguin, 1972), 3: 82.
43 Bell, 'The Alphabet of Justice: Reflections on *Eichmann in Jerusalem*', *Partisan Review*, Vol. xxx, 1963, p. 424.
44 Frederick S. Burin, 'review of *Eichmann in Jerusalem*', p. 122.
45 Arendt's book sparked widespread controversy even before its publication. All sorts of implausible accounts of her argument and motives were given. On a Freudian analysis it was suggested that she contended that the Jews had a death wish and they killed themselves. Her motivation for the claim was self-hatred.
46 Jacob Robinson, *And the Crooked Shall be Made Straight*.
47 Robinson, *And the Crooked Shall be Made Straight*, p. 59. He accused Arendt of being almost completely ignorant of the way international law emerges, and of its jurisdiction, and condemns her for criticising competent jurists devoted to ensuring the operation of the rule of law in the international sphere (p. 100).
48 Walter Lacquer, 'review of *And the Crooked Shall be Made Straight*'.
49 Lionel Abel, 'The Aesthetics of Evil', *Partisan Review*, Vol. xxx, 1963, p. 215.
50 Bell, 'The Alphabet of Justice', p. 432.
51 Bell, 'The Alphabet of Justice', p. 423.
52 Bell, 'The Alphabet of Justice', p. 424.
53 Bettelheim, 'Eichmann', p. 27.
54 Bell, 'The Alphabet of Justice', p. 428.

55 Adam Morton, *On Evil* (London: Routledge, 2004), p. 80.

56 Arendt, *Eichmann in Jerusalem*, p. 247.

57 Raimond Gaita, *A Common Humanity*, pp. 153–4.

58 Johnson, *On Arendt*, p. 48.

59 Arendt, *Eichmann in Jerusalem*, p. 277.

60 Arendt, *Eichmann in Jerusalem*, p. 287.

61 Arendt, *Eichmann in Jerusalem*, p. 286.

62 Arendt, *Eichmann in Jerusalem*, p. 277.

63 Arendt, *Eichmann in Jerusalem*, p. 279.

64 G. E. Moore, *Principia Ethica* (Cambridge: Cambridge University Press, 1903), p. 208. Also see S. I. Benn, 'Wickedness', *Ethics*, 95, 1985, p. 208.

65 Arendt, *Eichmann in Jerusalem*, p. 287.

66 Immanuel Kant, 'Of the Indwelling of the Bad Principle along with the Good, or On the Radical Evil in Human Nature', in *Kant's Theory of Ethics*, trans. T. K. Abbot (London: Longman, Green and Co., 1927), p. 343. For a discussion of Kant's views see Benn, 'Wickedness', pp. 797–8.

67 Barry Clarke, 'Beyond the Banality of Evil', pp. 424–8, and Benn, 'Wickedness', pp. 802–4.

68 Benn, 'Eichmann "pleaded that he simply obeyed orders"', in 'Wickedness', p. 802; Clarke, 'the rules under which he subsumed particulars were given to him by superiors', in 'Beyond the Banality of Evil', p. 429.

69 Immanuel Kant, *The Critique of Judgment*, trans. James Creed Meredith (Oxford: Oxford University Press, 1952), p. 152.

70 Bridget Cotter, 'Arendt and "The Right to Have Rights"', p. 97.

71 Arendt, *Origins of Totalitarianism*, p. 290.

72 Seyla Benhabib, *Another Cosmopolitanism*, p. 25.

73 Bonnie Honig, 'Another Cosmopolitanism? Law and Politics in the New Europe', in Seyla Benhabib, with Jeremy Waldron, Bonnie Honig and Will Kymlicka, *Another Cosmopolitanism* (Oxford: Oxford University Press, 2006), pp. 106–7.

74 Arendt, *Origins of Totalitarianism* (New York: Harcourt, Brace and World, 1973), p. 195. Also see Shiraz Dossa, 'Human Status and Politics: Hannah Arendt on the Holocaust', *Canadian Journal of Political Science*, 13: 1980, pp. 309–23.

75 Arendt, *Origins of Totalitarianism*, p. 194.

76 Arendt, *Origins of Totalitarianism*, pp. 190–2.

77 Arendt, *Origins of Totalitarianism*, p. 300.

78 Arendt, *Origins of Totalitarianism*, p. 319.

79 Arendt, *Origins of Totalitarianism*, pp. 296–7.

80 David Boucher, *The Limits of Ethics in International Relations: Natural Law, Natural Rights and Human Rights in Transition* (Oxford: Oxford University Press, 2009).

INDEX